WE CHOSE TO SPEAK OF
WAR AND STRIFE

WE CHOSE TO SPEAK OF WAR AND STRIFE

*The World of the
Foreign Correspondent*

John Simpson

B L O O M S B U R Y
LONDON · OXFORD · NEW YORK · NEW DELHI · SYDNEY

Bloomsbury Publishing
An imprint of Bloomsbury Publishing Plc

50 Bedford Square
London
WC1B 3DP
UK

1385 Broadway
New York
NY 10018
USA

www.bloomsbury.com

BLOOMSBURY and the Diana logo are trademarks of Bloomsbury Publishing Plc

First published in Great Britain 2016

British Library Cataloguing-in-Publication Data
A catalogue record for this book is available from the British Library.

Library of Congress Cataloging-in-Publication Data has been applied for.

ISBN: HB: 978-1-4088-7222-2
TPB: 978-1-4088-7223-9
EPUB: 978-1-4088-7225-3

4 6 8 10 9 7 5 3

Typeset by Newgen Knowledge Works (P) Ltd, Chennai, India
Printed and bound in Great Britain by CPI Group (UK) Ltd, Croydon CR0 4YY

MIX
Paper from
responsible sources
FSC® C020471

To find out more about our authors and books visit www.bloomsbury.com.
Here you will find extracts, author interviews, details of forthcoming
events and the option to sign up for our newsletters.

To Rafe, who is to me what Du Fu's son was to him:
嬌儿

MEMORIAL

We spoke, we chose to speak of war and strife –
a task a fine ambition sought –
and some might say, who shared our work, our life:
that praise was dearly bought.

Drivers, interpreters, these were our friends.
These we loved. These we were trusted by.
The shocked hand wipes the blood across the lens.
The lens looks to the sky.

Most died by mischance. Some seemed honour-bound
to take the lonely, peerless track
conceiving danger as a testing ground
to which they must go back

till the tongue fell silent and they crossed
beyond the realm of time and fear.
Death waved them through the checkpoint. They were lost.
All have their story here.

James Fenton

CONTENTS

PREFACE

[Ms Merritt and Ms Lloyd-Roberts at the headquarters of the Sisters of Our Lady of Charity]

Lloyd-Roberts: Good morning, my name is Sue Lloyd-Roberts, I'm here from the BBC and this is Mary Merritt, a former Magdalene Laundry worker.

Unidentified representative of the order: You've already sent in a request and I think you've got your answer to that request.

Lloyd-Roberts: No, we've been refused an interview but we have some very important questions to ask.

Transcript from BBC *Newsnight*,
September 2014

YOU COULD SEE RIGHT from the start that it wasn't going to be the usual kind of commemoration service. People trooped in quietly and sat down, without saying much to each other. Often these media gatherings are a chance for everyone to talk loudly and show off, and maybe score a point or two off someone else. Here, though, the mood was different. Nash's masterpiece, All Souls, Langham Place was as full as I'd ever seen it for an occasion like this, but normally there would be an expectant buzz of conversation, almost an enjoyment about the whole thing, as though it was part of a last performance by the person we were commemorating. There would be a sort of half-expectation that they might come on stage soon, the same as ever, and cheer us all up and give us something to laugh about.

I've been to plenty of memorial services like this, and I hope that one day there'll be one for me – that people will sing the hymns loudly and enthusiastically, and laugh at the reminiscences of the hare-brained things I've done, then troop out in jolly mood at the end, clapping each other on the back and saying, 'Fancy a spot of lunch somewhere?' That, after all, is the finest way to be remembered: with affection and amusement, in an atmosphere of camaraderie.

The service for Sue Lloyd-Roberts wasn't like that at all. She had died of leukaemia at the age of sixty-four, at the height of her powers, as beautiful and witty and spikily charming as she had been when I first met her, thirty years earlier. No one in All Souls can have felt that this was a life which had reached its logical, dignified end. On the contrary, everyone must have felt a sense of unfairness, of potential not fully realised, of personal loss. When the last strains of a song Sue had loved, 'Bye-bye Miss American Pie', had faded away, and the congregation was standing up reluctantly to leave, my wife, who had known Sue as well as I did, turned to me with her eyes full of tears and said, 'I don't want to talk to anyone.' I felt the same. We actually did have a lunch to go to, but when we got to the restaurant we both found it hard to shake off the sense of gloom that hung over us. One of the sunniest people either of us had ever known had been taken out of our lives.

Sue was born in 1950, and never entirely lost the cut-glass accent (modified by a delightful lisp) which she learned at home in Belgravia and at Cheltenham Ladies' College. She went on to St Hilda's, Oxford, where she worked on the student magazine *Isis* with Tony Hall, the future director-general of the BBC. She was a lifelong socialist, and always maintained an unshakeable sympathy with the underdog. Throughout her career, first at Independent Television News and then at the BBC, she did some of her very best reporting on human rights issues, from the Soviet bloc in the 1970s to Burma in the 2010s.

There've been too many untimely deaths in recent years. Among others, Marie Colvin of the *Sunday Times*; John Harrison, John Schofield, Kate Peyton, Brian Hanrahan and Brian Barron of the

BBC; Terry Lloyd and Gaby Rado of ITN; James Forlong of Sky News; Rick Beeston of *The Times*; Daniel Pearl, James Foley, Steven Sotloff: all died at the height of their powers, killed by disease or violence or accident or the pressure of the job, and the friends and admirers who went to services of commemoration for them felt very much the same as those who went to the one for Sue Lloyd-Roberts.

Still, other things being equal, foreign correspondents tend to live at least as long as any other section of the community, and by no means all commemorations are gloomy affairs. Sir Charles Wheeler died, full of honours, in 2008 at the age of eighty-five. Dick Beeston of the *Daily Telegraph*, the father of Rick, died at eighty-eight. The man who's generally regarded as the founder of the profession, William Howard Russell, was eighty-six when he died, having reported on the Crimean War, the Indian Mutiny, the American Civil War and the Franco-Prussian War. Martha Gellhorn, who smuggled herself onto a hospital ship in order to reach the D-Day beaches, ended her life peacefully in Chelsea at the age of eighty-eight; only a year or so before, she had visited Brazil to write an article on the murder of street children by the police. Clare Hollingworth of the *Daily Telegraph* and the *Guardian*, who reported from the Polish border on the outbreak of the Second World War, is 104 at the time of writing and, though very frail, still turns up most days at the Foreign Correspondents' Club in Hong Kong. Not every foreign correspondent, fortunately, dies before their time. Even Nathaniel Butter, the great-great-grandfather of British journalism, whose story appears in the next chapter, lived to be eighty-one, dying in 1664.

This book is intended to be various things: in particular, an affectionate celebration of a trade which, I fear, is on its way out. I would also like to think that over the course of the stories I tell in the following pages it will constitute a kind of guidebook to the origin, development and practice of the foreign correspondent's profession. What it isn't, is an exhaustive history. I have followed the advice of Lytton Strachey in his bitchy but influential book *Eminent Victorians* in 1918, where he declared that the author of such a wide-ranging account shouldn't attempt an overall approach, but should adopt what he called 'a subtler strategy': 'He will row out over the great ocean of material, and lower down into it, here and there, a little bucket, which will bring up to the light of day some characteristic specimen, from those far depths, to be examined with careful curiosity.'

This is, of course, very much the approach of the journalist; so I don't feel that, as a journalist myself, I need to apologise for following it. All the same, the bucket I have lowered in the source material of foreign reporting has allowed all sorts of valuable samples to escape. This isn't the kind of book in which everyone gets their paragraph; and even if it had been, it would probably have left out plenty of deserving cases. My hope is that it will create a composite picture of the experiences and varied approaches of foreign correspondents in such a way that it can act as a kind of how-to-do-it guide. For this reason I've thrown in a few experiences of my own, because I felt they illustrated particular points that needed to be made.

Over the years many of us have no doubt gone into a bookshop, spotted a book about some subject we've been personally connected with, and done a so-called 'Manhattan name-check' on ourselves: that is, looked ourselves up in the index. And in a large variety of cases we've found that we haven't rated a mention. I know very well how that feels, and I'm sincerely sorry to have inflicted this slight modicum of pain on anyone else. All I can say is that I haven't left anyone out on purpose, or through malice.

Among the noteworthy people I have lacked the space to mention at length are Herbert Matthews, one of the most famous of the foreign correspondents of the *New York Times*, who played just as important a part in the reporting of the Spanish Civil War as Ernest Hemingway and Martha Gellhorn, whom I *have* mentioned, and Denis Johnston, the Irish writer and protégé of Yeats and Shaw, who worked as a correspondent for the BBC from El Alamein to Buchenwald. I haven't found room for the friendship and rivalry between Alan Moorhead of the *Daily Express* and Alex Clifford of the *Daily Mail*, which symbolised some of the very best of wartime journalism. I've also had to leave out the delightful Anglo-Irish peer, Eddie Ward of Reuters and the BBC, who tossed a coin with Richard Dimbleby in North Africa to decide where they should go; as a result Dimbleby headed westwards, and went on to cover El Alamein and D-Day, while Ward made for Tobruk and was taken prisoner of war when it fell. Immediately after being released Ward managed, by a combination of charm and fierce determination, to get an interview with Admiral Doenitz, who was still running what was left of Hitler's Germany.

Worse, in some ways, I've omitted an extraordinary and able range of television news correspondents, who were at the peak of the profession from my own time: they include Michael Sullivan, one of the finest writers I have ever worked with; Keith Graves, a dominant force in foreign reporting; Michael Nicholson, whose work helped ITN to become the best television news organisation of its time; Mark Austin, whose coolness and charm have made him an archetypical foreign correspondent as well as one of Britain's best news presenters; Tom Bradby, who was injured during riots in Jakarta while he was ITN's Asia correspondent, and eventually became royal correspondent and then presenter of the main ITN news; John Humphrys, with whom I worked with great enjoyment in Southern Africa in the 1970s, and who has remained a close friend ever since; Gavin Hewitt, whose commitment and endurance I've admired for much of my own career; and David Sells, a correspondent of great understanding and humanity, from whose work I learned a great deal over the years.

I have shamefully left out the entire foreign reporting team of *Channel 4 News* in Britain, whose work I regard as among the best in international television. To leave out any mention of Lindsey Hilsum, Matt Frei, Alex Thomson, Jonathan Rugman and Jonathan Miller is therefore more than a little perverse. I've not included

John Irvine, one of the present ITN correspondents whom I admire greatly, nor Bill Neely, formerly of ITN and now of NBC News. I have mentioned Christiane Amanpour of CNN, whose sharpness and sympathy have always been outstanding, but I haven't alas had room to go into the achievements and impressive qualities of her colleague, CNN's senior international correspondent, Nic Robertson. I haven't managed to fit in the experiences of many of my colleagues and friends at the BBC either. I hope they, and all the other foreign correspondents who deserved a mention here and haven't received one, will find it in their hearts to forgive me.

As we left the memorial service for Sue Lloyd-Roberts, my wife and I chatted for a while with Emily Buchanan of the BBC. I remember watching her one evening in our office as she got ready for a trip to West Africa to cover the first big outbreak of Ebola. She was plainly worried about the dangers, but she refused to let them stop her from going; and once she got there, she showed tremendous humanity as she followed the fate of the victims of the disease. It is, as Martha Gellhorn, one of my great heroes, once put it, not how tough you talk that defines you, but the degree to which you overcome your fears.

I have written this book on the hoof, in true foreign correspondent fashion, in places as varied as Kabul, Baghdad, Beijing, Singapore, and the Libyan capital Tripoli; in the depths of the Kenyan bush with Ian and Jane Craig of Lewa Downs; in the grand sitting room of the Mount Nelson Hotel in Cape Town, one of the world's great watering-holes; and finally at a delightful hotel at Ayers Rock in Australia, where the manuscript was at long last finished. Thanks to the help of a dozen or more colleagues, whose experiences will appear in the pages to follow, the writing of it has been a genuine pleasure.

At the risk of sounding like an Oscar winner, I must express my great gratitude to my agent, Julian Alexander, who has guided my writing with such wisdom over the years; to Mark and Gina Nelthorpe-Cowne, for whose guidance I am deeply thankful; to my editor at Bloomsbury, Michael Fishwick, for his insight and patience, and to his colleague Anna Simpson for getting it all together so smoothly and with such kindness; to Malcolm Balen of the BBC, who read the manuscript and spotted a couple of egregious errors; to the people at the Bodleian and London Libraries for their help and support; and to the staff at the News Café and at the Vaults in Oxford, at which pleasant places the bulk of the writing was done.

And finally, with much love, to my wife Dee, a foreign correspondent in her own right for the Johannesburg *City Press*, and to my son Rafe, who will probably be too sensible to become a foreign correspondent when he grows up.

If indeed such a job even exists by then.

Ayers Rock/Uluru,
Central Australia,
June 2016

ONE

A Glamorous Existence?

To those intrepid ones who went across the seas to be
the eyes and ears of America. . .
To those forthright ones who early saw the clouds of war
while many of us were seeing rainbows. . .
To those clear-headed ones who now stand like recording angels among the dead and dying. . .
To the Foreign Correspondent – this motion picture is
dedicated.

On-screen preamble to *Foreign Correspondent*,
directed by Alfred Hitchcock, 1940

WE ALL HAVE A tendency to think that other people lead more
interesting lives than we do. A Formula One champion driver,
an Oscar-winning actor and an MI6 agent have each told me over
the years how much more exciting my job was than theirs; while I, of
course, knowing how diminished and controlled the life of a foreign
correspondent has become, assured them that it wasn't.

I've sat beside a beautiful, well-known model and watched as
she pulled off her shoes and showed me what eight years of photo-
shoots and excessively high heels had done to her feet. I've listened
to a world-renowned rock star telling me how sick and tired he'd
become of life on the road and the company of the other members
of his band; not to mention the girls who still, he said wearily, imagine he'd prefer a night with them to sitting at home with his wife on
a couch by the fire, with his dog curled up on the mat. Glamour is
the quality we infuse into other people's lives, not our own.

So it is with the job of the foreign correspondent. We get on a lot of planes, we sleep in a lot of hotels, we see a lot of things other people don't see, and we meet a lot of intriguing people. Sometimes it's dangerous. Yet it isn't as exciting and fulfilling as other people assume, or as we expected when we first launched ourselves into the job. The glamour vanishes the instant you try to reach out to touch it.

I confess, though, that it was this perceived glamour that made me yearn to be a foreign correspondent. I was twenty-three, and shackled to a sub-editor's desk in the BBC radio newsroom at Broadcasting House, in the West End of London. Around me were people who seemed only a little lower than the angels, possessing the kind of savoir-faire that someone like me from rural Suffolk and south London could never hope to emulate. They strode around the third-floor corridors at Broadcasting House like demi-gods, charming the secretaries with their compliments and the bosses with their stories from the inexpressibly fascinating places they'd just come back from.

One lunchtime in the BBC Club bar at the Langham Hotel, opposite Broadcasting House, I gripped an orange juice (I was a teetotaller in those days) and stood silently on the outer fringes of a small gathering of worshippers around a tough, ebullient character in his forties, his faced pitted with long-dead acne, who was paying a fleeting visit to London from the Far East. 'I've got this simply enormous bed, you see – the bloody BBC won't pay for me to have a suite, so I have to have an ordinary bedroom, and the bed fills up the place. Anyway, over my head there's a bell-push. I press it once, and a gin and tonic appears. If I press it twice, a girl appears. And if I press it three times *two* girls appear.'

The worshippers collapsed with ingratiating laughter. I stood there and thought with the seriousness of youth about what he'd said. I didn't necessarily want to be him, sprawled on his gigantic *World of Suzie Wong* bed in the tropical heat: I could never imagine myself so cynical, so worldly-wise. But his life seemed wonderfully exotic, and he appeared to be utterly liberated from the petty rules and regulations that controlled the life of a junior sub-editor.

When I started at the BBC in 1966, I understood nothing whatever of the complex hierarchies around me. Apart from anything else, it took me some time to realise that the oldest members of the staff around me in the radio newsroom were usually the ones who had clung on longest and had failed to move onwards and upwards.

'Be careful,' said one tall, scholarly character with thin, straggling white hair, a stoop, a stained tie, a disturbing lump on his forehead and a pawky, subtle wit, 'if you don't get out of here pretty soon, you'll end up like me.' I didn't want to end up like him, even though I liked him immensely; apart from anything else he put me up for membership of the London Library, to which I have belonged ever since. So I took his advice, and was out of there within eighteen months. Of course, big organisations being what they are, I immediately found myself locked up in another prison, but at least it was a different one, equipped with a new set of chains.

It soon became abundantly clear to me that everyone I came across carried their own legend around with them. In a place like this, you were who you announced yourself to be. There were those who just wanted to be comfortable, and wore cardigans and old, soft shoes to prove it. There were clever, pushy young men and women whose very way of dressing and speaking and walking into an office declared that they were going somewhere. And there were those a decade or so older who had never quite got anywhere. They had been caught by the unexpected falling of some invisible barrier, and for some reason had never managed to work their way round it.

And there were the foreign correspondents. Among them was a magnifico who had recently given up a posting in Washington and was now the diplomatic correspondent: an important job, which in those days meant he was on practically every television and radio bulletin. He was gentle and unpretentious (you spot these things quickly when you're new and utterly unimportant) and I had to nag him to describe what chatting with President Eisenhower had been like, or to retell the story of the day Kennedy had been shot. After Christopher Serpell's death I discovered he had worked under Ian Fleming in naval intelligence during the

Second World War: even more glamour. He treated me no differently from the way he treated the head of news or the exalted producers he worked with; and he put up with my dopiness and inadequacy with patience and occasional quiet humour.

Christopher's deputy was constructed rather along the same lines as himself; no doubt he had chosen him for that reason. David Willey was slightly built and handsome, and pleasant to the rest of the staff, and had the general appearance (so my young Californian wife, who worked in the same department, maintained) of a Greek god. This naturally annoyed me until I understood that his charm was genuine. I still have the memory of emerging from my office one morning and bumping into David as he was hurrying along the corridor in his white linen suit with a yellow and red striped tie rucked up and out of place, on his way to the airport to catch a plane to somewhere as glamorous as he was: Paris? Beirut? Buenos Aires? I can't now remember, but he told me matter-of-factly, and seemingly without any desire to engender envy.

After Cambridge, David had gone to work at Reuters, and had reported for several years from the war in Algeria before going to East Africa, Vietnam and China. In the instant of opening my office door and bumping into him, my own future was settled. How could anyone not want a share in that sort of life? For decades now, David has been the BBC's correspondent in Rome, covering the activities and travels of successive popes; something he continues to do. I last saw him recently at breakfast on the terrace of a hotel in Ischia, as elegant and good-looking as ever. We'd both been staying there for an international get-together, and I silently congratulated myself on my choice of a role model, more than forty years earlier.

Until that point I'd had no real idea what sort of job I should aim for in the BBC. I knew I didn't want to go back to being a sub-editor, having just managed to break away, and being a producer on a radio current affairs programme didn't seem particularly to my taste either, but that was about it. On seeing David Willey, though, I understood what I wanted: it wasn't a specific job, it was an attitude – an air of freedom, a release from the daily routine. I had sufficient self-awareness to understand that being a foreign correspondent wouldn't make me handsome or glamorous like David, but I thought (rightly as it turned out) that it would be completely liberating. While I was in London, in the presence of my bosses, I had to jump through immense numbers of hoops; abroad, I would be a free agent.

Like David Willey, I could go to exciting and dangerous places and come back with things to say about them that other people would be interested in hearing. And it wouldn't be about how many times I had to ring to get a girl or a gin and tonic delivered to my room; it would be about witnessing things that were important. As David bustled down the corridor that day, heading for the airport, I felt that everything had been settled.

The BBC being the BBC, it didn't prove easy. It took two more years, after my moment of epiphany, to become a foreign correspondent in my own right; and even then I was only sent to Ireland, which, though satisfyingly dangerous at the time – as dangerous, indeed, as David Willey's Algeria had been – wasn't as foreign as I'd wished. They spoke English, and used sterling, and lived in houses that looked very much the same. But southern Ireland had a sovereign government and no love whatever for Britain, and for three years it became my kingdom. I fought for its interests at BBC meetings, raged over British misunderstandings of its politics and geography, and put in for a larger staff and more money, as foreign correspondents always do. And as the BBC always seems to do, it found ways of cutting back on my pay ('Dublin doesn't constitute a demonstrably foreign capital, so unfortunately we're unable to pay you the full emolument that a correspondent in, say, Paris could expect.' 'We'll look at the position again, come the summer.' 'Unfortunately we won't after all be able to give you the extra increment we've been discussing, because in the meantime a general freeze on rises of all kinds has been introduced. While we are on the subject of money, your statement of accounts seemed to differ by a matter of £1–2s-9d from our understanding of the correct position. Kindly make good this shortfall as quickly as possible.')

Until I became a foreign correspondent I had rather liked the BBC and the people who ran it. Afterwards, I found myself engaged in frequent hand-to-hand combat with it over a range of issues; and although I continued to admire its principles and defended its interests as fiercely as before, I caught frequent glimpses of a much less pleasant side of it than I would have if I'd stayed in London. Every foreign correspondent I know, for whatever news organisation they might work, seems to have the same attitude. It's something about the distance from headquarters, I think: the organisation treats you more impersonally because it doesn't see you face to face, and you dislike it more as a result.

Was being a foreign correspondent really a profession then, and is it now? The British lifted the word, and the concept, from the French in the nineteenth century, cutting it down from the original expression *'profession libérale'*. The accepted professions, which include medicine, the law, the Church, engineering, even estate agency and accountancy, are based on proper educational training: you have to undergo courses and examinations to get a qualification, and only then can you start to practise. True, there are nowadays plenty of courses in journalism at universities and colleges of higher education, but these are not exclusive gateways to the newspapers, magazines, news agencies, radio or television. I know plenty of people who studied journalism at Cardiff, or Westminster, or Roehampton, or various other universities; but I also know equally large numbers who drifted into journalism because they were good at writing, or simply got lucky. Among my journalistic colleagues over the years there have been a nuclear physicist, two barristers, an army captain, a farmer and a failed New York banker.

I have described elsewhere how the BBC hired me because it assumed that I had achieved a first in the English tripos at Cambridge; I didn't lie to the appointments board about it, but my director of studies had written a letter on my behalf promising that I was highly likely to get one, and the board gave me the job on the assumption that I had. Since no one actually asked me, I didn't have to admit that, because I'd spent so much time editing the magazine *Granta*, I'd actually got a 2:2 – what British students would later call a Desmond, after Archbishop Desmond Tutu of South Africa. The BBC had, in other words, bought a pig in a poke.

I never trained at any stage to be a journalist, and never even learned to do shorthand. This caused me profound difficulties when I had to cover long and hugely important IRA trials in Northern Ireland and the Republic, since every reported word counted; but I managed to muddle through without any obvious disasters.

Journalism is an odd-job calling, not a profession. To be honest, I prefer it that way; too much training, organisation and filtering can't be a good idea if the aim is to attract free spirits. Once, when I was lucky enough to be the chancellor of one of Britain's newest universities, we invited the wife of the then prime minister to open a new faculty. Neither her husband nor she were admirers of mine; in fact, her husband's press secretary had revealed not long before in his published diaries that the prime minister had referred to me privately as 'that sanctimonious wanker'. For the sake of the university, though, I behaved politely. Not so the prime minister's wife, whom I had to host at a gathering of students from the media studies department. 'I don't know what you're doing, studying journalism,' she told them crossly. 'It's not a profession, like the law is. It's just something that gives you the opportunity to tell any truth or lie you choose.'

At that stage, early in the new century, people used to sign up for media studies in large numbers, apparently believing that this was the way to clean up the body politic. The students were shocked to hear her attack the subject they'd chosen to study, and at the end they trooped out in silent gloom. I'm not a particular defender of the nobility of journalism, but I thought it was unpleasant and tactless of her to speak to the students like that, and rather than see her again I decided to make myself scarce for the rest of her visit to the campus. Unfortunately, just when I thought it was safe to come out of hiding, I bumped into her. 'Oh, there you are,' she said, with a strange, imploring note in her voice. 'Was I really a bit too hard on the media students?' In the normal way I might have replied politely; not now. 'Yes,' I said. 'They're doing the subject because

7

they're idealistic, and you've smashed their illusions.' A tear stole down her cheeks, and I could see she had wanted me to tell her that everything was all right. I felt awkward, but the fact was that she had chosen the wrong audience to share her views of journalism with. So I didn't.

Still, she was right, in a way. Journalism isn't a profession; it's not even properly monitored or controlled. Journalists have always behaved badly, whether they are hacking phones to listen to private messages, as happened with the *News of the World* and the *Sun* and (though no charges were brought) the *Daily Mirror*, or badgering the hurt and stricken with crude questions, or sneaking into places where they are not supposed to be. And in case you think this is just something that came into British life as a result of Rupert Murdoch, here is an extract from a 1911 biography of the pioneering war correspondent William Howard Russell by John Black Atkins, a thoroughly upright and usually rather po-faced correspondent on the *Manchester Guardian*. For all his principles, Atkins clearly has a sneaking admiration for the man:

> One daring representative of a daily paper, which was consid-
> ered the organ of fashionable life, was notorious for the audacity
> with which he penetrated secrets held to be sacred by the offi-
> cial customs of the time, and it was reported that once he was
> detected on board the Royal yacht in disguise when the Queen
> and Prince Consort were on an excursion, and was obliged to
> continue his journey in a dinghey [sic] towed behind.

Journalism isn't a science, any more than it's a real profession. Instead, it's an omnium-gatherum of opinions, ideas, personal spite, propaganda, and sincere efforts to explain what's really going on. There are relatively few newspapers where the boss's whims are not translated into daily news coverage. If he or she dislikes refugees, or the European Union, or a particular political party or politician, depend upon it – they will be targeted on a daily basis, under the flag of truth and honesty. We would like our newspapers to provide us with honest insights into the world around us, but in reality we just plump for one that has roughly the same opinions as we do.

Precisely because journalism is such a hotchpotch of intentions and values and abilities, any newspaper or broadcasting organisation has to possess a moral backbone if it is to keep its head out of the dirty waters we all swim in. Surely, the only real point of working as a journalist is to be honest and, where necessary, outspoken. Charles Wheeler, who served as the BBC's Delhi, Washington and Brussels correspondent, as well as presenting various current affairs programmes, was magnificent in this way – a real example to young correspondents like me. Once, when the director-general of the day came to address a group of foreign correspondents who were angry about some particular issue (I've forgotten what it was, but it was probably about money and conditions), Charles went for him in front of everyone.

'Charles,' said the head of news reprovingly, 'you really can't speak to the director-general like that.'

'What do you mean?' Charles exploded. 'You pay us to ask the fiercest questions of presidents and prime ministers all over the world, but when we're in the presence of our own director-general we're supposed to be all meek and shut up?'

Sitting in the audience, I started to applaud, but stopped directly people glared at me. I might feel galvanised and inspired by Charles Wheeler's moral courage, but I didn't necessarily want to emulate it at that moment.

———

Do foreign correspondents have links with intelligence organisations? Some unquestionably have: the British Secret Intelligence Service, often known as MI6, made the necessary arrangements for the *Observer* to take on Kim Philby as its Beirut correspondent, after he was outed as a Soviet agent. There's no doubt that various other journalists have had some kind of relationship with SIS; its information is usually excellent, though in my brief experience it's reluctant to dish it out in any serious amounts.

After I had spent six months in Baghdad in the run-up to the Gulf War of 1991 I wrote an article in the *Spectator* saying I was surprised that no hawk-faced character from SIS had rung me out of the blue to see if I'd got anything to tell them. A few weeks later I was invited to lunch with the head of the organisation, but over the first course of salmon and cucumber it became pretty obvious that he had better information than anything I could match. I knew what life on the ground in Iraq was like, but SIS wasn't interested in that: they wanted contacts in Saddam Hussein's inner circle, and they obviously had someone in their pay who was pretty close to him.

Over the cold roast beef I explained that it never did journalists any good in reputational terms to be linked to intelligence organisations, and he took that in good part. By the coffee and *petits fours* stage I felt confident enough to say that, although I wouldn't reveal any details of our conversation, I would be writing about the experience of having lunch with 'M' ('C' in real life). He liked that, and I had a pleasant note from him (not in green ink) after I'd described in the *Spectator* what lunching with the spooks was like. It may have helped that I explained how good their claret had been. My feeling was that you only get into trouble for the things you hide, not the things you're open about.

For the same reason, when an attractive Czech woman whom I'd met in Prague in the early 1980s (she was a receptionist at my hotel) made contact with me later and suggested a cosy little meeting in relatively liberal, though still communist, Hungary, I wrote about it at length in the American magazine *Harper's*; but only after it had become painfully clear that Czechoslovak intelligence was behind the entire scam. They'd tried it out on at least one BBC broadcaster before, I found, only he'd foolishly tried to keep it secret.

So my advice is to say as much about these things publicly as you can, without breaking any confidences. That way, no one can use them against you; though of course if you really were working for MI6 or the CIA, I suppose it would be a clever form of cover to reveal some of the harmless details. That's the trouble with the secret world, you see: it's like a Russian doll within a doll within a doll...

Kim Philby used to keep a framed photograph of Mount Ararat on his desk at SIS headquarters. It showed a larger peak and a smaller one, side by side. If you saw it from the Turkish (i.e. NATO) side, the larger peak was on the left; if you saw it from the Armenian (i.e. Soviet) side, it was on the right. Philby's photo was taken from the Soviet side. It was a silent, jokey indication which side he was really on, but no one at MI6 ever spotted it. If they had, he would no doubt have explained it away smoothly enough.

I've known various spooks over the years, and one or two of them have been good friends. Still, I think it's essential not to get professionally involved with them. Both spies and journalists are concerned with finding things out; but while spying is about keeping things secret, journalism is about opening them up. The two simply don't mix.

Some foreign correspondents fall into the job by chance, like William Boot in Evelyn Waugh's *Scoop*, who has the same surname as a genuinely glamorous character the Editor intends to appoint. Some have known for years that this is the job they want. Robert Fisk, who famously writes from Beirut on Middle East affairs for the *Independent*, was hooked on the idea from the moment he watched a rerun of the Alfred Hitchcock film *Foreign Correspondent*, which came out in 1940. It happens not to be one of Hitchcock's better efforts; the lead character, Huntley Haverstock, played by Joel McCrea, is distinctly wooden, and the plot is an absurd one which concentrates more on espionage and adventure than on the role of a journalist in the run-up to the Second World War; and it treats correspondents with a quite absurd degree of reverence – as the quotation from the film, which appears at the start of this chapter, shows.

Nevertheless, you can see why the young Robert Fisk was attracted to it. Hitchcock has completely bought into the glamour of the foreign correspondent legend. Haverstock, a tough American crime reporter, joins forces in London with a British journalist ('Scott ffolliott') played by the smooth, witty actor George Sanders: ffolliott explains that ever since one of his ancestors was beheaded, the family has chopped the capital letter from its surname. Like Fisk, I saw the film when I was in my early teens, but it was the sophisticated and jokey George Sanders whom I liked, not the dull, earnest Joel McCrea. The very term 'foreign correspondent' brings a whiff of glamour with it, like the smell of an expensive cigar which some passer-by is smoking in the street. We associate it with trench coats, with hats elegantly pushed back on heads, with well-cut suits, and with being on first-name terms with the head waiters of good restaurants.

Not everyone reacts to this notion of the foreign correspondent with enthusiasm, of course. There was a controller of BBC2, now thankfully long gone, who when asked to renew a programme called *Correspondent* for another season, rejected it outright. The title, she said, was horrendous; it reminded her of Old Etonians in linen suits. She plainly had Scott ffolliott in mind. In fact, only a very small minority of the people who appear in these pages is an Old Etonian, and the linen suit, though popular enough in the days of Graham Greene and Ian Fleming, is less likely to feature in the journalist's wardrobe now than it did in the past. If you fly overnight in the back of the plane to, say, Nairobi wearing a linen suit, you're likely to look like something out of the ironing basket when you arrive. It certainly won't be the kind of thing you can wear on camera, or turn up in at the information ministry to get your accreditation.

Anyway, the entire picture is increasingly outdated nowadays. The money which once funded the suits, the cigars and the restaurants has long since evaporated. Most newspapers have largely sacked their foreign correspondents, relying instead on one or two staff members, one in, say, the United States and the other perhaps in the Middle East. The rest of their foreign coverage depends on local stringers, news agencies, and people sent out from London. When one leading British newspaper reported the result of the

2015 presidential election in Argentina, its story was written from Washington, only a couple of thousand miles closer than from London.

Nowadays the BBC, the German network ARD and Reuters news agency have the largest number of foreign correspondents, and all of them have had to make fierce cutbacks in recent years. Newspapers which used to be known the world over for their international reporting – *The Times*, the *New York Times*, the *Guardian*, the *Daily Telegraph*, the *Washington Post* – are now increasingly reliant on agency coverage; and the news agencies themselves have been forced to cut back. As for newspapers like the *Daily Mail* and the *Daily Express* which, hard though it may be to imagine such a thing, once used to be known for their lively and informed foreign reporting, they now seem to depend largely on rewriting stories gleaned from the internet; often adding in egregious mistakes and misspellings.

Other habits traditionally associated with the foreign correspondent are fading too. Back in the 1990s, a Serbian friend of mine, Dragan Petrovic, went to the local airport to meet a well-known British correspondent, a woman. He recognised her the moment she came through customs, and hurried forward to help with the luggage. Would she, he asked, like a coffee?

'Let's get one thing straight,' she rasped.

He was appalled. Had he come on to her too strongly? Was she going to rip him apart for suggesting they should waste time on a coffee when there was work to be done?

'First of all, I don't drink coffee, I drink Scotch. And secondly, where can I buy fags?'

This correspondent may no longer smoke, but she certainly still drinks Scotch. Yet most people who work in journalism nowadays sit at their desks throughout their lunchtime, eating a sandwich and drinking bottled water as they continue to work at their desk-top computers. The more adventurous may drink their water 'sparkling' (an ad man's word, if ever there was one). Alcohol is becoming widely disapproved of; and scarcely anyone still tells admiring stories about people who work under its influence.

Here, however, is one. I used to know a foreign correspondent – it's better, even at this late date, not to mention his name – who was on a duty visit to London from his base abroad, and was called in one evening to write a piece for the next day's paper about some looming crisis. When he'd finished he went out boozing, yet his sense of duty impelled him to drop in at the office half an hour before deadline time. He was far gone in drink, but the foreign editor managed to make him understand that the entire basis of his story had changed, and that a couple of important new developments, complicated in nature, had occurred.

'I'll do a rewrite,' said my friend thickly.

The next thing he knew, it was four in the morning and he was lying face down on the old stained carpet under the desk he had been using. He got up and staggered over to the sub-editors' desk, full of remorse and muttered promises. They gazed at him wonderingly; they remembered, as he did not, that he had rewritten his story meticulously and with complete accuracy, had finished it just in time to meet the deadline, and had then passed out under his desk the moment after handing it to them.

Today it seems to be completely unacceptable to tell this story in any spirit of admiration, though as a fairly light drinker myself I feel there is something almost Homeric about it. Here again, times have changed. Until the 1990s it was normal for journalists to drink at lunchtime, then drink more at dinnertime, and have a last couple of rounds before they left for home. At the BBC, when I joined it, the newsroom where I worked divided into two schools: one drank at the Coach and Horses, and the other at the George. I didn't go to either pub. This was noticed, and disapproved of.

'How can you fit in properly if you don't take a drink at lunchtime?' someone asked me. 'I really think you ought to come along to the old George.'

I never did fit in properly, though I'm not sure how much harm it did me in the long run.

In Michael Frayn's 1967 novel *Towards the End of the Morning*, which did for sub-editors what *Scoop* did for foreign correspondents, most of the staff on the paper (it is presumably the *Guardian*) head straight out for the pubs and restaurants at lunchtime. There are no women in their number.

> One by one and two by two the sober, responsible men emerged from the main door again to go out for lunch. The Foreign Editor, the Literary Editor, the Diplomatic Correspondent, and the Rugby Football Correspondent made up a party to share a taxi to the Garrick. . . The senior advertising men, swishing rolled umbrellas, strolled grandly off to sip hock at El Vino's. The Editor shuffled out, unnoticed by anyone, and caught a number fifteen bus to the Athenaeum.
>
> At the Gates of Jerusalem, just around the corner from Hand and Ball Court, Bob and Dyson found Bill Waddy, the News Editor, with Mike Sparrow, Ralph Absalom, Ted Hurwitz, and Andy Royle. It was that sort of set that went there. . .

You'll notice that the grandest figures (the Editor only excepted) go to the Garrick, then as now one of the more exclusive private members' clubs in London, and that they include the Foreign Editor and the Diplomatic Correspondent. The people in charge of domestic news, by contrast, head round for the local pub. At that time, every national broadsheet and broadcasting organisation regarded foreign news as being innately superior to domestic news. Nowadays they still do, marginally, although in most newsrooms domestic political reporting has become entrenched as the most important branch of the service.

In television, especially, the amount of foreign news which is broadcast is often seen as a key indicator of the seriousness of a news broadcast. When Tony Hall, who later became director-general of the BBC, was head of news in 1990 he decreed that the editors of the *Nine O'Clock News* should strive for a fifty-fifty balance between home and foreign news. It almost never managed to achieve that, partly because the overriding domestic news of the time was the fall of Margaret Thatcher and the resultant civil war in the Conservative Party. Soon, Hall's instruction was quietly forgotten. But it was a gallant effort, all the same.

Foreign news is classier than home news, not simply because it seems more complicated and often involves other languages and difficult names, but because it costs more. There are air fares and hotel bills for the correspondent, the producer and the cameraman, and all the varied charges that a television team is faced with; and there is excess baggage to pay for lighting cases, a tripod and the battery chargers, which sometimes costs an outrageous amount. Nowadays, though, one cost rarely appears: the cost of transmission from a foreign television station or facilities house. With the advent of wifi and the internet, we can now – ludicrous though it may sound to some – *email* our reports to London from almost anywhere in the world. It's a little reminiscent of the way the South African government sent the enormous Cullinan Diamond to London to be part of Edward VII's Crown Jewels in 1905. A big fuss was made as a diversion about sending the diamond by sea, accompanied by a posse of security guards, but the South Africans actually packed it in a wooden box and posted it. It arrived a few weeks later in complete safety.

Emailing a news report can involve problems, though. In the place where my team and I stay in the troubled Libyan capital, Tripoli – it's the only hotel of any size that is still open – a wifi service exists, but upstairs in the bedrooms the signal is distinctly unreliable. So in order to send our report to London my producer, Peter Leng, usually has to hang around in the gloomy, deserted lobby, peering at his computer screen for half an hour or more until the report has finally gone through. Whichever unfortunate sub-editor was given the job of hanging over the telegraph machine at the *Daily Telegraph* or the *Daily News* in the 1870s and '80s, waiting for some immensely long despatch on the latest battle in Zululand or Afghanistan, must have suffered just as much as a television producer in London now does as a foreign report comes in right at the last moment.

———

At this point, a basic definition. The foreign correspondent, in the strict sense, is a reporter who is based in a foreign country and regularly sends back news to his or her organisation. As I will try to demonstrate, foreign reporting has remained surprisingly unchanged in the 400 years the news business has been in operation.

I have been a foreign correspondent in this sense myself, though only between the years 1972 and 1978. I was based in Ireland, Brussels and Southern Africa, and ever since, although my working base has been London, I've lived in Paris and Dublin and now Oxford, and travelled to all the world's continents, Antarctica excepted. I've reported on everything from the plight of uncontacted tribes in the Amazon to the destruction of the African elephant, taking in the Iranian revolution, the Tiananmen Square massacre, the fall of the Berlin Wall, the end of apartheid and the various wars of the late twentieth and early twenty-first centuries along the way: all things I have written about at tedious length in other books. So I'm in no position to be too precious about my definition of who is and who is not a foreign correspondent; and the people whose experiences fill these pages are more often habitual travellers like me, rather than settlers in some foreign spot with their books on the shelves, their pictures on the wall, and their children at the local school.

Foreign correspondents of the traditional kind, who are sent by a news organisation to live in some significant foreign capital for three years or more, have become a species as endangered as the silver-backed gorilla. Nowadays, when you go to these places, you are much more likely to find young men and women who have thrown up their jobs in their own countries, bought a copy of a book like *The World on a String*, by Alan Goodman, John Pollack and the admirable CNN reporter Wolf Blitzer, and are renting a small flat in some cheap neighbourhood while they strengthen their grasp of the local language and send back reports to as many different outlets as they can find. As a way of documenting this tendency, the blurb for Goodman, Pollack and Blitzer's book cannot be bettered; even though it makes journalism sound like muscle development:

> Young reporters need not spend years struggling in obscurity
> to land coveted foreign assignments. In fact, technological

advances and cost-cutting at major media companies have created unprecedented opportunities for enterprising journalists to succeed abroad as freelance correspondents – stringers – for newspapers, magazines, radio, television, wire services, and internet outlets.

The World on a String: How to Become a Freelance Foreign Correspondent is the step-by-step manual that describes how to:
* choose your region wisely
* select the right equipment
* establish vital editorial contacts at home and abroad
* make ends meet while filing stories to various media
* prepare for the risks of reporting from war zones
* work effectively with distant editors.

Increasingly, in the second decade of the new century, those distant editors seem less concerned with off-the-wall stories that might interest and inform their readers, listeners and viewers, than with the dire concept of 'coverage'; which essentially means, the range of subjects that their organisation is absolutely obliged to report on. 'Coverage' is a defensive, minimalist, negative approach, which has driven out the old buccaneering notion of discovering new stories and breaking them wide open. 'Yes, but what exactly are we going to get if we agree to this?' is a question which today's foreign correspondents are asked with depressing frequency when they propose an expedition to some interesting place. Money has become so tight in the news business that there is no room for failure, nor for the so-called fishing trips that used, more often than not, to produce valuable results.

In this book I'm concerned mostly about that older kind of journalism, which made the names of a hundred foreign correspondents. Fortunately, the buccaneering spirit still exists. There are surprisingly large numbers of young, enterprising people who are prepared to give up everything that is safe and reliable in order to discover what is really going on in the world outside. And there are also various more senior figures who carry on the tradition. One can perhaps stand as an example for all of them.

In the 1980s and '90s the *Independent* was the best newspaper in Britain, and – many felt – in the world. Now, after various changes of ownership and some fairly disastrous business decisions, the *Independent* has ceased to exist as a physical entity and can only be found on the internet. Even in this reduced form, it can call on the talents of some of the finest correspondents in world journalism. There is Robert Fisk, whose highly opinionated but always interesting articles have a readership which is almost distinct from the newspaper as a whole. There is Patrick Cockburn, whose insights into some of the most dangerous places on earth, mainly in the Middle East, are unrivalled. He has written movingly about the polio he suffered from as a child, which has left him with a serious and painful limp; yet I have watched with admiration as he works in Baghdad and Kabul and other places where most other journalists would be too scared to go; and his analysis, based on this fearless personal knowledge of the situation, is unrivalled.

And then there is Kim Sengupta. Kim is the foreign correspondents' correspondent. He arrives in the latest trouble spot and is already filing while the rest of us are still trying to convince the foreign desk to let us go. Short, tough, with thinning yet still bristling hair, he always strikes me as a force of nature, a fierce engine of enquiry and investigation. Highly sociable, he is always ready to exchange information and contacts, and yet his stories always seem to have an extra element of fact which you either knew about but didn't realise was important, or never quite found out. There are a lot of my colleagues who are worthy of admiration, but I find myself admiring Kim Sengupta more than most.

He read politics and economics at London University, then after a six-month stint at a local paper, the *Romford Observer*, was given a contract, and then a job, by the *Daily Mail*. After that – his early career sounds like a tour of Fleet Street in its final years – he went to the short-lived *Today* newspaper. From there, in 1996, he was hired by the *Independent*, which had then reached its apogee, and over the years since then has worked his way through the atlas of conflict reporting: Afghanistan, Iraq, Israel/Palestine, the Balkans,

Sri Lanka, Syria, Libya, Egypt, Tunisia, Somalia, Darfur, Mali, Kashmir, Sierra Leone, Ukraine, Georgia and Northern Ireland. The list of places is impressive enough, but it's the quality and gutsiness of Kim's work which is quite extraordinary, accompanied by a gruff modesty which once typified a whole era of foreign reporting. You could imagine Kim getting on uproariously with a lot of the people I have included in this book.

'One of the more memorable stories I covered was also one that was rather unwanted,' he says in his usual understated way; 'the blowing up of our hotel in Baghdad in November 2005.'

There had been rumours going the rounds for weeks that the insurgents were planning to blow up one of the hotels where foreigners were staying. There were various of them, since most of the Western journalists who spent time in Baghdad lived outside the American-controlled Green Zone; though this didn't stop some of the less well-informed writers from explaining away their reluctance to go to Baghdad by claiming that you couldn't see anything worth reporting because you were obliged to live in the Green Zone or had to be accompanied on occasional forays outside by American troops.

None of this was true. The BBC, for instance, rented a house near the *New York Times* and Reuters news agency. At the time of writing, the BBC is still there; and the house has been home for many of us over the years. It was protected from any direct attacks, though it sometimes suffered from nearby bomb explosions. The outfits which could afford to rent houses were better funded than most of the British, French and American newspapers whose correspondents would come in and out, and spend two or three weeks at a time in Baghdad. We had full-time security people, often former Royal Marines or ex-SAS or Paras, and trusted local helpers. If you worked for the *Independent*, as Kim did, you couldn't afford such luxuries, and the newspapers found it cheaper and more convenient to put their journalists up in a hotel, usually the Hamra, and sometimes share drivers, translators and security men with other correspondents. At that time dozens of bombs were going off and hundreds of people were being killed every week. Just being in Baghdad was shockingly dangerous. When he heard the rumour of a coming attack, Kim Sengupta looked around for another hotel, but the Hamra had a good safety record and seemed well enough protected.

Not so. At 8.20 on the morning of 19 November a truck packed out with explosives was driven into the blast wall at the back of the hotel, smashing it to bits. The plan was for a second truck with even more explosives on board to drive through the gap into the hotel complex and blow itself up; that would have brought down the building, killing those inside. It became a fairly common tactic. But the first truck had been packed with so much ordnance (around 400 pounds, it was later estimated), that it gouged out a crater in the ground too deep for the second truck, a two-and-half-ton flatbed with a thousand pounds of explosives on board, to be able to get through. As a result the second driver blew up his explosive load, and himself, a little way from the main hotel building. Many of the adjoining houses collapsed, and more than sixty people died – mostly hotel employees and their families. The journalists, who were the real targets, escaped the worst of the explosion; Kim Sengupta among them. As he later described it in a letter to me:

> I was lying in bed reading when the blasts took place. The windows exploded and a horizontal shower of jagged glass flew across the room over me. My lethargy had saved me: I would have been seriously injured or worse if I had been up and about: I only got some cuts and bruises instead.
>
> There was wild gunfire which always seemed to follow bombs in Baghdad at the time. We went out after it had died down and found bits of the bombers' bodies: a piece of scalp in the swimming pool with thick black bristly hair; a penis in a rose bush.

It was often hard at this time to know which group had carried out a particular bombing. There was an atmosphere in Baghdad which reminded me of the slogan of the ultra-right in the Spanish

Civil War: 'Long live death'. Why should Western journalists have been targeted? At this stage (things changed later) they weren't seen as an enemy; they were thought to be useful in telling the outside world what was going on. The local American commander, Brigadier General Karl Horst, educated and well informed, arrived with some of his men and examined the wrecks of the two lorries and the damage they had wrought. Standing in a puddle made by the shattered water pipes, Kim and his colleagues asked him why the Sunni insurgents would want to do this.

'What makes you think it was the Sunnis?' the general asked; and he told them he thought the bombing had been organised by some leading figures in the interior ministry who were fed up with the kind of reporting people like Kim were doing at the time about death squads run by the mostly Shi'a government:

> Just a few days earlier there had been uproar after we had described how 169 beaten and starving captives had been found in an underground prison run by the Shia Badr militia, which controlled part of the Interior Ministry. Bayan Jabr, the Minister of the Interior, was himself a former Badr commander.

In the extraordinarily convoluted conditions of the time, the attack could well have been organised by some middle-man who had persuaded a couple of Sunnis to drive the trucks. It was noticeable that no one claimed responsibility for the Hamra bomb: that was rare at the time.

Most Western journalists in Baghdad were content to report the explosion and move on to other things; there was no shortage of death and destruction to cover. Kim, in his characteristically stubborn way, wasn't prepared to let it go. With the help of one or two others he carried out an investigation into what had lain behind the attack. Though it was difficult and sometimes dangerous, he felt in the end he had discovered the identity of the man responsible for ordering the attack. It was a senior government figure.

After a lot of reflection, Kim decided not to write the story. If it had appeared, he would have gone home safely enough at the end of his tour of duty; but the people who had helped him, plus his Iraqi fixer and his drivers, would have been left in Baghdad with no protection whatever. A man who had decided to blow up an entire hotel filled with foreign journalists wouldn't have thought twice about killing off a few Iraqis.

Still, Kim didn't forget about it. Some years later he met this man, who was still an influential member of the Iraqi government, at a diplomatic reception in London:

> Fuelled by several gin and tonics earlier in the evening, I told him, while reminiscing about Baghdad days, that there was a strong rumour he had been the one who had organised the Hamra bombing. There were sharp intakes of breath all around us, and the Iraqi minders tried to usher the VIP off.
>
> He, however, waved them away. Unfazed, coolness personified, he pinched the bridge of his nose as if trying hard to recall; and then he asked, 'Remind me again, which month was the Hamra bombing?'

Not every foreign correspondent has Kim's grit and determination, but most of them seem to share his freebooting approach to life and his sociability. In writing of their lives and experiences I have concentrated mostly on English-speaking correspondents, because I know them best. But it would be easy to fill another book with stories about leading French, Italian and Russian correspondents – often the bravest and best-travelled foreign reporters of all, in my experience. Far from the influence of the health and safety departments which every news organisation now seems to employ, foreign correspondents are able to demonstrate their independence of mind, and to dig out the stories which are their lifeblood. It's all very much in the spirit of James Elroy Flecker's poem 'The Golden Journey to Samarkand':

> We are the Pilgrims, master; we shall go
>   Always a little further; it may be
> Beyond that last blue mountain barred with snow
>   Across that angry or that glimmering sea.

Those four lines are, I'm told (for I've never been there to see them for myself), inscribed at the base of the clock tower at the 22 Special Air Service (SAS) barracks in Hereford. But there's another stanza from the poem which has a particular attraction for the foreign correspondent, the archetypical seeker after things which people and governments want to keep hidden:

> We travel not for trafficking alone;
>   By hotter winds our hearts are fanned:
> For lust of knowing what should not be known
>   We take the Golden Road to Samarkand.

And if that's not glamorous, I don't know what is.

TWO

Palaeojournalism

MIRTH: But how like you the newes?
CENSURE: O, they are monstrous! Scurvy! And stale!
And too exotick! Ill cook'd and ill-dish'd!
Ben Jonson, *The Staple of News*, 1625

IN THE BEGINNING, FOREIGN news was the only news that was fit to print.

The first example we know of in English of a daily newspaper dates from 1620. As a result of an order by Queen Elizabeth I's Privy Council back in 1586, no domestic news could be printed for public circulation, so the earliest news-sheets which appeared in England concentrated exclusively on what was happening abroad. For news about events at home you had to rely on gossip, private letters, the work of balladeers, sermons and official pronouncements. The differences with today's news reporting could scarcely be greater; and yet it's remarkable how many of the journalistic habits and practices of our own day were established right from the very start; rather as the late Elizabethan and Jacobean theatre established traditions which we can still see in the theatre today.

The man who founded English journalism was a printer called Nathaniel Butter. He followed his father into the book trade, and in 1608 published the first quarto of Shakespeare's *King Lear*. From the evidence of his work over the years, Butter seems to have been a lively-minded, innovative character, and he was often prosecuted and punished for challenging officialdom. In 1620 he was in gaol for publishing a pamphlet which claimed the Holy Roman

Emperor, Ferdinand II, had been born of an incestuous relationship; there was always a distinctly tabloid streak in Nathaniel Butter. While he was inside, something arrived in London from the Netherlands to catch the attention of the population: a news-sheet, written in an approximation of English, published in Amsterdam by a Dutch map-engraver called Pieter van den Keere, and sent to London for sale. The word used to describe it at the time was *coranto*, which was associated with 'courier' and 'current'. The first edition which is known to survive is dated 2 December 1620, and is a single folio sheet.

As it happens, it contains news of international importance, about the run-up to an event which would affect Europe for centuries to come: the battle of the White Mountain, outside Prague. When the battle took place, the Catholic Emperor Ferdinand (whom Nathaniel Butter had slandered) wiped out the forces of the Protestant Frederick V of Bohemia. Frederick's wife was the daughter of James I of England and VI of Scotland, which meant that Britain was disturbingly close to getting involved in what became the Thirty Years' War. At the White Mountain, Bohemia lost its independence for 300 years.

The lead story in this first surviving English *coranto* is datelined Prague on 5 November, and was written just before the battle took place: 'Three days agone are passed by, a mile from this Cittie 6000 Hungarians (chosen out Soldiers) under the General Rediferens, which are gon to our Head-camp, & the Enimie lieth yet near unto ours…' Pieter van den Keere's language has clearly been picked out of a Dutch–English dictionary. Still, despite its grindingly awkward phrasing, this is the first known despatch in British journalism.

In the spring of the following year, 1621, the first English-produced *coranto* appeared. Printed by Thomas Archer, whose workshop was in Pope's Head Alley, Cornhill, it was just a translation from the Dutch. A few months later, in September, Archer was thrown in gaol for publishing his *corantos* without a government licence.

At this point Nathaniel Butter, newly out of gaol, applied for and was given a licence to publish *corantos* of his own, from his bookshop at the Pied Bull near St Austin's Gate, an alleyway lead-ing into St Paul's Churchyard in London. Characteristically, he had spotted a gap in the market.

The Pied Bull became a major clearing house for information. If you wanted to know what was happening in the outside world, this was where you gravitated. Some extremely knowledgeable people hung out there, among them John Pory (1572–1636), who qualifies as Britain's first foreign correspondent.

A Cambridge graduate and a Member of Parliament, Pory was one of the early seventeenth century's great travellers. At first his journeys took him to France, the Low Countries and Italy, and over the following years he settled in Constantinople. After that he grew even more adventurous, and crossed the Atlantic to Virginia, where he was secretary to the governor, Sir George Yeardley. He stayed there from 1619 to 1621, then went back two years later to be the first speaker of the Virginia Assembly. In 1624 he returned to London, where he had a large circle of friends: Richard Hakluyt, John Donne, William Camden, Sir Robert Cotton, and, later on, John Milton. One of his books was a source for Shakespeare's *Othello*, while Ben Jonson based *The Masque of Blackness* on another.

There were various well-informed correspondents around at the time: John Chamberlain (1553–1628), for example, had an equally wide range of friends and informants, and was a shrewd observer of the world. He went to St Paul's Cathedral every day, and wandered round the nave and aisles networking with people who came there because they too were interested in what was going on. The sellers of pamphlets and news-sheets also hung out in the cathedral, sell-ing their wares, and the book-stalls outside in St Paul's Churchyard offered more pamphlets and the latest books. The cathedral and its surroundings constituted a kind of stock exchange of news and gossip, and a friendly, inquisitive man like Chamberlain was good at listening to people with information to impart, and passing it on to others.

On 24 September 1621 the visitors to Nathaniel Butter's Pied Bull would have found a brand new item of interest on sale: his first news-sheet. Entitled *Corante, or, News from Italy, Germany,*

Hungarie, Spaine and France, and signed 'N. B.', it was printed on one side only, and consisted of a few short paragraphs. Soon, though, Butter became more ambitious. He gave up single news-sheets in favour of something more like a modern magazine. It is the size of a quarto book, though unbound, and contained anything from eight to twenty-four pages. This was easy to carry around, and became known as a 'newsbook', or a 'book of news'.

Butter had an orderly mind, and from the start he numbered and dated his editions; something no one else seems to have thought of doing. He also introduced the headline to European journalism.

Nouemb. 16. 1622   Numb. 7

A
CONTINVATION
OF THE NEVVES OF
this present *Weeke.*

Wherin are fully related, the going of the
Emperour and the Princes of *Germany,* to the
Dyet of Regenspurgh, *with the Imperiall Gifts.*

The Embassage of *Bethlem Gabor,* and the old
Count *Thourne,* to solicite the great Turke for
aide against the Emperour.

With the resolute holding out of the Siege of *Glatz.*

Together with the Articles granted to Generall V E E R E, *upon* yeelding up
of MANHEIM Castle.

And a particular Iournall of Count M A N S F I E L D S
proceedings in the Bishopricke of *Munster,* with
some other Occurences.

LONDON,

Printed for Nathaniel Butter, Nicholas Bourne, and
William Sheffard, 1622.

Butter knew how to attract a readership. On 15 July 1622 he announced:

> The strangling and death of the great *Turke*, and his two sonnes.
>   With the strange preservation and deliverance of his uncle
> Mustapha from *perishing in prison, with hunger and* thirst, ...
>   A wonderfull story, and the like never heard of in our
>   *moderne times.*

At the end of the newsbook is a promise that the next week's edition will contain more details of this story.

Butter was meticulous about correcting his mistakes. After a report about an attack by the Prince of Orange on the town of Cleves, in Westphalia, this appears: 'Errata. In page 8 for, hath razed the Castle and Towne down to the ground: read, hath razed the Castle downe to the ground.'

Soon, he was a familiar and significant figure in London, and attracted the attention of the cantankerous Ben Jonson. In 1625 Jonson's satire, *The Staple of Newes*, appeared on stage, with Nathaniel Butter lampooned in it as Cymbal, the manager of the news exchange. Perhaps Jonson gave him the name because he was loud and discordant.

The play contains the first account in English of a newsroom, as well as the first references to correspondents, foreign and domestic. (The domestic correspondents would have fed their material into Butter's news exchange, but only the foreign news could be printed at this stage.) Act 1, scene 4 is set in Butter/Cymbal's newspaper office:

> REGISTER: What, are those Desks fit now? Set forth the Table,
> The Carpet and the Chayre: where are the *Newes* That were
> examin'd last? Ha' you fil'd them up?
> CLERKE: Not yet, I had no time.
> REGISTER: Are those Newes registred
> That *Emissary Buz* sent in last night
> Of *Spinola, and his Egges?*
> CLERKE: Yes Sir, and fil'd.
> REGISTER: What are you now vpon?
> CLERKE: That our new *Emissary Westminster* gaue

us, of the *Golden Heyre.*
REGISTER: Dispatch, that's newes indeed, and of
importance.

The 'emissaries' are correspondents, and 'Emissary Westminster' is
clearly Cymbal's political correspondent. Emissary Buz is one of his
foreign correspondents. Buz's main job would have been to report
on the doings of Ambrogio Spinola, the Genoese aristocrat who
served as one of the King of Spain's finest generals. *The Staple of
Newes* was, suitably enough, bang up to date. In June 1625, immediately before the play opened in London, Spinola had captured
the strategic Dutch town of Breda. What his eggs were, is anyone's
guess: some sort of explosive, maybe?

The scene continues with a take-off by Jonson on the way people
have become addicted to news.

REGISTER: What would you haue good woman?
WOMAN: I would haue Sir,
A groatsworth of any Newes, I care not what,
To carry down this *Saturday,* to our *Vicar.*
REGISTER: O! You are a Butterwoman, aske Nathaniel
The *Clerke,* there.
CLERKE: Sir, I tell her, she must stay
Till *Emissary Exchange,* or *Paul's* send in
And then I'll fit her.

These emissaries are two more correspondents, one based at the
Royal Exchange and the other at St Paul's, the main centres for
gossip and information in London. 'Butterwoman' and 'Nathaniel'
are jokey references to Nathaniel Butter. 'Send in' sounds like
the agency's jargon for 'file a report'. Butter's achievements and
fame were hard bought. He was gaoled again in 1627, by which
time the news business was proving increasingly difficult and
dangerous. In October 1632 the Privy Council ordered Butter
and his partner, Nicholas Bourne, to stop publishing their weekly
newsbooks, because the ambassadors of France and Spain had

complained about the stories they had published. Butter was experiencing the kind of political problems which editors down the ages have known.

Soon England was heading irrevocably into civil war. Butter had to mortgage many of his copyrights, and, once fighting broke out, he was tried for sedition and imprisoned yet again. By 1649 he was forced to get rid of his prime location at the Pied Bull, and set up shop in down-market Cursitors' Alley. Two years later the Stationers' Company used its poor fund to get him out of prison. He turned up with embarrassing regularity at the company's meetings, pleading for help, and in 1662 was on the waiting list for Sutton House, an almshouse for the old and poor. He never got there. On 22 February 1664, shortly after his eighty-first birthday, one of the newspapers (now free to publish again) announced the passing of the inventor of the British news industry: 'Nath. Butter, an old stationer, died very poore.'

The first British foreign correspondent in the modern sense was a charming polymath, Henry Crabb Robinson (1775–1867), who became better known for his friendships than for his reporting. *The Times* took the innovative step of sending him to report from Germany and Denmark at the height of the Napoleonic Wars. By this time Robinson had developed a dazzling range of contacts including William Wordsworth, Samuel Taylor Coleridge, Charles and Mary Lamb, William Hazlitt, Robert Southey and William Blake in England, and Johann Wolfgang von Goethe, Friedrich Schiller and Johann Gottfried Herder in Germany. And although he had little formal education, Robinson became one of the founders of University College, London.

He was born in 1775 in the pleasant Suffolk town of Bury St Edmunds, the son of a reasonably well-to-do nonconformist. Since this meant he was barred from going to any of the big public schools or to university, he was articled to a lawyer in Colchester. When the

French Revolution broke out in 1789 he was delighted, though the news of the execution of Louis XVI and Marie Antoinette changed his mind. All the same, he was an instinctive radical, a democrat, and a lifelong defender of human rights. He spent five years in Germany from 1800, studying and travelling, then moved to London and went to live with a friend of his, John Dyer Collier, a reporter on *The Times*.

The editor of *The Times*, John Walter, was only thirty, but he had already established an impressive independence for the paper. He infuriated Pitt, the prime minister, by refusing to support the government. Walter's father, John senior, had been editor before him, and had printed as much continental news as he could get hold of, realising that at a time of such international turmoil, foreign news would be good for sales.

John Dyer Collier convinced Walter junior that Robinson's fluent German and easy manner would make him a good foreign correspondent; and Walter offered to send him to Altona to cover events there for *The Times*. Altona is nowadays a pleasant suburb of Hamburg, but from 1640 to 1864 it was the capital of the Danish province of Holstein. It was a useful listening post, and Robinson's main job was to cover the military and diplomatic manoeuvrings of Napoleon and the Russian Tsar, Alexander I.

Robinson was habitually short of money, and he jumped at the offer. It was the first time a British citizen had been based abroad specifically to work as a foreign correspondent. He wrote his stories about the politics of central and northern Europe in a daily letter to his editor, and sent it via the Royal Danish Post. A week or so later, the letter would reach the offices of *The Times* in Printing House Square, Blackfriars, and would appear in the paper the following day.

Robinson reported from a distance on the battle of Friedland, in which Napoleon demolished the Russian army of Alexander I, and on the punitive Treaty of Tilsit which followed. Soon afterwards British forces landed in Denmark, and the authorities in Altona were ordered to arrest every British citizen. Robinson was tipped off by a friend, and insisted on warning every one of his fellow countrymen in the town before getting out himself, posing as a teacher. He reached Hamburg, and found he was wanted for espionage by the authorities there. He escaped to the neighbouring state of Mecklenburgh, where he was safe for a while. Soon, though, while Robinson was taking a swim in the sea, the reigning Duke of Mecklenburgh-Schwerin (one of his many contacts) hurried down in person to warn him that 10,000 French soldiers had landed and that he was in grave danger. The duke pulled him out of the water, and Robinson, after thanking him profusely and drying off, escaped to Stockholm. The very first British foreign correspondent had started his journalistic career in a way that large numbers of his successors over the years would recognise: that is, by a combination of chance and some useful contacts, and a touch of excitement.

John Walter, his editor, was delighted with Robinson's efforts. He offered him a post as 'a sort of Foreign Editor', translating stories from the international press and writing articles about foreign affairs. At £500 a year his salary was generous, and for good measure Walter made him the paper's drama critic, a job he found particularly congenial. But directly the uprising in Spain against the French broke out in 1808, Walter offered him a second foreign posting. 'Who so fit to write from the shores of the Bay of Biscay,' his letter said, 'as he who had successfully written from the banks of the Elbe?'

Robinson was reluctant. He was just starting to get to know and appreciate Coleridge and Wordsworth, and his social and literary life in London was blossoming. Finally, though, he accepted, and a ship called *The Black Joke* took him to Corunna at the end of July 1808. He was occasionally invited to a formal *tertulia*, or social gathering of the local gentry:

> The ladies sit with their backs against the wall on an elevated floor. . . The gentlemen sit before them, each cavalier on a very small straw-bottomed chair before his *dama*, and often with his guitar on which he klimpers, and, if report say true, by aid of which he can make love undetected. . .

As well as being a lively writer, Robinson had the other key quality which every correspondent requires: luck. Just as he was developing some good sources among the local Spanish nobility and the British officers who were advising the Spanish army, the story began to heat up. The French, in overwhelming numbers, advanced on Corunna and found the British forces much weakened by sickness. General Sir John Moore, a Glaswegian, staged a brilliant fighting retreat, but was struck by a cannonball during the final battle outside Corunna. He stayed alive long enough to know that he had won a key victory, which allowed the British army, Dunkirk-like, to withdraw undefeated and fight again elsewhere. His fate used to be known to generations of British schoolchildren because of the poem 'The Burial of Sir John Moore after Corunna', by Charles Wolfe:

Not a drum was heard, not a funeral note,
    As his corse to the rampart we hurried;
Not a soldier discharged his farewell shot
    O'er the grave where our hero we buried.

This campaign was Henry Crabb Robinson's first really big story, and his despatches were read eagerly back at home:

6 January 1809: On whichever side we look, we see cause for distress; the enemy advancing in the front, Portugal abandoned to the right, the Asturias defenceless to the left, and in the distance uncertainty and obscurity.

8 January: The peril is drawing nigh, and the apprehensions and fears of the unmilitary are therefore increased... There is a strong sentiment in favour of the English troops, notwithstanding their retreat. This has relieved our minds of a great embarrassment...

11 January: Famine stares us in the face.

Robinson behaved with courage throughout. He bought a cargo boat and sheltered refugees on it, remaining on shore until the last British civilian had been taken off. The British ships were fired on by the French, but he got away safely.

His reports had made *The Times* required reading back at home. All the same, office politics – one of the foreign correspondent's greatest problems – had made his position more difficult. His friend Collier had fallen out with the editor, John Walter, and was about to become a reporter on the rival *Chronicle*. Walter remained friendly with Robinson and was grateful to him for what he'd done, but had no more work for him as a foreign correspondent.

He went back to being foreign editor, though after his exciting experiences in Corunna it can't have held much interest for him. After a few months he resigned. He wanted a change:

> I left my post in good spirits. My acquaintances were become numerous and respectable. . . My income, tho' narrow, amounted to an independence, and I had acquired a confidence in myself. Not that I ever thought highly of my talents – but I was conscious of possessing what will often supply their place – high animal spirits, strength of body and good health.

He walked out of journalism at the age of thirty-four, and went to the Middle Temple to train as a lawyer. Nowadays, if Henry Crabb Robinson is remembered for anything, it's for his reminiscences of his impressive collection of literary friends. But he had most if not all the qualities which make a first-class correspondent. He got on easily with people, even awkward, cantankerous characters like Wordsworth and Blake. He was a good listener who observed and wrote with sharpness and clarity.

Even at the end of his life, sixty years later, he was an excellent host, selecting his guests with great care to make sure they got on with each other. People such as Matthew Arnold, William de Morgan and Walter Bagehot remained with him until the end. He died in 1867 at the age of ninety-one – fifty-seven years after abandoning the profession of foreign correspondent which he had single-handedly created.

It took a major war between Russia on one side and Britain, France and Turkey on the other for a British journalist to become famous across the world.

William Howard Russell was one of the finest journalists who ever wrote a dispatch; yet he had no training whatever for the job. As he said, and as we are still inclined to say, 'he fell into it'. He was born in 1821, the son of a Protestant father and a Catholic mother, in Jobstown, Tallaght, then a village outside Dublin. When his parents left to start a business in England, William stayed in Ireland with his grandparents and went to Trinity College, Dublin.

In 1841 he was still uncertain what he should do in life. At that point his cousin Robert Russell, whom William had never previously met, was sent to Dublin by *The Times* to organise the coverage of the coming elections in Ireland, which were to prove critical for the balance of power at Westminster. Robert sought out his cousin: 'You will have a pleasant time of it if you will do the work – letters [of introduction] to the best people, one guinea a day and your hotel expenses. Will you start next week?'

The luck which never seems to fail the successful correspondent had made its appearance. Russell didn't hesitate, and headed to Longford to report on the campaign there.

He arrived late, and so missed the rioting which had taken place earlier in the day; but he had the bright idea of going round to the local hospital to see the aftermath.

The BBC's Kate Adie did precisely that in June 1989 when the Chinese army started firing at demonstrators around Tiananmen Square, and the results of her enterprise were shocking and memorable. Russell was probably the first journalist in history to have tried out this tactic, and he was always proud afterwards of his flash of imagination. He talked to the injured on both sides – another characteristic of his lifelong approach – and got a fairly clear picture of what had happened.

That night he went to a dinner at the Tory headquarters and was listening to a rousing speech from the local Protestant clergyman when some of the opposition roughs started throwing bricks and paving stones through the window. In spite of all the distractions he demonstrated another key ability: he managed to file his report, an article several hundred words long, for *The Times*. It was excitable, inclined to stress the first person singular, and didn't worry much about political objectivity; but it still has a fine sense of drama:

> I have this moment returned from a visit to the Infirmary and never was I more affected than I was by the horrid sights I witnessed... I regret to say I have to record an atrocious attack made this day upon a harmless young gentleman named King, who, while standing near his own house in the middle of the day not twenty yards from the barracks, and within a hundred yards of an immense force of military and police, was attacked by a number of pitiless miscreants, beaten, trampled under foot, and left helpless on the road. He is now, or rather his inanimate body is, lying in the Infirmary, his life despaired... It being extremely dangerous to leave the parts of the streets lined with the military, I cannot procure accurate information as to the state of the suburbs; in fact, I have been warned that I am a marked man.

Any number of leading reporters of my generation cut their teeth on the troubles in Northern Ireland from 1968 onwards, among them Max Hastings, Robert Fisk, Gerald Seymour, Keith Graves, Martin Bell, Michael Sullivan, John Bierman, Michael Nicholson, Peter Taylor, Jonathan Dimbleby and Denis Murray. I myself spent five years reporting on the troubles from 1970 onwards. Every one of us, and all the others who deserve mention, could have written an equivalent of William Howard Russell's despatch, though hopefully with fewer 'I's and less partisanship. All the same, *The Times* was delighted with it: 'Your work is capital, a most effective description.'

He made his way to London, where his cousin Robert advised him to learn shorthand. Once he had done that, the editor of *The Times*, J. T. Delane, offered him a job as a reporter in the House of Commons press gallery. He started work in 1842. But there was a problem: *The Times* would only pay him when Parliament was sitting. In the recesses he was out of a job.

He was rescued by Irish politics. Daniel O'Connell, 'the Liberator', was campaigning in Ireland for the repeal of the union with Great Britain, attracting vast crowds wherever he went and often whipping them up to great heights of passion. What made Russell such a powerful reporter, right from the start, was his ability to sum up his subject in broad terms, while including the small, telling detail:

> I have never heard any orator who made so great an impression on me as O'Connell. It was not his argument, for it was often worthless, nor his language, which was frequently inelegant. It was his immense passion, his pathos, his fiery indignation. At first sight one was tempted to laugh at the green cloth cap, with the broad gold band set on the top of his curly wig – his round chin buried deep in the collar of a remarkable compromise between a travelling cloak and a frock, green and ornamented with large gilt buttons; but when he rose to speak with imperious gestures for silence, and was 'off', in a few minutes the spell began to work; the orator was revealed.

Anyone who has reported politics in Ireland, north or south, knows how intimate a world it is. The politicos, the journalists, the followers, the thugs, all know one another. Reporting public appearances by the Reverend Ian Paisley in the early part of the Northern Ireland troubles could be a frightening business. 'There are three gentlemen here from the BBC sittin' here in the front row,' he would say, pointing at us. 'I'm tellin' you now, I don't want a hair of their head touched.'

The crowd would always roar with laughter: this meant that Paisley would have deniability for anything that might happen afterwards. As a result you could usually expect to be roughed up, or at least given a kicking. At his rallies Paisley was particularly keen to point out Martin Bell, who was the leading BBC television reporter covering Northern Ireland. 'Mr Bell of the BBC has been reporting untruths yet again,' he would say, and the audience would hiss and groan. The untruths might be an entirely accurate account of some act of violence carried out by Paisley's supporters at a previous rally, or they might simply be a more realistic estimate of the size of the crowd (usually supplied by the police) than Paisley's own followers liked.

A hundred and thirty years before Ian Paisley roared at Martin Bell over the microphone, William Howard Russell had similar problems with Daniel O'Connell: '[H]e did not bridle his tongue when he had to speak of the organs of "the base, bloody and brutal Whigs". "Let Mr Russell past, boys!. . . The young gentleman, I daresay, does not like being a *Times*-server after all" (laughter).'

Once, as we headed out to yet another one of Paisley's meetings, I asked Martin Bell if he was nervous. In those days I was much in awe of Martin, and I find I jotted down his reply in my notebook afterwards: 'They can be pretty frightening,' he said, 'but you always have to remember that your job is to tell people back home what these things are like – it isn't to be nice to the people here.'

I felt better after that. The important thing wasn't to protect my own skin; it was to report what was going on.

In January 1844 Russell got into serious trouble with *The Times* because he ruined the paper's expensive efforts to get exclusive coverage of the result of O'Connell's trial for sedition. There was intense competition between the various London newspapers over the story and, at that time, before the advent of the telegraph, the only way to get the story to London was to take it there physically. *The Times*'s great rival in London, the *Morning Herald*, accordingly hired a small steam yacht and kept it waiting in the port of Kingstown, now Dún Laoghaire, to whisk their correspondent across the Irish Sea to Holyhead, and thence to London by train. *The Times* went one better: it found a newly built steamship, *The Iron Duke*, which could make the journey much faster.

The jury took hours to reach its verdict; but in the end the foreman announced that Daniel O'Connell was guilty. Although Russell had laid on a special train at the nearest Dublin station, the delay had given the station master the impression that it wouldn't be needed that night, and he had allowed the driver to go off for a beer. In the end the station master found him, and the train moved out. Russell was the only passenger, with his bags, a large notebook full of drawings and jottings, and a light overcoat. It was gone midnight when he reached Dún Laoghaire, and there was no one to meet him at the pier; the *Iron Duke*'s crew had also got it into their heads that nothing would happen that night. It took them an hour to gather together and get up steam, but they made excellent speed across the Irish Sea, and Russell was soon on board another special train, from Holyhead to London.

He was exhausted and his boots were painfully tight, so he kicked them off. The next thing he knew, the train had arrived at Euston and he was being shaken awake by the office messenger of *The Times*. The messenger looked at Russell's discarded boots. 'You put them on in the cab,' he said, and added: 'They [the editorial staff] are in a dreadful state waiting at the office!' It took Russell the entire cab journey to get just one of his boots on, so when they reached Printing House Square, he had to hop out of the vehicle. A man who was hanging around there came up to him and whispered: 'We are glad to hear they've found O'Connell guilty at last.' Russell, distracted by his boot problem and assuming the man was a fellow employee of *The Times*, replied artlessly: 'Oh, yes! All guilty, but on different counts.' Then he hopped into the office and handed over his copy to the editor. By 4.20 in the morning, with everything finished, Russell slipped out to a nearby hotel to get some sleep.

He was awakened at noon by an angry note from *The Times*: 'You managed very badly. The *Morning Herald* has got the verdict!'

Although the *Herald* had been soundly beaten in the race across the Irish Sea, it had stationed one of its reporters outside Printing House Square to wheedle the result out of Russell. It then put out a reasonably accurate guess about what had happened, and undercut the exclusive which *The Times* had spent so much money obtaining.

Delane warned Russell that he was lucky not to be sacked. Then he gave him a piece of advice: 'Keep your lips closed and your eyes open. Never speak about your business. Commit it to paper for the editor, and for him alone.'

A hundred and thirty years later, in what was then Rhodesia, Brian Barron, one of the best foreign correspondents the BBC ever had, told me why he was turning down an invitation to dinner that night with the team from ITN. 'We've got to get up really early to go to Bulawayo for a story. Someone's bound to let it slip at dinner. That way the ITN guys will know we're going to do something, and they might even guess what it is, and get there first. So never tell anyone anything, is my advice.'

I never forgot it.

William Howard Russell stayed with *The Times,* and over the years that followed he covered many interesting, but not particularly important, stories. One evening in February 1854 he was sitting at his desk at Printing House Square when a messenger came over to him and said the editor wanted to see him straight away.

Russell discovered, when he sat down in Delane's office, that he was to be sent on what sounded like an enjoyable voyage to the Mediterranean. The British government wanted to demonstrate its support for France and Turkey in their dispute with Russia over the control of the major sites in the Holy Land, and it had been decided to send a detachment of the Coldstream Guards to Malta to make the point. Everything would, Delane said soothingly, be made as easy and as comfortable for him as possible, and his pay and allowances would be generous. Russell was worried about losing the occasional briefs he received as a part-time barrister, but Delane had his answer ready: 'There is not the least chance of that; you will be back at Easter, depend upon it, and you will have a pleasant trip.'

Did Delane know that a major war was coming? Nobody else at that point seemed to, including the British, French and Russian governments, so the answer is presumably not. But Delane was known for his shrewd judgement, and at that stage he had been editor of *The Times* for thirteen years (altogether he was in the post from 1841 to 1877); instinct clearly told him to be prepared. He gave Russell whatever assurances he needed to hear, knowing that Russell's inclination as a journalist was to go anyway.

Shortly before he left London, a group of Russell's friends from the Garrick Club gave him a farewell dinner in a private room at the Albion pub in New Bridge Street, just round the corner from Fleet Street. The faces around the table included those of Charles Dickens and William Thackeray, who were working on the serialisation of *Hard Times* and *The Newcomes* respectively. The guests sang songs and recited comic verses in Russell's honour. 'These particular verses fell below even the standard observed by the warm-hearted but inefficient rhymesters who generally step in on valedictory occasions,' commented Russell's biographer, J. B. Atkins, severely.

From Valletta, Russell wrote his wife the kind of letter which foreign correspondents usually do write to their partners at times like this: 'I am glad to be able to tell you it is generally believed that our troops will never see a shot fired.'

He was wrong. The crisis deepened, and Russell sailed on to Gallipoli, sending back despatches about life with the British army. Even before there was any fighting, he spotted signs of gross mismanagement and a shocking lack of preparation for dealing with the sick and wounded. At first he wrote about it privately to Delane, but at last he broke into print: 'Let us have an overwhelming army of medical men to combat disease. Let us have a staff, full and strong, of young and active and experienced men. Do not suffer our soldiers to be killed by antiquated imbecility.'

The result of these reports was predictable: Lord Raglan, who was in overall command, refused to give official recognition to Russell and the rest of the press, or to assist them in any way.

If Russell had kept quiet about the inadequacies of the army's organisation, Raglan might have started to offer him some help.

But Russell never hesitated. His reporting, over the following months, would do immense damage to Raglan, the War Office and the Cabinet, and eventually brought down the government of Lord Aberdeen. Throughout, Delane gave him every support.

The day before the first battle, at the Alma, Russell was hauled in front of General Pennefather. 'By —, sir,' said the general, 'I had as soon see the devil!' But Russell's charm soon started to work. 'You're an Irishman, I'll be bound,' Pennefather said. 'Are you from Limerick?' 'No, sir; but my family are.' 'Well, goodbye. . . There will be wigs on the green today, my boy, so keep away from the front if you don't want to have your nose cut short.'

None of the senior officers wanted to have Russell around, and he was always being waved away. Afterwards, Russell always felt that this had prevented him from observing the battles properly. Yet there never is a right place to report on a war. The most any individual correspondent can do is to describe what he or she has seen, and pick up the rest afterwards. It was extraordinarily difficult for him to work out what was going on, and in the early stages of the war Russell had no idea about the effect which his despatches would have, back home in Britain: 'I did not then grasp the fact that I had it in my power to give a halo of glory to some unknown warrior by putting his name in type.'

Russell, charming, funny and without any form of snobbery, was as welcome in the tents of the ordinary private soldiers as he was among the officers – and eventually among the generals. He had a ready sympathy for the injured and sick on both sides, and told his readers in detail about the sufferings of the Russians, Turks and French when he came across them on the field of battle or in hospital; while his descriptions of the privations endured by British soldiers helped to change the entire way the army was run.

But the quality which made Russell the force he soon became was an unstoppable determination to find out precisely what was going on; and because he got his information from everyone, from the generals to the private soldiers, he wrote with real insight. At Balaclava in October 1854, he watched the Charge of the Light Brigade from the heights above the battlefield. But directly it was over he rode down to the vast plain where the charge had taken place, talking to the wounded and the survivors and trying to comprehend the whole inexplicable business. The men who had taken part in it had no clear understanding themselves of what they had been through; his sense of it, gained from several hundred yards away, was often better than theirs. He went from tent to tent, trying to find out what had happened to friends and acquaintances of his who had taken part in the charge. He found the survivors deep in a sense of anger and gloom; it had been 'all for nothing', they kept telling him. 'They had not the least idea,' he wrote, 'of the immense kudos they had gained for ever.'

Back at his own tent at headquarters, on the broad ridge above the battlefield, he found the staff officers arguing about what had happened. It was now evening, and the mail would be leaving in a few hours' time. Russell was exhausted. He had eaten nothing since morning, and was suffering from a particularly bad headache. Above all, everything he had seen and heard made him deeply depressed. Yet he had to write his report. It was the biggest story of his entire career.

Russell's writing conditions were difficult. He shared the tent with several officers, who were all just as exhausted as he was and were desperate to sleep. He had to sit on his horse's saddle because there were no chairs, and write on his knees by the light of a candle stuck in a wine bottle. He said later that he carried on until the candle 'disappeared in the bottle like a stage demon through a trap door'.

He wrote around 4,000 words in all, though not all of what he wrote appeared in print at the time. The despatch, which was packaged up with several others of his, went by sea and railway, and took nineteen days to reach London. It just made it into the second, London, edition of *The Times* on Monday 13 November 1854, but Delane decided that it should appear again in Tuesday's paper, so that the rest of the country could read it.

As ever, the first few pages of the paper were devoted to adver-
tisements, and to lesser items of mostly domestic news. The top
news of the day was carried in the middle pages. Russell's latest
despatches appeared on page seven, the main news page, under the
headline: THE WAR IN THE CRIMEA, and bylined simply: (FROM OUR
SPECIAL CORRESPONDENT).

There is no indication at the top of page seven that a major
battle had been fought, and that one of the most exciting and
disastrous attacks in British military history had taken place. The
page begins with Russell's despatch of 19 October, which deals
with the continuing siege of Sevastopol. This is followed by two
more despatches on the same subject, dated 20 and 21 October.
They are interesting enough, but of no great importance. His
despatch of 25 October, about the battle of Balaclava and the
Charge of the Light Brigade, follows three-quarters of the way
down the fourth of six columns.

But even though to modern eyes the article seems to have been
buried after the halfway mark, Russell's opening words would have
galvanised his readers' attention instantly:

THE CAVALRY ACTION AT BALAKLAVA
    October 25.
If the exhibition of the most brilliant valour, of the excess of
courage, and of a daring which would have reflected lustre on the
best days of chivalry can afford full consolation for the disaster of
today, we can have no reason to regret the melancholy loss which
we sustained in a contest with a savage and barbarian enemy.

Having explained the principle that cavalry should never be used
in a charge against enemy guns without the support of infantry,
Russell launches into his account:

[T]here was a plain to charge over, before the enemy's guns
were reached, of a mile and a half in length. At 11.10 our
Light Cavalry Brigade rushed to the front... [T]he Russians
opened on them from the guns in the redoubt on the right,
with volleys of musketry and rifles. They swept proudly past,

glittering in the morning sun in all the pride and splendour of war. We could scarcely believe the evidence of our senses! Surely that handful of men are not going to charge an army in position! Alas! It was but too true – their desperate valour knew no bounds, and far indeed was it removed from the so-called better part – discretion.

The cavalry charged in two long lines, going faster and faster as they approached the Russians:

> At the distance of 1,200 yards the whole line of the enemy belched forth, from 30 iron mouths, a flood of smoke and flame, through which hissed the deadly balls. Their flight was marked by instant gaps in our ranks, by dead men and horses, by steeds flying wounded or riderless across the plain. The first line is broken, it is joined by the second, they never halt or check their speed for an instant; with diminished ranks, thinned by those 30 guns, which the Russians had laid with the most deadly accuracy, with a halo of steel above their heads, and with a cheer which was many a noble fellow's death-cry, they flew into the smoke of the batteries, but ere they were lost to view the plain was strewn with their bodies and with the carcasses of horses.

From his vantage point Russell could see the flash of their sabres as they charged up to the guns and cut down the gunners. Then they turned, and rode back:

> ...to our delight we saw them returning, after breaking through a column of Russian infantry, and scattering them like chaff, when the flank fire of the batteries on the hill swept them down, scattered and broken as they were.... At 11:35 not a British soldier, except the dead and dying, was left in front of those bloody Muscovite guns...

That night, in his haste and exhaustion, Russell often just copied out word for word the notes he had made as he watched the charge, not bothering to change the present tense he found there ('The first line is broken, it is joined by the second...').

46

His sense of passionate involvement grabbed the full attention of the British nation back home. The humorous weekly *Punch* carried a cartoon in its next edition entitled: 'Enthusiasm of Paterfamilias on reading the Report in the *Times* of the Grand Charge of British Cavalry'. The father is standing in front of the fireplace, holding his copy of *The Times* and brandishing a poker excitedly. His wife and one of his daughters are sitting at the breakfast table in tears, but the other six children are in various stages of enthusiasm, and the only son, aged around ten, waves a breadknife with one hand and half a broken plate with the other.

At home in Lincolnshire, Alfred Tennyson read Russell's despatch in *The Times* and turned the details he found in it, from 'a mile and a half' ('Half a league, half a league, half a league onward') to 'sabring the gunners there' and 'not, not the six hundred', into one of the most recited poems in the English language. Russell's name and reputation were made for life.

Still, Russell didn't fit into the new technological era, which opened with the arrival of the telegraph in the 1860s. During the Franco-Prussian War, in particular, he was scooped again and again by the rising star of British journalism, Archibald Forbes, who was eighteen years younger. *The Times* was often furious with Russell, but he was far too important to sack. Still, his bosses sent him some angry letters which showed that they were not at all in awe of his reputation. Correspondents today often have the same experience.

In the Crimea 160 years later, in 2014, I was badly scooped by one of ITN's best correspondents, after Russia's decision to annex the territory from Ukraine. James Mates's team, working on their own for just a couple of daily news programmes, had been free to make their own decision about where to base themselves, and they had rightly chosen the unattractive inland capital of Crimea, Simferapol. The contingent from the BBC, which had to service thirteen different BBC outlets, headed across the

Crimean peninsula to base itself in Sevastopol, an hour and a half farther on from Simferapol. Sevastopol, with its delightful harbour and the Black Sea behind it, was regarded as the best possible backdrop for all the live reporting we had to do for television, and for cheapness' sake we were all instructed to stay there together.

It proved to be unwise. A UN delegate flew in to Simferapol to see if a political agreement was possible, and ITN arranged to interview him. But when a crowd of pro-Russian thugs realised that the UN man was in town they surrounded his car and banged on its roof, and he managed to escape to a café. There, James interviewed him while the mob continued to bay outside. Perhaps in the overall scheme of things it wasn't hugely important, but it was superb stuff, tailor-made for television. And since I was stuck in Sevastopol, ninety minutes' drive away, the entire incident was over and done with before I had even heard about it.

The next morning there was a tremendous fuss at the BBC in London, and the brand new boss of news sent me a sulphurous email telling me to pull my socks up. I was deeply embarrassed by my failure of the night before, but after thirty-two years as a senior figure in the BBC's foreign news reporting I didn't enjoy being ticked off quite so fiercely.

As we drove along the Crimea's rutted, bumpy roads I tapped out an answering email to him on my mobile phone, ending with the words 'Don't EVER write to me like this again.' I might have toned the message down if I had had time to reread it; but we hit a particularly deep hole in the road and I pressed 'send' by accident. The boss in question took it very well, and we've been good friends ever since.

———

Archibald Forbes, the author of the Franco-Prussian War scoops, might have beaten Russell again and again, but he wasn't as good or conscientious a writer, and he seemed to have less empathy with the people he reported on. He was a driven man, and for him and for his paper, the *Daily News*, getting the story back first was more important than ensuring it was accurate, or readable, or emotionally moving.

Years later, in 1899, Forbes wrote to Russell explaining how he'd got one of his biggest scoops at the older correspondent's expense, back in 1870. They had both been with the Prussian army as it advanced on Paris. Forbes found out everything about the siege artillery which the Prussians were planning to use against the forts round Paris, and sent over a complete despatch before the first shot was fired; he told the *Daily News* to set it up in print, but to hold it until he telegraphed the paper to let them know the bombardment had begun.

He had made another arrangement, this time with the Prussian crown prince, no less. When the time came for the guns to open fire, the prince told Forbes exactly when and where he was going to give the pre-arranged signal to the gunners. Forbes watched from a distance as the prince raised his arm, then lowered it; and as he did so Forbes bellowed out to a telegraph operator who was stationed close by, to send a pre-prepared message to the *Daily News* in London. It read simply 'Go ahead!'

Poor old Russell, whose grasp of technology was thoroughly out of date and whose style was florid and wordy, waited until the bombardment of Paris was properly underway before sitting down to write his despatch, which then had to be telegraphed at full length. Forbes beat him by an entire day.

Yet fame, for journalists, is often independent of the ups and downs of their professional life. People remember you for your big moments, and seem not to pay much attention to your relative failures. William Howard Russell's reputation and his air of authority endured for the rest of his life. His fame was due in part to his legendary ability to make people like him; when Queen Victoria's eldest son, the easy-going and raffish Prince of Wales, went on a royal progress to India in 1876, Russell was sent to cover it, and they struck up a friendship which lasted until Russell's death in 1907. After the prince became king in 1901, Russell, who was already a knight, was made a Commander of the Royal Victorian Order. At Buckingham Palace, Russell hobbled gamely up the steps to the throne on his bad legs.

'Don't kneel, Billy – just stoop, stoop!' whispered Edward VII. It was the ultimate accolade.

THREE

Genesis of a News Story

At 10 A.M. Jacopo, at No. – Calle de la Cruz, handed me a
telegram: It read, 'Come to Paris on important business.'
The telegram was from Mr James Gordon Bennett, jun.,
the young manager of the 'New York Herald'.

Henry Morton Stanley,
How I Found Livingstone, 1872

STORIES CAN BEGIN IN any number of ways. The editor can get an
idea in his bath, and mention it at the morning meeting; and the
senior editorial staff will fall over themselves to praise its wisdom
and, in later discussions with reporters and producers, will give the
impression it is their own.

Someone just back from somewhere can pass on an idea or a
suspicion which sounds attractive; though it can fall to dust when
you examine it with any rigour. You can find some mention of
something interesting in a foreign newspaper – the *Moscow Times*,
perhaps, or the *South China Morning Post*, or the Johannesburg *City
Press* – but someone else may well have seen it and got there first.
And then there's the sort of story which unfolds in front of your
eyes. That's the best and most reliable kind.

In August 1990 I had just arrived with my then girlfriend in the
southwest of France, at a particularly attractive hotel with a fine
swimming pool, an underused tennis court, and (by all accounts) a
first-class chef. We came in late, promising ourselves a swim, a set or
two of tennis and an excellent lunch the following day; but we woke
up to hear the radio telling us that Saddam Hussein had invaded

Kuwait during the night. I had a tense conversation with the hotel manager, but managed to prise almost our entire down-payment from him before we caught the midday plane back to London. Very soon after that I started a long stint in Baghdad.

Sixteen years later, on Boxing Day, I was relaxing with my wife Dee and year-old son Rafe in South Africa, at the charming seaside resort of Nature's Valley – a place that felt like being back in the 1950s. Lounging in a hammock in the sunshine, I answered my mobile phone to find that Saddam Hussein was about to be executed in Baghdad. My wife's mother, Adele, was staying with us, so Dee asked her to look after Rafe while she gallantly drove me the 200 miles to the nearest airport. After dropping me off she had to drive back on her own in the dark: not something that is generally advised in rural South Africa. While Adele was watching over Rafe, a boomslang, one of Africa's most venomous snakes, came slithering into the house, but after looking around for a while, it headed harmlessly out again – so everything ended well.

Less so for Saddam, of course. I reached Baghdad in time to watch him hang – an ugly, savage spectacle, which made me, like many others, feel sympathy for him rather than for those Iraqis on the scaffold who mocked him as he died. It didn't help, either, that the exultant American soldiers I came across in the following days continued to believe, in spite of all the evidence, that Saddam had been behind the 9/11 bombings.

———

In a turbulent, decaying part of Kinshasa, the capital of the Democratic Republic of Congo, a long and bumpy taxi drive brings you to the former city bus station, built in the days when the city had buses. The structures look increasingly rickety now, their roofs gaping, the metal rusting, and birds squabbling noisily under the eaves. What's left of the buses is still there, but their tyres and engines and seats have long ago vanished, and the glass in the windows has mostly been broken. The skeletal remains of the vehicles have now been colonised by squatters, who sit in front of them all day long gossiping and watching their children play, while their washing flaps on improvised lines and lean-tos with makeshift awnings give them shelter from the powerful sun. A notice declares, in words that are increasingly hard to make out, that these buses were the gift of the European Union. It's years since the European Union realised that its gift was helping to sort out Kinshasa's housing problem, not its transportation, and no more buses have been donated since.

If you walk past the squatters in the buses and across an open field, which is used partly as a rubbish dump and partly as a latrine, you find yourself heading towards the magnificent Congo River; and close to its bank there is a curious light green human figure, ten feet long, which seems to be raising its arm towards you as it lies on its front. It is hard to make out from a distance, especially since you have to spend a lot of time watching where you're stepping, but, closer to, it becomes even more strange.

It's a larger than life-sized statue in bronze which has been cut off at the ankles, and stretched out full length on a decaying boat. The figure is wearing a solar topee and a tropical suit, and when he was standing upright his right arm was raised in greeting. Now that he is lying down, the arm, raised over his head, makes him look as though he is swimming freestyle and is in mid-stroke. The man is Henry Morton Stanley, foreign correspondent and explorer, and the boat he is lying on is the one he sailed in down the Congo. That was one of his many achievements: proving that the river was navigable from the town which later bore his name, Stanleyville, and is now called Kisangani, to the capital, Léopoldville: now Kinshasa.

The authorities in Kinshasa have never decided what to do about Stanley's statue. When I visited it, a soldier with a rifle was standing guard over it, and had to be bribed to allow me to take photographs. He was presumably there to make sure that metal thieves didn't take the statue away; though why the local authorities haven't locked it up somewhere secure isn't clear. Perhaps it's for the same reason that they haven't replaced the EU buses.

Stanley was in many ways an unattractive character. He could be a brutal taskmaster to his African servants, and he seems to have supported his boss, King Leopold II of the Belgians, in the grossly cruel treatment of the Congolese people, who were forced to engage in the rubber and ivory trades and were liable to have their hands or feet cut off if they failed to fulfil their quotas.

Stanley, who was became one of the nineteenth century's greatest foreign correspondents and explorers, came from a background of the utmost poverty and deprivation. Born John Rowlands in the Welsh town of Denbigh in 1841, he was the son of an unmarried eighteen-year-old girl who abandoned him as quickly as she could. He was brought up mostly in the local workhouse, where he was frequently abused by the bigger boys and possibly raped by the headmaster. Still, he was clever, and became a pupil-teacher. In 1859, at the age of eighteen, he emigrated to the United States, and a chance meeting at the port of New Orleans, where he landed, brought him a degree of affection which he had never previously received. A local man called Henry Hope Stanley took him in and treated him as his own son; in gratitude, the boy adopted his name. Soon, though, Henry Morton Stanley was swept up by the American Civil War, managing to fight on both sides, one after the other. It was only after the war ended that he was able to follow his dream, and began working as a journalist.

His newspaper, the *New York Tribune*, took his work seriously enough to send him abroad as a foreign correspondent. In Madrid, on 16 October 1869, he received the summons from his editor which would eventually make him the most famous journalist in the world. Here is Stanley's account of the episode, in his staccato, urgent style:

> Down came my pictures from the walls of my apartments on the second floor; into my trunks went my books and souvenirs, my clothes were hastily collected, some half washed, some from the clothes-line half dry, and after a couple of hours of hasty hard work my portmanteaus were strapped up and labelled 'Paris'.
>
> At 3 p.m. I was on my way.

Arriving in Paris the following night, he went straight to the Grand Hotel where James Gordon Bennett, the paper's owner, was staying, and knocked at the door of his room. Bennett was in bed.

'Who are you?'

'My name is Stanley.'

'Ah, yes! Sit down; I have important business on hand for you.'

Bennett hopped out of bed and started to explain.

He was an interesting, complex man who was born in the same year as Stanley and had taken over the *Tribune* from his father. A sportsman and something of a playboy, he organised the first tennis match in America and captained the winning boat in the first transatlantic yacht race. He also drank heavily. Late one evening, at a party given by the wealthy parents of his new fiancée, he staggered in and started urinating into the fireplace (or, according to an alternative account, into the piano), right in front of his prospective parents-in-law. That was the end of his engagement.

Now, as he threw on his dressing gown, Bennett launched straight into the subject which had been obsessing him:

'Where do you think Livingstone is?'

'I really do not know, sir.'

'Do you think he is alive?'

'He may be, and he may not be.'

'Well, I think he is alive, and that he can be found, and I am going to send you to find him.'

'What! Do you really think I can find Dr Livingstone? Do you mean me to go to Central Africa?'

'Of course you will act according to your own plans, and do what you think best – BUT FIND LIVINGSTONE!'

Stanley objected that it would cost at least £2,500:

'Well, I will tell you what you will do. Draw a thousand pounds now; and when you have gone through that, draw another thousand, and when that is spent, draw another thousand, and when you have finished that, draw another thousand, and so on; but, FIND LIVINGSTONE.'

Yet, oddly, Bennett didn't seem to be in any particular hurry about this. Sitting there in his dressing gown he told Stanley that he wanted him to go and cover a weird shopping list of stories first, beginning with the opening of the Suez Canal. After that he was to report on Sir Samuel Baker's proposed expedition up the Nile, then go to Jerusalem, and on to Constantinople.

Bennett went on: 'Then – let me see – you might as well visit the Crimea and those old battle-grounds, then go across the Caucasus to the Caspian Sea; I hear there is a Russian expedition bound for Khiva.'

After that Stanley was to travel through Persia to India, with a detour to Baghdad. Only when he had done some reporting in India would he finally be free to cross to Zanzibar and start the search for Livingstone. James Gordon Bennett, whose very name became a joke, was a megalomaniac in the manner of Beaverbrook, Northcliffe or Evelyn Waugh's Lord Copper. The power that having a lot of money and owning a newspaper confers is rarely good for a person's character or judgement. Yet in this case Bennett turned out to be triumphantly right, both about the ultimate story and about the abilities of the man he was sending to cover it.

'That is all. Goodnight, and God be with you.'

And with that Bennett climbed back into bed. Faced with such an extraordinary list of prerequisites, it was well over a year before Stanley had sufficient leisure to turn his attention to the main purpose of his elaborate tour. Still, he was lucky: during that time Livingstone remained lost, and no one else was crazy enough to try to find out what had happened to him. Stanley followed his instructions and, as we will see, scored perhaps the greatest scoop of all time.

Nowadays journalists, like politicians and all sorts of other people who were once regarded with admiration, are more often than not regarded as liars and cheats; and anyone who listened to the evidence given at the Leveson tribunal into phone-hacking will find that easy to understand. The best that the rest of us can say – those of us, that is, who don't tap people's phones, or steal the photographs of murdered daughters from their bereaved parents' mantelpieces, or pay masseuses to video their clients, or pose as young women in order to induce junior ministers to send them selfies of their private parts – is that we try to behave according to some ethical system.

Yet it's a long time since journalists were well regarded. Certainly there was little respect for them by 1938, the year when Chapman & Hall published a handsome novel bound in swirling maroon and black, with a dust cover which purports to be a cutting torn from the front page of a newspaper: the *Daily Beast*. The dust cover reads:

S C O O P
by Evelyn Waugh

There is a picture of the author, smiling enigmatically, with the caption 'Photograph of Mr. Waugh received by wireless late last night'. The rest of the supposed newspaper cutting is made up of text in journalese – or, rather, what Chapman & Hall's designers thought journalese sounded like. The result is pretty excruciating, and one can only imagine Evelyn Waugh's vicious reaction when he read it for the first time:

> Press Peer coaxed by Society Beauty – Big chance for Small Town Boy – Threat of war in Africa's most glamorous hinterland – News-hawks race for story across uncharted continent – Goat butts black – Mystery financier outwits Reds – Boot makes good – Editor's Ordeal – Lord Copper personally welcomes the future – These are only a few of the thrills revealed exclusively to a *Daily Beast* reporter yesterday by thirty-four-year-old novelist Evelyn Waugh. 'I hope it sells a hundred thousand,' said Waugh, 'but I shall be very pleased with half that number. Two or three of the characters seem to me quite funny. There is a good deal of plot and a happy ending.' 'It is stupendous,' said hundred-years-old publishers, Chapman & Hall. 'Epoch-making, intoxicating. We have published nothing comparable to it this week.'

In all of this, the only phrase which sounds entirely convincing is 'hundred-years-old publishers'. The blurb creaks with an outmoded effort to be funny. Chapman & Hall, founded in 1834, had once published William Howard Russell's friends Charles Dickens and William Thackeray, but it had declined sadly in the twentieth century under its managing director Arthur Waugh – one of whose few achievements was to publish the novels of his son Evelyn. Soon after *Scoop* came out, Chapman & Hall merged with Methuen. After that its disappearance into the oubliette of old publishing companies that have failed to keep up with the rest of the world was greatly speeded up, though the Chapman & Hall name still exists as an imprint for books on science and technology: a bit of a comedown for the publishers of *Great Expectations* and *A Tale of Two Cities*.

Scoop, however, was brilliant, and quite extraordinarily and lastingly amusing. Like tabloid journalists, passages like these lurk in the memory and refuse to go away:

> Shumble, Whelper and Pigge knew Corker; they had loitered of old on many a doorstep and forced an entry into many a stricken home. . .

> William and Corker went to the Press Bureau. Dr Benito, the director, was away, but his clerk entered their names in his ledger and gave them cards of identity. They were small orange documents, originally printed for the registration of prostitutes. . .

> 'Why, once Jakes went out to cover a revolution in one of the Balkan capitals. He overslept in his carriage, woke up at the wrong station, didn't know any different, got out, went straight to a hotel, and cabled off a thousand-word story about barricades in the streets, flaming churches, machine guns answering the rattle of his typewriter as he wrote, a dead child, like a broken doll, spread-eagled in the deserted roadway before his window – you know. . .

> 'Well, they were pretty surprised at his office, getting a story like that from the wrong country, but they trusted Jakes and splashed it in six national newspapers. That day every special in Europe got orders to rush to the new revolution. They arrived in shoals. Everything seemed quiet enough, but it was as much as their jobs were worth to say so, with Jakes filing a thousand words of blood and thunder a day. So they chimed in too. Government stocks dropped, financial panic, state of emergency declared,

army mobilized, famine, mutiny and in less than a week there *was* an honest to God revolution under way, just as Jakes had said. There's the power of the press for you.

'They gave Jakes the Nobel Peace Prize for his harrowing descriptions of the carnage...'

Once you've read *Scoop*, it becomes impossible to take the function and practice of journalism entirely seriously, ever again. A hundred and twenty years ago, journalists wrote books called *Glimpses Through the Cannon-Smoke*, or *Camps, Quarters and Casual Places*. After the First World War, front-line correspondents such as Philip Gibbs wrote guilt-ridden confessions about their failure to give a full picture of the fighting, like *More That Must Be Told*. But *Scoop*'s mocking of the ways of journalism proved deeply infectious. Once the Second World War was out of the way, titles like Edward Behr's *Anyone Here Been Raped and Speaks English?* became usual. It was now the absurdity of foreign reporting, not its heroism, which was in fashion, and that attitude has proven to be a lasting one. Today, no one who writes about it can afford to be too admiring of journalism or journalists.

One of the outstanding figures of Fleet Street came to embody this sense of the absurd, thanks to *Scoop*. William Deedes was a gentle and modest man, whom it was a pleasure to meet and talk to. He listened to the most junior person in any group (it was sometimes me) with apparent interest and respect. Betraying the slight lisp that was so well parodied in *Private Eye*'s 'Dear Bill' column, week after week, he would gently agree with what was said and put forward something to reinforce it from his own hugely longer experience. As a guest on the satirical television series *Have I Got News for You* he took the jokes of the other panellists with modesty and charm.

Bill Deedes led a remarkable life. He remains the only newspaper editor to have been a cabinet minister, and carried on writing about international affairs until two weeks before his death in 2007 at the age of ninety-four. His last column was about the war in Darfur.

With characteristic spite, Evelyn Waugh spotted Bill Deedes's gentleness and naïveté and skewered him as the hapless William Boot, *Scoop*'s unheroic hero. (It was Waugh who remarked savagely, when his equally spiteful friend Randolph Churchill went into hospital to have a benign tumour removed, that it was typical of the pointlessness of modern science to take Churchill and extract the only benign thing about him.) Deedes always said that he had spent part of his life brushing aside the charge that he was the model for Boot, but even he had to accept that his inexperience as a reporter 'might have contributed a few bricks to the building of Boot'.

A former editor of *The Times*, Sir Peter Stothard, has suggested that Boot was modelled in part on William Beach Thomas, a former countryside columnist for the *Daily Mail* who for obscure reasons was put forward by the *Mail* as its chief war correspondent on the Western Front in the First World War. His gung-ho style and his determination to give the impression that he was always right up on the front line instead of being safely at the rear, made him loathed by huge numbers of fighting soldiers. All the same, the character and innocence of Boot belong to Deedes, not to Beach Thomas. Deedes's simplicity and lack of any kind of guile or front provided Evelyn Waugh with a clear target; not something he could easily resist.

In 2003 Deedes published *At War with Waugh: The Real Story of* Scoop, a concerted attempt to deflect once and for all the charge that he was the model for Boot. Yet, right from the first words, Deedes's deadpan, loose, innocent style, so different from Waugh's tightly phrased barbs, simply reinforces the identification:

One sunny morning early in August 1935, I was summoned from the *Morning Post*'s reporters' room by H. A. Gwynne, editor since 1911, and asked if I was willing to go as the newspaper's correspondent to Abyssinia, where war with Italy seemed inevitable.

Directly, and without meaning to, Deedes leads us into Waugh territory – what the writer and polemicist Christopher Hitchens, writing about *Scoop*, called 'Absurdistan':

> Gwynne had been a Reuters war correspondent in the South African war along with Winston Churchill, Edgar Wallace and others, and so had plenty of avuncular advice to offer. A dead correspondent, he reminded me cheerfully, was useless to his newspaper. A finger of whisky in the water bottle killed bugs in doubtful water. Above all, as a representative of the *Morning Post*, I must look the part, acquire the proper kits, and so on.

Deedes, who was only twenty-two and had never been further than Switzerland, nodded, uncomfortably aware that he knew nothing whatever about Abyssinia. Gwynne sent him to see the paper's news editor, Mervyn Ellis, who seemed to know equally little about the country or its conditions, but said it was likely that those who reported the war from the Abyssinian side would be cut off by the advancing Italians and must be prepared for a long siege. 'That line of thought,' says Deedes in words that condemn him for ever as William Boot, 'led to a lively shopping spree'.

There is always a joy in buying gear for an expedition. As a journalist, you know that you can get the kind of equipment you have always wanted but could never afford on your own. In preparing for filming trips in the Arctic, or the Amazon, or the Sahara, I have gleefully bought tents and sleeping bags and special torches and gadgets to deter insects and strain drinking water (without using whisky), or triple thermal socks, or gloves of some new and magnificent material to protect my fingers from the cold – ineffectually, as it turned out in the Arctic, since I had to be medivaced out after getting frostbite on all my fingers.

When Deedes writes about the equipment he bought at Austin Reed in Regent Street, with Mervyn Ellis alongside him, egging him on, it is all deeply reminiscent of Boot:

> We were persuaded to buy, among other things: three tropical suits, riding breeches for winter and summer, bush shirts, a sola topi, a double-brimmed sun hat, a camp bed and sleeping bag, and long boots to deter mosquitoes at sundown. To contain some of these purchases we bought two large metal uniform cases and a heavy trunk made of cedar wood and lined with zinc to keep ants at bay.

Here is Evelyn Waugh's parody:

> William... acquired a well-, perhaps rather over-, furnished tent, three months' rations, a collapsible canoe, a jointed flagstaff and Union Jack, a hand-pump and sterilising plant, an astrolabe, six suits of tropical linen and a sou'wester, a camp operating table and set of surgical instruments, a portable humidor, guaranteed to preserve cigars in condition in the Red Sea, and a Christmas hamper, complete with Santa Claus costume and a tripod mistletoe stand, and a cane for whacking snakes. Only time brought an end to his marketing.

And of course there were the famous cleft sticks, recommended to Boot by the paper's ludicrous proprietor, Lord Copper, to be used by native runners carrying his despatches. 'We can have some cloven for you,' says the store assistant brightly. 'If you will make your selection I will send them down to our cleaver.'

'William, hesitating between polo sticks and hockey sticks, chose six of each; they were removed to the workshop.'

Boot has to fly to Paris, then catch the train to Marseille: 'His luggage, which followed the taxi in a small pantechnicon, made him a prominent figure at the office of the Air Line... They telephoned to Croydon [Airport] and ordered an additional aeroplane.'

And here is Bill Deedes: 'What troubled my mind then, to the exclusion of almost everything else, was how I might contrive to convey a quarter of a ton of luggage in six separate pieces from

London to Addis Ababa.' It took two heavily laden taxis to get him and his gear from his house to Victoria station.

How did Evelyn Waugh come to know about Bill Deedes's equipment? That becomes clear from *At War with Waugh*, though with his characteristic innocence Deedes lets it pass without comment. When he reached Addis Ababa, he writes:

> Stuart Emeny, a senior reporter on the *News Chronicle* I had come to know well from stories we had covered together in England, met the train with Evelyn Waugh and our own local man, Salman. I found they had made most satisfactory arrangements on my behalf. These enabled me to leave the station without a finger being raised by immigration or customs.

As he watched Deedes's cases being carried off the train and piled up on the platform, the idea for William Boot's hapless foray into the world of the foreign correspondent must surely have been forming already in Waugh's mind.

———

Clare Hollingworth was sixty-seven when I first met her, on the tarmac of Bucharest airport in 1978; to me, in my early thirties, she seemed ancient – too old, I thought patronisingly, to be still working as a foreign correspondent. Directly I glimpsed her energy and formidable intelligence, I changed my mind: she had more drive and more stamina than I did. And in spite of her poor eyesight, as she peered through lenses as thick as the bottom of a beer bottle, I could see how attractive she must have been a couple of decades earlier. She was extraordinarily charming and perceptive, and full of wonderful stories.

As our friendship grew and we agreed to travel together across communist-ruled Romania in search of news, I listened in open admiration to her tales of Mao's China and Stalin's Russia, of spies and traitors and sudden arrests. Even my camera crew, who had seen and heard just about everything that had happened during their working lifetimes, were fascinated. But the tale that interested us all the most was her start in journalism, and how she happened to be the only journalist who witnessed the start of the Second World War.

Clare always sounded immensely grand, her drawling sentences peppered with little snippets of French – *'Jamais de la vie'*, *'Je t'assure, mon brave'* – but she was born in Knighton, near Leicester, the daughter of a travelling salesman who worked for a local shoe manufacturer. Her great-nephew, Patrick Garrett, who has written a biography of her, *Of Fortunes and War*, notes that on the day she was born, 10 October 1911, an uprising broke out in Wuchang which would bring about the overthrow of the last imperial dynasty in China – the country where she would one day do some of her most distinguished work, reporting on the communist successors to the emperor.

In 1933, at the age of twenty-two, Clare became engaged, but her fiancé broke it off. To get over him she went to Switzerland and enrolled at an institute of international affairs in Geneva, before returning to England to take a job with a branch of the League of Nations Union. She studied at the School of Slavonic and Eastern European Studies, married her first husband, and went with him to live in Prague; she could see that a good story was unfolding there. By early 1939 she was in Poland, rescuing around three thousand refugees from the hands of the Nazis. In doing so, she fell foul of British officialdom, and MI6 seems to have told the organisation she was working for that it shouldn't employ her. She went back to London, with the aim of becoming a journalist.

Some time earlier, in Geneva, Clare had met a journalist from the *Daily Telegraph*, a man with the splendid name Trilby Ewer. After listening to his stories about foreign correspondents, Clare had decided that this sounded like the life she wanted to lead. Ewer may well have helped to get her an interview with his newspaper in London.

Finance houses now occupy the magnificent Elcock, Sutcliffe and Tait building at 135–141 Fleet Street, built in 1928 for the *Daily Telegraph*, with its Graeco-Egyptian columns. At the time its proud owners described it as 'the most modern, up-to-date newspaper office in the British Empire', equipped with the latest lifts which could rise six floors in eight seconds. Its front hall was, and still is, splendidly proportioned, 'a grand room two storeys high, dignified by great bronze doors, huge hanging lamps of bronze and frosted crystal, [with] white marble walls...' At the far end of the first-floor corridor was the office of the editor, a man who by tradition worked in splendid isolation, meeting very few people. When the *Telegraph* was founded in 1855, soon after Russell's initial triumphs for *The Times* in the Crimea, the rules specified that 'the Editor cannot be seen by anyone', and even his staff could only communicate with him in writing.

Now, although she was a complete newcomer to journalism and was still only twenty-seven, Clare was ushered into the editor's office for an interview. It is tempting to wonder whether there was something more than Clare Hollingworth's own feminine attraction and her ability to impress people like Trilby Ewer; was MI6, in spite of its treatment of her in Poland, actually helping her to get a job as a journalist for its own purposes?

The man behind the ultra-large desk was Arthur Watson: in his late fifties, large, balding, bespectacled and impressively moustachioed. He had been in the job for nearly forty years, and had a reputation for being shrewd in both his journalistic and personal judgement. He certainly showed exceptional flair now. Clare's only relevant experience was the four months she had spent working with refugees along the Polish border, yet instead of giving her any kind of training Watson hired her on the spot as a 'stringer', or freelance, working to the *Telegraph*'s Berlin correspondent, Hugh Carleton Greene: Graham's brother, and a future director-general of the BBC. Then he sent her to see the news editor, Bob Skelton.

Clare Hollingworth's meeting with Skelton was something along the lines of William Boot's fictional meeting with Mr Salter:

'I don't suppose that after what Lord Copper has said there is anything more you want to know.'

'Well, there is one thing. You see, I don't read the papers very much. Can you tell me who is fighting who in Ishmaelia?'

'I think it's the Patriots and the Traitors.'

'Yes, but which is which?'

'Oh, I don't know *that*. *That*'s policy, you see. It's nothing to do with me...'

Clare knew perfectly well who was likely to be fighting who in Europe. Nor did Skelton advise her to go and buy 'kit' for her mission, as Mr Salter did with Boot. All he did, apparently, was to give her a briefing on the logistics: the times she would be expected to file, the telegraphic addresses, and the *Telegraph*'s all-important style manual, which laid great stress on the words and expressions that should never be used. Today's *Telegraph* style manual bans, among other things, 'autopsy' (Americanism), 'bid' (when we mean attempt), 'blasted', 'bloodbath', 'boardroom antics', 'boffin', 'breathtaking', 'bubbly' (both for champagne and for young women).

That evening, back at her flat in Buckingham Palace Road, Clare started packing – but quickly realised that the various suitcases she owned were too big for the aircraft which was to take her to Berlin the following day. Unlike *The Beast* with Boot, the *Telegraph* wasn't planning to go to the expense of chartering an extra plane for her luggage. Harrods, however, had a late-night delivery service, and sent over a modest suitcase from what it boasted was 'the most wonderful selection of Travel Kit in the country'.

Exactly a week before Germany invaded Poland – the news event with which Clare Hollingworth would always be associated – she left for Warsaw via Berlin in a silver Lockheed aircraft; Patrick Garrett's research inclines him to believe it was the very plane which had flown Neville Chamberlain to Munich the year before. As it started to descend towards Tempelhof, on the outskirts of Berlin, 'I felt as though my insides were dropping faster than the plane,' she wrote later in her memoirs. There were only two other passengers on the flight, both of them journalists like Clare. Time and again in the career of every foreign correspondent, you seem to find yourself on an empty plane going to places which everyone in their right mind is trying to get out of. This was Clare's first experience of a process which would repeat itself in her life frequently over the years.

She had good reason to feel nervous: she had been warned that her name appeared on a German blacklist as a result of her refugee work in Poland, and that the Gestapo were watching her. The Gestapo believed, too, that British journalists usually worked for MI6. On top of all this, the Nazi regime had a particular dislike for the *Daily Telegraph*. Goebbels, Hitler's chief of propaganda, had accused it of taking 'the leading place in the press campaign against Germany'.

The Lockheed taxied in, and an official with 'the expression of a prison-warder' (Clare's words) appeared in the doorway. The three journalists were led away to a holding pen. She wrote afterwards that she was more nervous during the hours she was held at Tempelhof than in any of the fighting that was to follow.

Their bags, books and papers were taken off them: 'We sat like three fowls on a perch, wondering whose necks would be wrung. The airport clerks glared at us through a window; every now and then an official would come and give us an extra scowl of his own. It made conversation difficult.'

Perhaps the German authorities, in these last days of peace, decided that imprisoning three British journalists would be more trouble than it was worth. For whatever reason, their onward flight to Warsaw was authorised and with huge relief they left Berlin behind and flew on towards Poland. Theirs was one of the very last British civilian flights on this route for nearly six years. A few hours later Hermann Goering, who doubled as aviation minister and head of the Luftwaffe, banned all non-military flights over German territory.

They landed in Warsaw that evening, and Clare went straight to the Hotel Europejski. Soon the hotel would be destroyed, but it was reconstructed after the war along precisely the same lines. At the time of writing, it is being rebuilt yet again, but until recently you could still eat in the restaurant where Clare Hollingworth had dinner that evening with her new boss. Hugh Carleton Greene was, in the words of one of his colleagues, 'fair, curly haired, has a grin like a half-moon, immense feet at the ends of long legs and arms that dangle about'. He also possessed great charm, which, thirty years later, would turn lowly people like me at the BBC into his devoted followers. Now, in the dining room of the Europejski, this charm was directed at Clare. To be responsible for a wholly inexperienced young woman journalist with a world war about to break out might have irritated plenty of bureau chiefs. Greene, however, remained kind and full of support and good advice; Clare regarded him with great affection ever afterwards. He told her his plan: he would stay on in Warsaw, while she headed to Katowice in the southwest – the area where she had been working just a few weeks before.

They moved on to the Bristol Bar, which also survived until the current remodelling of the hotel. That night it was jammed until five in the morning with 'journalists, ambassadors, senior officers, gigolos, war-contractors, courtesans, and spies. . . The medley of figures, jostling, hugging, whispering, laughing, composed a scene as mixed and tumbled as a dream. . .'

This was Clare Hollingworth's introduction to the foreign correspondent's life. Instantly, she was in her element.

For the best part of twenty years, the best known name in British television reporting was that of Kate Adie. 'Now that Kate Adie's here,' said a soldier in a newspaper cartoon, 'the war can start.' Once I went into a shop in Oxford Street in London and was greeted by a young salesman. 'Hello, haven't I seen you on television?' 'Possibly,' I answered warily. 'Don't tell me, it's the news, isn't it?' I said it was. 'So – a kind of Kate Adie of your day, were you?' I smiled politely, paid for the things I'd bought, and left.

Soon after the invasion of Iraq in 2003, the *Radio Times* carried out a poll of its readers to find out which news correspondent they thought had done the best job during the fighting. I came second, with around thirty per cent, but Kate got almost double that, leaving me far in her wake. Which was fine, except that she'd retired from active news reporting two years earlier, and had played no part whatsoever in the coverage on the ground in Iraq. Yet the viewers, the people all our efforts are directed towards, were certain she had been there, because they had come to expect that she would be. In television, as in so much else, perception is all.

The business of fixing your name and face in the minds of the public is a haphazard one. There are broadcasters who have worked steadily and well for years, yet continue to go unrecognised. As the BBC broadcaster Brian Hanrahan discovered when he was caught up in the reporting of the Falklands campaign in 1982, making a breakthrough in the consciousness of a nationwide audience requires at least two elements to come together at the same time. For a start, you have to be on camera when something of real significance is going on. Viewers have to care deeply about the subject you're reporting on, and must be watching with intensity and concern. Secondly, you have to say or do something that attracts real attention and lodges firmly in the mind of the audience.

Brian Hanrahan was on board *Ark Royal* when the very first sortie by RAF Harriers against the Super Étendards of the Argentine air force took place. No one watching at home really knew how good the British planes were, or how well they would perform in combat. The television audience for that news broadcast was phenomenally large, and Brian's report from *Ark Royal* by telephone managed to provide the answer to the question in everyone's mind, while getting round the often intrusive military censorship: 'I'm not allowed to tell you how many British aircraft took part, but I can say that I counted them all out and I counted them all back.'

It was clever and deeply satisfying, and the next day people in offices and shops and schools everywhere in Britain were quoting what he had said. From that moment on, people were able to put a name to Brian's face and voice. He did plenty of excellent reporting in the years before his untimely death in 2010 at the age of sixty-one; apart from anything else, he was one of the first reporters to clamber onto the narrow top of the Berlin Wall on the night in November 1989 when it ceased to divide Germany. His report then was quite extraordinarily memorable, but the fact that he had achieved such fame seven years earlier brought added attention for everything he did.

In Kate Adie's case the process was rather similar, and happened over the same general period. In the early 1980s Britain might have a woman prime minister, but on television in particular, women weren't involved in reporting combat in any direct way. At the end of April 1980 a group of six Iranian Arabs, possibly in the pay of Saddam Hussein's Iraq, invaded Iran's consulate overlooking Hyde Park in London. They took twenty-six people hostage and threatened to kill them. The SAS, under the command of Lieutenant Colonel Michael Rose, who was later knighted for his efforts and became a general, was given the task of bringing the siege to an end. The world's broadcasters set up live cameras which were trained on the embassy building. Everyone was watching, with a considerable degree of tension.

Kate Adie was a general reporter for BBC television news at the time. It was an interesting and attractive job, but reporters usually found themselves being elbowed aside by more senior correspondents when stories became important. In this case, though, it was a Sunday evening when the SAS decided to move in. Kate, as the reporter on duty, had the story to herself. BBC1 interrupted the broadcasting of the final of the World Snooker Championship, and as people all over Britain heard that something was happening, they turned on their televisions to hear her clear, precise voice explaining what was going on. She wrote later, in her book *The Kindness of Strangers*:

> I stuck to telling what I could see, though my imagination was racing. . . I just described the scene, and kept going, realising that this was a marathon but without a script. I kept saying to myself, keep it even, keep it cool, and stood rigid with concentration. The drama should be on screen, not in me. I had no idea I was broadcasting to one of the largest audiences ever – and a good thing too.

There was a boldness to her style which people always found compelling, and when she told them something they tended to believe it implicitly. By that evening, Kate Adie's name and face had been permanently imprinted on the minds of the British people.

Six years later, she reinforced this all the more strongly. She started to specialise in Libya, a difficult country with an insane leader and a highly eccentric government. Colonel Gaddafi's officials, though, gave her more than one visa. It paid off when the United States, under President Reagan, decided to make Libya the scapegoat for the bombing by an extreme Palestinian group of a bar in Berlin, in which an American serviceman died. Libya, as far as any expert could make out, had had nothing whatever to do with the bombing, though Colonel Gaddafi's regime was certainly nasty and irresponsible. Striking at countries which looked formidable but were in fact too weak to retaliate became a speciality of Republican presidents from Reagan to George W. Bush: it satisfied a desire to show that America was still strong, without actually incurring any great risk of retaliation.

Kate was already in Tripoli when the American bombs and missiles started falling. The attacks, several of which were launched from bases in Britain with the full approval of Margaret Thatcher's government, were carried out without much care, and many civilians were killed and injured. The hospitals were full of casualties, and Kate, following William Howard Russell's example nearly a century and a half earlier, headed there and started filming. Gaddafi's officials, who were useless enough in normal times, made themselves scarce. Kate Adie, and the other Western journalists who were in Tripoli, were able to see for themselves what had happened, and how many people were injured: 'I stuck to reporting what I had seen – which amounted to extensive damage to residential areas and a large number of civilian casualties – plus a direct hit on Gaddafi's headquarters, two miles from the district we had visited.'

Back in Britain, the response was furious. Many people disapproved of the raids, and of British support for them. But the Thatcher government, probably sensing that the American air strikes had been hastily planned and were not particularly well justified, attacked the BBC's reporting loudly and long, and some

newspapers – Rupert Murdoch's *Sun* and the *Daily Mail* in particular – echoed and reinforced the government's approach.

There were accusations that the BBC had been taken in by the
Gaddafi regime's dirty tricks; that the bodies weren't genuine; that
Kate Adie had been an instrument, willing or otherwise, of Libyan
propaganda. Slowly, though, public opinion rallied round the
BBC, partly because of Kate, who had become immensely popular in Middle England. The *Mail* and the *Sun* went quiet, and Mrs
Thatcher started to back-pedal. Norman Tebbit, the chairman of
the Conservative Party, lacking her instinct for the public mood,
came out with a carelessly researched dossier attacking the BBC's
reporting. The BBC emerged from it stronger, and Kate Adie was
a public hero.

FOUR

Getting There

I hereby declare that data provided in the application
form are full and correct. Subject to the receipt of visa,
I pledge to leave the territory of the Russian Federation
before the visa expiration date. I am aware that valid visa
does not automatically allow to enter the territory of the
Russian Federation.

Official application form for a Russian visa

IT WAS, CURIOUSLY, THE English, so insistent in later centuries
on their right to travel anywhere they wanted without a passport, who seem to have been the first to introduce the visa system.
In 1414, during the reign of Henry V, Parliament passed an act to
introduce a document which would allow English people travelling
abroad to prove who they were and where they came from. By 1540
the document was known as a *passe-port* because it permitted the
person holding it to pass through the ports.

In the second half of the nineteenth century, travel by train across
international frontiers became so commonplace that the old system
of border control broke down, and the French government decided
to abandon it altogether. Prussia's invasion of France brought the
whole unwanted paraphernalia of identity checks and government
permissions back again for a time, but once the Prussians left, the
passport system was relaxed across much of Europe for the rest of
the nineteenth century. Only with the outbreak of the First World
War were passports generally reintroduced; and although the period
of peace after the fall of the Soviet empire in 1991 encouraged the

European Union, in particular, to open up its internal borders, the activities of extreme Islamists and the pressure of migrants from Africa and Asia made that increasingly difficult to maintain. Every time an immigration official at an airport looks at the front of your passport and hands it back without opening it, you're benefiting from the afterglow of a mood of international self-confidence which has now faded.

In 2015, according to a study of visa requirements, British and German citizens could travel more freely than anyone else on earth: they could enter 173 countries and dependent territories without needing a visa. (There are 195 countries in the world, according to the United Nations, but no one can agree on how many territories there are.) Finland, Sweden and the US came second in the travel requirements list, being free to travel to 172 countries. Most other EU passport holders, plus citizens of the former British dominions, and rich countries like Japan, followed in third, fourth or fifth places. Citizens of Afghanistan had the worst access around the world, since only twenty-eight countries would let them in without visas. Iraqis came next, with thirty-one countries accepting them without visas. Then followed Pakistan and Somalia (thirty-two countries), North Korea, Angola, Iran, Sudan and Syria (from thirty-eight to forty-one countries). The picture is clear, and pretty understandable: the poorer your country, the less democratic or the more affected it is by terrorism, the more likely it is that you will need a visa to travel abroad.

Visas are the pinch point of a country's control over foreign correspondents. If you offend the government, or some senior and influential member of it, you can stand outside the gate waiting to be let in for a very long time: possibly even for ever. In 2003, in the run-up to the invasion of Iraq by the United States and Britain, I was desperately anxious to get to Baghdad to cover it. But the most senior Iraqi official in charge of foreign journalists, a fat-headed character whose year of study at Edinburgh University hadn't fully perfected his English, misread something I wrote for a Sunday newspaper back in 1991, at the end of the first Gulf War, and took it as a personal insult. He remained in the job for the next twelve years, serving Saddam Hussein faithfully, and blocked my return pretty effectively – even though I did manage to get into Iraq a few times despite him.

As it became clearer and clearer that President George W. Bush would not be dissuaded from attacking Saddam Hussein, I sent message after message to this character, asking for a visa. I even continued after the invasion had begun, but there was no joy. What I didn't realise was that a colleague of mine was going to see the official on a fairly regular basis, urging him not to let me in. I suppose he thought I was some sort of threat to him; such is the bitchiness of the profession. He has now left the BBC, I'm glad to say.

There was an odd sequel to this episode. A new man was put in as Saddam's information minister: Mohammed Saeed al-Sahaf, who became known around the world as 'Comical Ali' for the absurd claims he made at his frequent press conferences during the invasion. I knew him, and eventually managed to get a message to him just before the invasion started, asking him for a visa. Eventually, just as I was about to enter northern Iraq, which Saddam Hussein no longer controlled, I got al-Sahaf's reply: I had been given a visa after all. Yet even before I could make the arrangements to get to Baghdad – not at all easy at that point – I had another message from him, telling me not to come. As a result I had to get to Baghdad the hard way, by road via Saddam's home town of Tikrit; in the course of which my team and I were bombed by the Americans, and our translator, a delightful young man called Kamran, was killed.

Some weeks after the invasion was over, al-Sahaf contacted me and (a certain irony, this) asked for help in getting a visa to Britain, plus political asylum. I knew I wouldn't be able to swing this, and asked him why I should do it.

'Because I saved your life.'

I started yelling down the line that because he had refused me a visa, our translator had been killed and my life had been greatly endangered in a 'friendly fire' incident; but he interrupted me to explain. At his weekly audience with Saddam, he had read out the list of foreign journalists to whom he had given visas. When he got to my name, Saddam exploded with rage: 'This man is my enemy,' he shouted.

Al-Sahaf was terrified; you upset the president at your peril. The problem was that I had made a film about Saddam for the *Panorama* programme a couple of months before, which wasn't exactly favourable to him. In fact, I don't know how you could make a programme about him that was favourable.

Then Saddam stopped raging and turned icy cold. 'I'll tell you what,' he said, according to al-Sahaf. 'Give him a visa, and we can deal with him when he gets here.'

Al-Sahaf went away, walking backwards out of the great one's presence (you should never, one of his colleagues told me, make eye contact with Saddam when you were talking to him, in case he thought you were challenging his authority). He knew what that meant: Saddam would have me killed. So he sent me the second message to say my visa had been cancelled.

Well, that was al-Sahaf's story, and since he imagined, quite wrongly, that I had the power to get him political asylum in Britain, you can see why he might simply have invented the whole thing. Still, it would explain those two odd messages, the one offering me a visa and the other, a few days later, cancelling it. Perhaps the whole episode belongs in that magical file marked 'Interesting If True'.

———

Journalists are subject to a welter of controls which don't apply to tourists or business travellers; the intention being, of course, to bar, or at least keep very close tabs on, correspondents who are thought to be hostile or too inquisitive – or who come from organisations the government doesn't like. I have been travelling to Iran ever since 1978. I learned Farsi, and wrote a couple of books which display a deep affection for the place. I have been given visas at times when Iran and Britain were at each other's throats, and although there have been long periods when I was refused entry, the authorities have always allowed me back eventually. Yet after the BBC started up a Persian-language television service in 2009, the supply of visas began to freeze up. The government of Iran is more liberal and open to outside influences nowadays, and British tourists are going to Iran in increasing numbers. Even British journalists are finding it easier to get visas: but not those from the BBC. For Iran, as for many other countries, the visa is an instrument of control.

South Africa, which until 2015 allowed European and American journalists to enter the country without any special documentation, now demands a letter of invitation, a copy of the applicant's CV, a copy of a hotel booking, a copy of the flight details, and full personal banking details covering the previous three months. India requires something rather similar. Russia and the United States both make intrusive demands of foreign journalists before giving them visas; the difference being that each Russian press visa lasts only a few months, while the American one lasts for much longer.

For correspondents who are planning to base themselves in a country for two or three years at a time, the rules are a little more elastic; though the host country can always threaten those who do not make the kind of reports it likes with withdrawing their accreditation – in other words, with throwing them out. This has happened to plenty of correspondents, whose careers haven't necessarily been damaged by it. Michael Buerk of the BBC was ordered out by South Africa's apartheid regime in 1987, and came back to Britain as a hero. Nevertheless, being thrown out of the country where you live and work is an unpleasant business, and the correspondent and his or her family are likely to feel the effects financially; foreign correspondents' living costs are usually paid in full or (increasingly) in part, while they are abroad, and they can often rent out their own houses back home.

The threat is nothing like so direct or frightening as physical violence, but it is something worth considering. As a result, foreign correspondents have to understand the red lines which exist in any country for those who report on its affairs, and be very certain that they are not going to be prevented from doing a good job because they are afraid of annoying the authorities.

India is hypersensitive about how Kashmir is reported; China about the Muslim unrest in Xinjiang and the private and business lives of its top politicians; Russia about corruption at the presidential level, and the way dissidents there seem to be killed off with disturbing frequency. It's not that correspondents based in Delhi or Beijing or Moscow dare not report such subjects; the governments involved are all relatively sophisticated and understand that they can't simply silence the foreign correspondents they have allowed into their country. But there are ways of doing these things with care and a degree of subtlety. As a result, for a foreign correspondent, the dividing lines between sensible caution, timidity, and outright dereliction of duty are delicate ones.

In 1976, when I was preparing to go to South Africa as the BBC's radio correspondent, I asked the head of news about all this, knowing how defensive the South African authorities could get about their dreadful system and the brutal way it was imposed on the non-white population. He told me to grade the importance of every sensitive story I did from one to ten. Anything below five I shouldn't worry about; from six or seven I should consult him if I wanted to; and from eight upwards I should just grit my teeth and report the story, regardless of the consequences. And, he added, don't bother your head about the consequences of what you report. (He meant the political consequences, not the effect on individual people's lives.) Anyone who wanted their reporting to have an effect of some sort on the policy of governments was a politician, not a journalist – and he was sending me to South Africa to be a journalist. During the year I was based there I had plenty of official warnings from the government in Pretoria, and some private threats, but I managed not to be thrown out.

Henry Morton Stanley had a shockingly difficult time as he made his way from the coast to the village of Ujiji, the area, now in modern Uganda, where Dr Livingstone had last been reported as living. Negotiating with the local chieftains along the way, African and Arab alike, was a long and often unpleasant business, since he was certain they were trying to rob him. He was uncomfortably aware that his stocks of cloth, which were the currency he paid for everything with, were being depleted fast. The heat was dreadful, and the insects huge and dangerous.

There was no reporting for him to do, since he was anxious not to alert the outside world to the fact that he was looking for Livingstone. Anyway, he wasn't sure Livingstone wanted to be found, and that worried him: 'My impression of him was that he was a man who would try to put as much distance as possible between us, rather than make an effort to shorten it, and I should have my long journey for nothing.'

It was a strange sort of search, therefore, set up entirely for the purposes of increasing a newspaper's circulation. In a way, Stanley's long and difficult journey was a foreshadowing of the kind of journalism we have become accustomed to in our own time: celebrity-hunting, not news. And yet everyone in America and Europe was genuinely fascinated to know what had become of Livingstone; Stanley's search and the words he claimed he used when he actually found Livingstone wouldn't be so familiar right around the world today if there hadn't been an intense interest in the purpose of his journey.

The details of the diary of the journey which he published later aren't somehow as interesting as they might be. Sir Richard Burton, who together with John Hanning Speke had been this way thirteen years before, in 1858, was interested in digging out the ethnographical and cultural facts about the people they came across, and sometimes the scabrous ones; while Speke was obsessed with the wildlife. Stanley was mostly just interested in Stanley. He lists his team in order and describes the various members of it as the expedition leaves for the interior, then adds: '[L]astly, on the splendid bay. . . myself, called Bana Mkuba, the "big master", by my people – the vanguard, the reporter, the thinker, and leader of the Expedition.' There was never anything wrong with Henry Morton Stanley's self-image.

As the kirangozi [guide] unrolled the American flag, and put himself at the head of the caravan, and the pagazis [porters], animals, soldiers, and idlers were lined for the march, we bade a long farewell to the *dolce far niente* of civilised life, to the blue ocean, and to its open road to home, to the hundreds of dusky spectators who were there to celebrate our departure with repeated salvoes of musketry.

His diary is taken up with the places they passed through, or had to stay in; the food and the insects; and the people he thought were trying to cheat him. At one stage they got caught up in a local war. But whereas Sir Richard Burton was sardonically interested in the local people, and wanted to know the finer details of their worship and diet and (especially) their sexual habits, Stanley just saw them as a nuisance:

> Perceiving that a little manliness and show of power was some-thing which the Wagogo long needed, and that in this instance it relieved me from annoyance, I had recourse to my whip, whose long lash cracked like a pistol shot, whenever they overstepped moderation. . . [W]hen they pressed on me, barely allowing me to proceed, a few vigorous and rapid slashes right and left with my serviceable thong soon cleared the track.

He kept his mission a secret even from the Europeans in his team, but he was always alert for any hint about Livingstone:

> At this camp, also, we met Salim bin Rashid, bound eastward, with a huge caravan carrying three hundred ivory tusks. This good Arab, besides welcoming the new comer with a present of rice, gave me news of Livingstone. He had met the old traveller at Ujiji, had lived in the next hut to him for two weeks, described him as looking old, with long grey moustaches and beard, just recovered from severe illness, looking very wan.

That cheered him up immensely:

> [S]omething tells me, I do not know what it is – perhaps it is the ever-living hopefulness of my own nature, perhaps it is the natu-ral presumption born out of an abundant and glowing vitality, or the outcome of an overweening confidence in oneself – anyhow

and everyhow, something tells me to-night I shall find him, and – write it larger – FIND HIM! FIND HIM! Even the words are inspiring. I feel more happy. Have I uttered a prayer? I shall sleep calmly to-night.

There is an innocence about Stanley when he writes secretly in his own diary that is actually rather engaging. After all the immense effort and the degree of suffering he's been through, the only thing he really cares about is to fulfil the mission Gordon Bennett gave him that night in Paris: 'I was impelled onward by my almost uncontrollable feelings. I wished to resolve my doubts and fears. Was HE still there? Had HE heard of my coming? Would HE fly?' Finally, they reach the outskirts of Ujiji and look down on the peaceful village below:

At last the sublime hour has arrived; – our dreams, our hopes, and anticipations are now about to be realised! Our hearts and our feelings are with our eyes, as we peer into the palms and try to make out in which hut or house lives the 'white man with the grey beard' we heard about when we were at the Malagarazi.

'Unfurl the flags, and load your guns!' [called Stanley.]

'One, two, three, – fire!'

A volley from more than forty guns roared out. After a while a black man in a white shirt with a turban of American cloth round his head toiled up the hill to speak to them. Characteristically, Stanley gets his question in first:

'Who the mischief are you?'

'I am Susi, the servant of Dr. Livingstone.'

'What! Is Dr Livingstone here?'

'Yes, sir.'

'In this village?'

'Yes, sir.'

'Are you sure?'

'Sure, sure, sir. Why, I leave him just now.'

'And is the Doctor well?'

'Not very well, sir.'

'Now, you Susi, run, and tell the Doctor I am coming.'
'Yes, sir.'

And, says Stanley, off he darted like a madman.

The moment of one of the greatest, perhaps *the* greatest, scoops in journalism was only minutes away.

———

William Howard Russell, without realising it, became the author of his own future failure. Not long after he came back from the Crimea, he gave a talk at the University of Aberdeen about his life as a foreign correspondent. In the audience was a tall, gangling young student from Morayshire called Archibald Forbes. Born in 1838, Forbes had no idea what he wanted to do when he graduated, but Russell's lecture decided him: he would be a foreign correspondent. In the years to come, he gave Russell a beating on many occasions, but he always claimed to have respect, even love for him. Russell's private letters give the impression he wasn't altogether convinced about that.

Russell had no military experience of any kind, but during his lecture he gave the impression that he thought this was useful for someone who wanted to cover foreign wars. As a direct result, Forbes joined the Royal Dragoon Guards as an ordinary trooper, but at the same time he started writing for a Liberal paper, the *Morning Star*, and had several essays on military subjects accepted by the prestigious *Cornhill Magazine*. He stayed in the army for nine years, then briefly started a newspaper of his own. In 1870, though, he was hired to cover the Franco-Prussian War, first by the *Morning Advertiser* and then for the paper he would stay with for most of the rest of his career, the *Daily News*.

Forbes grew into a heavily built, tough man, and though he often suffered from debilitating health problems they didn't prevent his covering, during the 1870s alone, the war in France, the Paris Commune, the Carlist wars in Spain, the Serbian-Turkish War, the Russo-Turkish War, the occupation of Cyprus, the Afghan War, the Zulu War, and (almost as exhausting) the Prince of Wales's visit to India. He always took a big interest in the ordinary rank-and-file soldiers – it's one of the most attractive things about him – and his articles and stories sometimes sound quite Kiplingesque. Indeed, Rudyard Kipling admired his writing, and as a young writer found inspiration for his own stories about British soldiers in Forbes's work.

At the same time Forbes was often outspokenly critical of the tactics of the generals he reported on. This sometimes made him deeply unpopular in the top levels of the British army, and with the politicians at home. With his craggy self-confidence and the assurance that first-hand reporting gave him, he didn't care.

In 1879 Forbes covered the Zulu War, which began badly for the British. He was often openly critical of the tactics of the commander, Lord Chelmsford, and wasn't surprised when these led to the disaster at Isandlwana when 22,000 Zulus wiped out a careless and over-confident detachment of 1,350 British and African soldiers – one of the worst defeats the British army had ever suffered. Forbes wasn't at Isandlwana, but he was on hand five months later when the British faced the pick of the Zulu army at their capital, Ulundi, on 4 July. All through the night the Zulus had sung ferocious songs and performed war dances, and the British soldiers, as they watched and listened from their positions on the outskirts of the town, showed real signs of nervousness, remembering what had happened to their comrades.

At dawn the British troops stood to and formed up in one single great square formation, and watched as a vast wave of Zulu warriors, commanded by their king, Cetewayo, came bursting out of the circular kraal of Ulundi and hurtled across the open ground towards them. The Zulus had few guns to match the British weaponry, but their extraordinary discipline, ferocity and huge numbers had enabled them to beat a modern force at Isandlwana. Archibald Forbes, calmly jotting down his notes in the centre of the British square, wrote that the Zulus' valour and devotion was unsurpassed by the soldiers of any period or nationality. Every time they charged they slaughtered British soldiers by the dozen, hurling their razor-sharp assegais into the red-coated ranks. When one section of the British square repulsed them, they would regroup and charge at another. The war artist Melton Prior was standing just behind the lines of soldiers, sketching the scene from inside the square. When the Zulus pulled back from that particular sector he pushed through the ranks and measured out the distance from the foremost British soldiers to the heap of Zulu bodies which had piled up there. It was nine paces.

In the end, the Zulus' determination began to falter. Chelmsford saw the moment had come to launch his cavalry. He shouted a command, the infantry moved aside to make a pathway, and a detachment of Lancers and the irregulars of Buller's Horse came charging through to the cheers of the foot soldiers. They hunted the Zulus into the rough ground on the edge of the battlefield and killed them in hundreds. The British victory was total.

One of Lord Chelmsford's staff told Prior that the general would wait until the next morning to send his despatches about the battle to his headquarters at Durban, and Prior passed the information on to Forbes. Instantly, Forbes realised this would be his big chance: if he left at once, he could take the news himself and get a brilliant exclusive. But it was dangerous: the nearest telegraph office was at Landsmann's Drift, 120 miles away, across territory which was hostile and unmapped. He told Prior he would leave in half an hour, and that if Prior could get his sketch of the battle ready in time he would take that too. Prior agreed, and got to work. Forbes, meanwhile, went to see Lord Chelmsford, and offered to take messages about the victory for him. Chelmsford agreed.

As Forbes swung his massive frame into the saddle and prepared to leave, an officer came up and offered him an even bet that he wouldn't get through. When Forbes took the bet on, the officer raised the stakes, saying he didn't expect to see him alive again. Forbes took it all in good part and rode off, while the soldiers and the other journalists cheered his courage.

What he did was extremely dangerous. It was already getting dark – this was the depth of the South African winter – and the trail he had to follow was the one left by the wagon wheels of the British forces on their march to Ulundi. It led past a number of kraals which the British had burned on their way through, so it seemed certain that some of the survivors would still be around. The night became darker and darker, and now Forbes could see groups of Zulus silhouetted against the burning remains of their huts. Behind him as he rode past he could hear angry shouts. From time to time the bush was so thick and the ground so dry that he had to dismount and search for the tracks of the British wagons.

Finally he lost the path altogether. He couldn't see any wheel ruts now, or even feel them with his hand as he knelt down. All he could do was to stop and wait in complete silence for the moon to rise: 'The longest twenty minutes of my life was spent sitting on my trembling horse in a little open glade of the bush, my hand on the butt of my revolver, waiting for the moon's rays to flash down into the hollow. Any instant might bring the enemy.' Even when the moon rose and Forbes could see the tracks again, he had to move slowly and quietly so as not to be spotted. Yet in the end he reached the British army's reserve camp at Etonganeni and told them the news of the victory.

The road was much better defined and there was less chance of meeting stragglers from the Zulu army, but Forbes wasn't out of danger yet; that night a British lieutenant and a corporal were killed on this stretch of the road, and Forbes was wise to race along at full gallop. But now there were British forts every fifteen miles, and he could get something to eat and drink there, and change horses. After twenty hours of hard riding – 'prolonged and arduous' was how he put it – he reached Landsmann's Drift. It had been a remarkable feat of horsemanship, which he owed to his experience as a trooper in the Dragoons.

Forbes's journalistic work was only now starting. He had to jot down a short version of the despatch to the *Daily News*, which he must have been working out in his head for much of the ride.

The telegraph operator clicked it out on his machine, and once it had been transmitted Forbes sent two other versions to the high commissioner for Southern Africa, Sir Bartle Frere, and Sir Garnet Wolseley, the army commander. Frere cabled his copy to London, and Forbes's despatch was read out in both houses of Parliament to great applause. *The Times* commented the next day that it had been 'a proud moment for the confraternity of special correspondents'; it had to make the best of the fact that it had been scooped by Archibald Forbes yet again.

Sending the short version to the newspaper was only the start of the job. Now Forbes had to get to Durban to file a full despatch. He rode to Ladysmith, where he borrowed a buggy and a span of horses, and eventually reached Pietermaritzburg. From there he caught a train to Durban, and during the journey he worked on his report. He arrived, after a total of fifty-five hours' riding and travelling, having not had a moment's sleep.

It was worth it: once again Forbes's long, detailed report for the *Daily News* scooped all his rivals. Melton Prior (known to his colleagues, because of his high-pitched voice and entirely bald head, as 'the Screeching Billiard-ball') benefited too, since Forbes mailed his sketch to the *Illustrated London News* from Durban. It got to London an entire week before the work of the other correspondents.

Forbes was in a state of complete exhaustion. He was only forty-one, but his health never entirely recovered from his exertions; and he effectively gave up the hugely demanding job of being a special correspondent, turning instead to lecturing and writing about his experiences. He died in 1900.

Forbes was funny and brave, and could write beautifully at great speed. He wasn't modest, and he was inclined to trumpet his opinions tactlessly. His colleagues often accused him, as plenty of other correspondents have been accused over the years, of appropriating other people's experiences and passing them off as his own. But Mark Twain called him the greatest war correspondent ever, and

Kipling agreed. Perhaps they were right. He certainly won his bet with the officer at Ulundi.

When Philip Pembroke Stephens was sent by the *Daily Express* to be its correspondent in Berlin in the late summer of 1933, he lasted less than a year. Journalists don't often make good heroes, but Pembroke Stephens was pretty exemplary, reporting what he saw rather than what the proprietor of his newspaper might want to hear; and he defied Hitler's secret police system in order to investigate the new realities of Germany for himself, giving his readers a thoroughly accurate account of life under Nazism.

The record of British reporting from Germany in the 1930s was not, in the main, a good one; American and French journalism was even worse. It was difficult to get press visas, and anyone who angered the German propaganda ministry was liable to be bundled out of the country and barred for good. In the end, only the *Daily Mail*, whose owner, Lord Rothermere, sympathised openly with fascism and admired Hitler, was able to send its reporters to Berlin with any great frequency; though to do them credit, even some of the *Mail*'s correspondents and foreign staff managed to get their carefully phrased anxieties about Hitler into the paper after the Nazi takeover in 1933. It was the *Mail*'s great rival, Lord Beaverbrook's *Daily Express*, which briefly managed to raise the standard of decent, accurate journalism inside Hitler's Germany.

Pembroke Stephens was a serious young man, educated at Gresham's School and Cambridge. Born in 1903, he succeeded in getting a desk job on the *Express*, and was still only thirty when he was sent to Berlin as the paper's resident correspondent at the end of 1933. His predecessor, Sefton Delmer, became one of Fleet Street's best-known writers in the decades to come. Delmer's technique was to get as close as he could to the Nazi leadership; Stephens, his successor, disapproved of this approach and preferred to concentrate on the effects of Nazism on the lives of ordinary people, and particularly Jews. He believed that good reporting was a matter of going to see things for himself, not of relying on official handouts.

Stephens was fortunate in having Lord Beaverbrook as his employer. Like Rothermere, who regarded the business of owning a newspaper as a means of promoting his own views, Beaverbrook regarded the *Express* as a megaphone for braying out his theories and ideas. Nevertheless, he was a mischievous character who enjoyed stirring things up. He liked to hire people with completely different political views from his own, because (as he once said) it added zest to the family's reading over the breakfast table. Beaverbrook came to share his friend Winston Churchill's view of Adolf Hitler as a dangerous and disruptive influence in world politics, though at first he seems to have regarded Nazism in Germany as a necessary counterweight to Soviet communism. Above all, Beaverbrook knew the sales potential of running a campaign; and Pembroke Stephens's reporting in Germany convinced him that campaigning against Nazi atrocities would sell newspapers. He was right.

The first big story Stephens reported on after his arrival in Germany was the effect of the worldwide Jewish-led boycott on German trade which had followed Hitler's assumption of power. In May 1934 he went to Hamburg ('a graveyard among cities') and sent back a vivid despatch about the decline of the shipping industry there, and of business in the city. This must have pleased the Nazi propaganda ministry, since Stephens stressed that the problem had been caused by Jewish interests abroad, and particularly in America. Perhaps Stephens wrote this story in order to provide himself with a little credit as far as the Nazi authorities were concerned, knowing that most of his reporting in the weeks and months to come would have to be deeply hostile. It was completely accurate: Hamburg had been badly affected, as Stephens's reporting showed, and the boycott was unquestionably to blame.

More than a year into Nazi rule, Germany had already become a fully fledged police state. After leaving Hamburg, Stephens stopped in Magdeburg, where he interviewed local people about a chemical plant which was being built there. The Gestapo arrested him as a spy, and he spent several days in gaol while they carried out checks on him. After he was released, he didn't allow the experience to intimidate him. In the small town of Arnswalde in Pomerania, which became part of Poland after the Second World War and is now called Choszczno, he started investigating the story he had come to Germany for. On Friday 25 May the *Express* ran it prominently on the front page.

NEW HITLER BLOW AT THE JEWS

PLAN TO SEIZE ALL THEY POSSESS?

VIVID DESPATCH BY PEMBROKE STEPHENS

'BEST THING YOU CAN DO IS DIE'

Reading it, you can sense Stephens's pride in his success at talking to a number of Jews, and in getting the news out: 'What is happening to the Jews left in Germany?... I have spent the past few days visiting districts where the Jews are reported to be suffering most keenly, to answer the question which so fascinates the world.'

Stephens admits that he has failed to discover precise details of the ill-treatment and murder of Jews, but he describes the way they are forced to live now:

> Friends of fifty years' standing do not greet their old Jewish friends when they meet them in the village: they look the other way.
>
> Jewish children are boycotted by former playmates as if they had the plague; farmers willing to borrow money from the small Jewish trader in democratic days do not take their debts seriously; customers prefer not to buy in Jewish shops, and storm troopers stand outside the doors of Jewish cinemas warning visitors away...
>
> Robbed of work, denied civic privileges in a country which despises them, what is the German Jew to do but follow the brutal advice of officials: 'The best thing you can do is to die.'

Given what was to happen over the next few years to those Jews who were still living in Germany – half a million, Pembroke Stephens estimates – this treatment seems relatively mild stuff. Yet his exclusive story was deeply shocking to the readers of the *Express*, since it was the first time any British newspaper had described what was happening to the Jews at first hand. The paper's editor, Arthur Christiansen, was a man with a remarkable news sense, and he knew that the owner, Lord Beaverbrook, would never complain about a scoop, whatever he might think about the Nazis. As for the editor of the *Mail*, he would probably have buried an article like that, or spiked it altogether, knowing that his proprietor, Lord Rothermere, would disapprove.

Six days later the Gestapo arrested Stephens. At police head-quarters he was, he said, 'locked up in a pen like a beast in a cage behind high wire netting', and was not allowed to make any tele-phone calls. Then he was taken to a prison: 'I heard the moans of a woman prisoner in pain, and saw a youth handcuffed to a detective being led away to his cell. Grim photographs of murdered men with bloodstained faces distorted in death grinned at me from the walls.'

Again, far worse was to happen in the following years, but this was new and horrifying to a British readership, and the article was reprinted across the world.

Stephens listened as a senior policeman read out a document to him; he was, it said, being expelled because he had conducted himself 'in a manner hostile to the State'. The police took him to the Belgian frontier and threw him out of Germany. He had been based there for less than nine months. Now he made his way to Amsterdam and was flown back to London to a hero's welcome. He had known all along what was likely to happen to him. In September 1933, when he first arrived in Berlin, he had written an article for the *Express* in which he promised he would always report accurately, whatever the consequences. Now, the *Express* of Saturday 2 June 1934 splashed his story under the headline 'My Expulsion By The Nazis': 'Events have proved my belief that it is impossible to tell the truth, the real truth, about Germany, and remain an accredited correspondent in Berlin.'

Beaverbrook immediately saw the opportunity for a campaign – something he loved – and the *Express*, much to the enjoyment of Winston Churchill and his friends, became Britain's foremost anti-Nazi newspaper. Stephens was given the space to write article after article attacking Hitler and his chief supporters: 'Menace to Europe: "Germany is the mad dog of Europe. She must be kept on a strong chain".' 'The Evil Genius of Germany – Goebbels the Jew-Baiter.' 'Austria's New Leader – He Believes Hitler Is "Crazed".' Yet as so many newspapers have found over the years, a campaign cannot be sustained at this level for long: the readers get bored. Even today's *Daily Express*, which bears no relationship to its former self, eventually gave up printing stories 'proving' that Diana, Princess of Wales, had been murdered.

As for Pembroke Stephens, he went off to cover the second Abyssinian War and the Spanish Civil War, where he was one of the first journalists to enter the city of Guernica after it had been bombed continuously for four hours in late April 1937 by the Condor Legion of the German Luftwaffe, sent by Hitler to support Franco's Nationalist forces.

He seems, however, to have learned a depressing lesson from his time in Germany: in his despatch he reported simply that the town had been burned, though a few days later he privately told the British ambassador to Spain that Guernica had been destroyed by air strikes, and that these were German tactics. Stephens asked the ambassador not to attribute the information to him, though, because he wanted to report from Franco's headquarters; the Nationalist line, in face of worldwide condemnation of the attack, was that the people of Guernica had set fire to their own town. Every foreign correspondent knows the problem, and has to deal with it as his or her own conscience dictates. But Pembroke Stephens, who had put his job and his personal safety on the line in Hitler's Germany, took the decision to muffle the news in Guernica, in order to keep on reporting. I know what my old head of news would have said: the Guernica story would have registered nine or ten on the importance scale, and reporting that the town had been destroyed by the Luftwaffe was so significant a part of it that Stephens should have concentrated on that.

Six months later, Stephens paid the ultimate price for his reporting. He went on from Spain to China, where the invading Japanese army was committing atrocity after atrocity. In November 1937, as he was watching the fighting from a water tower outside Shanghai, a machine-gunner fired at him and killed him with a shot through the head. He was only thirty-four. The Japanese actually apologised afterwards, saying that they had been shooting at snipers on the rooftops nearby.

A tough, heavy-drinking *Daily Mail* correspondent called Edward O'Dowd Gallagher, who later worked for SOE, the Special Operations Executive, throughout the Second World War, was close by when Pembroke Stephens was killed, and wrote the story of his death. In a characteristic gesture he sent it, not to his own newspaper, but to Stephens's.

'I couldn't scoop him on his own obituary,' he said.

The relationship between a country and the foreign journalists based there is a complicated one. Some correspondents, like Philip Pembroke Stephens in Germany, hate the place, or at least its government, and feel an urgent need to reveal its awfulness to the world. Other foreign correspondents endure the place where they are posted with as much patience as they can muster, waiting only for the opportunity to move on to another posting. And a third category adores the place they report from so much that they stay and stay, and become totally identified with it. Such a one was Alistair Cooke, whose chocolate-toned voice was heard on British radio for nearly sixty years, describing the weekly doings of the United States in *Letter from America* from 24 March 1946 to 20 February 2004, the longest-running speech programme on British radio. The last programme was broadcast only four weeks before his death at the age of ninety-five.

Alistair Cooke the radio voice was charming, smooth, deeply perceptive and witty. Alistair Cooke the man responsible for the broadcasts was often less than attractive. To the young producers who were responsible for putting his programme on the air, week after week, he could be savage and cutting. (They were almost

invariably young, because the job required no great skill or judgement to fulfil: Cooke was so immensely experienced a broadcaster
that he rarely made mistakes, and had a superbly honed style which
was all his own.)

A colleague of mine, who was in nominal charge of the programme,
broke in at one point to question, hesitantly and politely, Cooke's
grammar. It was something like a plural verb after a singular noun,
or maybe vice versa. I was sitting in on the session, because it would
be my unfortunate turn soon to act as Alistair Cooke's London
producer. My colleague was right, as it happens, but if you had any
sense you never questioned anything Alistair Cooke said.

Down the line from thousands of miles away, the chocolate
turned to acid. He was absolutely foul: 'How old are you? How
many years have you been working there? What makes you think
you can criticise my work just like that? I'll speak to your editor
about it right away.'

As it happened, our boss, a charming, elderly, overweight gent
with a name that had a faintly Dickensian sound to it and white
hair sprouting from various unexpected places around his face, had
endured years of complaints from his star performer. He'd been
listening on another loudspeaker, and now he came bustling into
the studio, pausing only to turn the fader down so Alistair Cooke
wouldn't hear him in New York.

'Don't worry, dear boy,' he said, smiling seraphically and looking
more like a character out of Dickens than ever. 'Poor old Alistair can
sometimes be a bit tetchy.' And he reeled off the names of various
grand, senior figures in our department who had felt the transatlantic lash over the years.

But although he may not always have been sweet-tempered,
Alistair Cooke wrote like an angel. This paragraph, taken pretty
much at random, was how *Letter from America* opened on 7 June
1970:

Every night the comfortable people who have no personal link
with Vietnam, and surely the anxious who do, settle down to
one of the three television networks that put on, at seven o'clock,

a half hour of world and domestic news. The other night one of their Vietnam correspondents poked his camera into a small jungle clearing in an unnamed and probably unpronounceable corner of Cambodia, and asked four or five American soldiers who were squatting there how they felt about crossing yet another Asian border, or should we say entering a new country? One of them smiled wanly and said, 'We ought to get back home where we belong, in Vietnam.' It was the only faint attempt at a joke. All the others were sad and sore. To put it mildly, they violently disagreed with the Commander-in-Chief, who, as you may recall, is the President of the United States. They not only had no taste for war in general, they thought the Cambodian adventure was a mess and a mistake.

Here, a few years later, at the height of the political scandal which had engulfed President Richard Nixon, is how Cooke opened a *Letter* about Watergate:

> Nobody has ever denied America a gift for melodrama, in its history as well as in the great popular literature it more or less invented: the movies. This leads Europeans, more than anybody, to expect melodrama all the time and to report even the gravest American political upheaval as some sort of comic horror film.

He adored America, but he was never blind to its failings. Though he had strong political opinions, you can read carefully through his stories about Vietnam and Watergate, right through to his reporting of the doings of George W. Bush, and never find any sign of bias.

'Alistair' was a name he adopted to make himself sound classier; his name at birth (in 1908) was Alfred, which was distinctly *démodé*. His father was a metalsmith in Salford, Lancashire, and Cooke went to Blackpool grammar school. He won a scholarship to Jesus College, Cambridge, where he set up a successful theatre group called The Mummers, and edited *Granta*. After studying at both Yale and Harvard on a scholarship, he initially returned to Britain. In 1937, though, he emigrated to America and became a

US citizen in 1941, shortly before Pearl Harbor. From 1947 to 1972 he was the New York correspondent of the *Manchester Guardian*, which later shortened its name to the *Guardian*. He wrote as beautifully as he spoke, and his broadcasts were always carefully scripted and re-scripted, so that you can still hear his voice clearly when you read his articles on the page.

Although he was primarily a commentator, he was also a superb reporter. In a Los Angeles hotel on 5 June 1968, shortly after midnight, he happened to be a few yards away from Robert Kennedy when he was murdered by Sirhan Sirhan. For my money, Cooke's account of it, broadcast by the BBC's *Letter from America* soon afterwards, is the best and freshest piece of reporting in this entire book:

> There was suddenly a banging repetition, of a sound that I don't know how to describe – not at all like shots, like somebody dropping a rack of trays. Half a dozen of us were startled enough to charge through the door, and it had just happened. It was a narrow lane he [Kennedy] had come through, for there were long steam tables and somebody'd stacked up against them these trellis fences with artificial leaves stuck on 'em, that they use to fence the dance band off from the floor.
>
> The only light was the blue light of three fluorescent tubes slotted in the ceiling. But it was a howling jungle of cries and obscenities and flying limbs and two enormous men – Roosevelt Greer, the football player, and Rafer Johnson I guess, the Olympic champion, – piling on to a pair of blue jeans.
>
> There was a head on the floor, streaming blood, and somebody put a Kennedy boater under it, and the blood trickled down like chocolate sauce on an ice cake. There were flashlights by now and the button eyes of Ethel Kennedy turned to cinders. She was slapping a young man and he was saying 'Listen lady, I'm hurt too', and down on the greasy floor was a huddle of clothes and staring out of it the face of Bobby Kennedy, like the stone face of a child, lying on a cathedral tomb.
>
> I had and have no idea of the time of all this, or even of the event itself, for when I pattered back into the creamy, green

genteel dining room I heard somebody cry 'Kennedy – shot' and heard a girl moan 'No, no, not again' – and my companion was fingering a cigarette package like a paralytic.

A dark woman nearby suddenly bounded to a table and beat it, and howled like a wolf, 'Stinking country, no, no, no, no' – and another woman attacked the shadow of the placid TV commentators, who'd not yet got the news.

Alistair Cooke may not have been popular among his younger colleagues, but he was one of the finest writers the BBC ever employed.

FIVE

Journeys

When George Bush senior invaded Panama in 1990, pursuing his uppity former CIA buddy General Manuel Noriega as a pretext for controlling the Panama Canal, the media reports made little mention of civilian casualties. My phone rang. 'I smell a rat,' said Martha [Gellhorn]. The next day she was on a plane to Panama. She was then in her eighties. She went straight to the slums of Panama City, and walked from door to door, interviewing ordinary people. That was her way. She estimated some 6,000 people dead from the American bombing that had accompanied Bush's invasion. She then flew to Washington and stood up at a press conference and asked a general: 'Why did you kill so many people then lie about it?'

John Pilger, speaking at the 12th annual award of the Martha Gellhorn Prize for Journalism, June 2011

THE SPEED WITH WHICH a foreign correspondent's material can reach headquarters seems to get faster by the year; or certainly by the quarter-decade. Friends of mine who worked in South Africa for the British, French or American newspapers in the 1970s used to praise the remarkable qualities of a man they all knew as 'Fingers' van der Merwe, a freelance telex operator who used to travel with them to places where news was breaking, and charge them per every hundred words to telex their material back to London, Paris or New York. 'Fingers' – we all stopped laughing at his nickname quite quickly, because we became so habituated to it – made a packet and was eventually able to retire on his thoroughly well-deserved earnings, having improved the working conditions of dozens of journalists beyond measure.

Now, of course, the fingers that send material back to the office at home are those of the foreign correspondents themselves. Their laptop is far and away the most important piece of equipment they have, and through a dongle or a Myfi – if you are reading these words only four or five years from now the equipment will be something even faster and more reliable – they can make sure that their despatch will be in their editor's hands almost as soon as they press the send button. Oddly, television news, which used to be one of the most instantaneous forms of journalism, can nowadays be rather slower than this. Of course, a great deal of the output of organisations like Al Jazeera or CNN or the BBC is live, and that can only be achieved with portable satellite equipment.

I have opened the *Ten O'Clock News* from the Zimbabwean bush, memorising the headlines and my introduction to my own report, lit by the headlights of our car and praying that the breakdown in our equipment, which had happened only seven minutes before we went on air ('Can you promise me that you will come up on time?' asked the editor of the programme, and I, crossing my fingers, did exactly that; fortunately the glitch was overcome and we did indeed come up on time) would be sorted out. It was a dodgy business altogether: we had crossed the South Africa–Zimbabwe border illegally, and the penalty laid down by the Zimbabwean criminal code for broadcasting without a government licence was seven years in prison. But it was all a great success, and my colleagues, Oggy Boytchev, Nigel Bateson and I celebrated back in Johannesburg with the best meal available; though in some ways Nigel's wife Sally had been the real hero of the episode, since she drove for six hours through the South African and Zimbabwean bush – something lone women are advised in the strongest terms not to do – in order to bring us a piece of equipment we needed.

Live broadcasting is a complex and difficult business; but in some ways the real art of working for television news abroad is still summed up in the edited report, well honed, sharply written and beautifully illustrated with the latest pictures, usually put together at extremely short notice in a hut or a hotel bedroom. Yet the cost of satelliting it is so great that we tend instead to send it by internet. And because we often work in places where the wifi signal is weak or intermittent, it can take a long time and be bad for the temper, the health and the digestion.

In 2014 the BBC producer assigned to work with me, Peter Leng, and a BBC cameraman, Duncan Stone, both of whose adventures will appear later, travelled with me to a town in northeastern Nigeria called Maiduguri. The extreme Islamist group Boko Haram was active around the edges of the town and sometimes inside it, and we had just come back from a town twenty-five miles away which had been almost wiped out by Boko Haram two days before. I had never seen such damage in my entire life. We were caught up in an angry crowd of survivors who were demanding protection from Boko Haram, and had to leave in a hurry. It was brilliant material, and was all the better because we knew our main competition had flown timorously into the relative safety of Maiduguri for three hours, done a few quick interviews, and flown out again.

We faced one major problem: how to send our edited report back to London. Internet communication was pretty haphazard in Maiduguri. Worse, as we were starting to transmit it by email, a savage electrical storm broke over the town. In the deafening darkness Duncan sat over the equipment, urging it on, and Peter paced up and down, talking to London whenever the line was up, and shouting imprecations when it wasn't. Not being able to help in any way, I just sat nearby, sheltering from the rain, and hoping for the best. In the end, about two-thirds of the report got through, and the rest had to be broadcast the following night. With nerves of steel, the editorial team in London ran whatever they could of our report, and cut it short with an apology when the pictures ran out. Television news isn't for the weak-hearted. As for us, drenched in the rain of north-eastern Nigeria, we had the profound satisfaction of knowing that we had beaten our opposition badly.

Every traditional British country house seems to have them, especially in the corridors leading to the lavatories. So do the grander and more old-fashioned pubs and restaurants. They portray characters in top hats or army helmets or cricket caps in a variety of attitudes, carrying canes or bats or guns, and there are enigmatic titles under them, which people must once have understood instantly but which are now mystifying: 'Stock Exchange', or 'HMS', or 'Rugby Football', or 'St Paul's School'. You can pick them up for £10 each from boxes outside secondhand booksellers, if you want them; not many people seem to nowadays.

The man who invented the idea of caricaturing the foremost people of the day, and who founded *Vanity Fair*, the magazine which gave them their collective name, was born in 1841, the illegitimate son of an early Victorian politician. This didn't hold him back. Thomas Gibson Bowles became a famous yachtsman, and the maternal grandfather of the Mitford sisters. But to historians of journalism, he is best known as the *Morning Post* correspondent during the siege of Paris in 1870. His coverage of the rigours and hunger suffered by the inhabitants was flown triumphantly out of the city by balloon and pigeon, while the frustrated Prussian besiegers wasted their bullets trying to shoot them down. Tommy Gibson was a jovial, high-living, self-confident kind of man with an attractive openness which make his account of the siege of Paris (published in 1871) a pleasure to read.

Characteristically, he was out sailing when France fought and lost the battle of Sedan. He had been on a fishing cruise off the Cornish coast, 'a deliciously lazy life between sea and sky', he writes, 'with a maximum of sun and a minimum of clothes'. When they reached Southampton he got dressed, went ashore to buy the newspapers, and found that Napoleon III had surrendered to the Prussians and France was now a republic. His dreams of continuing his cruise vanished instantly. With an instinct that every foreign correspondent, past or present, would recognise, he knew he had to go there at once:

> Should a Republic be established, should Paris be besieged, and I not there? Impossible. I must go. Go I accordingly did by the very next train to London, just managed to get a passport and

a *visé* by special favour, put ten pounds in my pocket, and took the night mail to Paris. I saw three or four people in town, who declared that I must be mad, and predicted horrors of all kinds. I have always found, however, that horrors grow much less horrible the nearer you get to them.

Any number of foreign correspondents, from William Howard Russell to Kate Adie and Marie Colvin, could have written – indeed probably have written – their version of those sentiments, and will for as long as the reporting of news lasts. It is the correspondent's equivalent of that line from 'The Golden Journey to Samarkand': 'For lust of knowing what should not be known. . .'

Tommy Gibson got his passport very quickly: by special favour, he says, which sounds as though he had a friend at the Foreign Office. But what about the *visé* he talks about? Where did he get that? It can only have come from the French embassy, where he presumably had friends too. The embassy would have been devastated at the news from France, but it would have wanted to encourage as many British correspondents as possible to go to Paris. Britain's attitude to France and Prussia was of real importance to both countries; and while British public opinion had tended to favour the Prussians at first, the savagery that was shown to Paris during the siege changed British attitudes sharply; perhaps the French diplomats sensed that something like this might happen, and wanted to help Tommy Gibson get there quickly, before the siege took hold.

Visé simply means what we nowadays call a visa. The word comes from the Latin phrase *carta visa*, 'document seen', and Gibson's *visé* is a French version of the Latin. It means essentially that the necessary paperwork has been submitted and has been approved as satisfactory, so that the passport holder can be allowed to enter. Only nine years earlier, in 1861, France had abolished both passports and visas, and many European countries had followed suit. Gibson presumably needed both, or thought he might, because Prussia had invaded France and would probably start to control the movement of foreigners.

Ahead of him lay an intensely difficult and testing time, emotionally and physically.

If a writer has any guts he should write all the time, and the lousier the world the harder a writer should work. For if he can do nothing positive to make the world more liveable or less cruel and stupid, he can at least record truly, and it is something no one else will do, and it is a job that must be done.

To anyone who had the good fortune to know Martha Gellhorn, the voice is unmistakably hers, with its directness, its sense of duty, its willingness to lay down the law, and its certainty that writing has a special, overriding value. She wrote this to a friend in 1940, when she came back to London to report for *Collier's* magazine on the unfolding war. She had last visited the city in 1938, when she had been disgusted by the complacency of the British and their unwillingness to confront the ugly future which she knew lay ahead. But coming back and seeing the efficiency and determination with which London was coping with the devastating nightly air raids, she changed her mind.

'I realised then that it was the only place in the world to be,' she once told me. 'And after the war I never really felt like going back to live in America because they didn't have any idea what had really been happening in the world. The people here did.' She sometimes lived abroad, and spent much of her time in her cottage in Wales, but London had become her true home. It was there that she ended her days in 1998.

At thirty-two she was only three years older than Clare Hollingworth, but was already an established writer and journalist. Her account of her travels through America's Depression-hit farmlands, published in 1936 as *The Trouble I've Seen*, gained her great attention in America and the friendship of Eleanor Roosevelt, the president's wife. Martha, beautiful, blonde and outspoken, became a highly successful and committed foreign correspondent when she went to cover the Spanish Civil War with Ernest

Hemingway, whom she married in 1940. (She was always reluctant to talk about Hemingway, beyond saying that marriage to him was 'a life-darkening experience'; but she told me that his dismissive, overbearing treatment of her in Spain, where he locked her into her own room in Madrid during an air raid 'for her own safety', was the beginning of the end for their troubled relationship.)

She was glad to be at the heart of things in London, reporting the war for *Collier's*; yet she found the controls that were already being placed on journalists irksome after the broad scope she'd had in Spain, when she could travel more or less where she wanted and say what she wanted to say. Nevertheless she could report more or less freely on the Blitz and on life in Britain, and she did this impressively well; she had contempt for her colleague Quentin Reynolds from *Collier's*, because 'he wrote as though he, rather than London, was being bombed'. The strength of her reporting was that she concentrated on portraying the lives and experiences of the ordinary Londoners she met. Her own difficulties and dangers didn't come into it; she never had any time for what she called the 'look at me' school of journalism.

The real problem came when she had to register as a war correspondent in order to visit the various theatres of war. This was impossible without accreditation, and that meant agreeing to submit everything you wrote to the censors: British in the first instance, and then increasingly American after the United States eventually came into the war. And anyway, women journalists weren't allowed to go to the front. Equally bad, from Martha's standpoint, was the intensifying effort by the Allied leadership to co-opt the press as part of its propaganda effort. General Eisenhower told the correspondents assigned to him that he regarded them as 'quasi-staff officers'; some of them were probably flattered by this, but it infuriated people of Martha Gellhorn's stature and independence of mind.

Nevertheless, she decided that she had no alternative but to take the official route. She bought a military uniform with a 'C' for correspondent sewn onto the breast pocket, and collected the accreditation papers which would give her the honorary rank of captain. But she quickly found ways of evading officialdom. When Ernest Hemingway eventually bestirred himself to stop drinking and fishing in Cuba and came to London at Martha's insistence to write about the war for *Collier's*, she lost her seniority, since Hemingway immediately became the magazine's chief war correspondent. Nevertheless, she still managed to go where she wanted, charming the lonely pilots she met into letting her fly with them even when she didn't have the necessary papers. Her attractions were obvious. In terms we would nowadays find pretty offensive, *Collier's* described her at this time as standing out 'among gal correspondents, not only for her writing but for her good looks. Blonde, tall, dashing – she comes pretty close to living up to Hollywood's idea of what a big-league woman reporter should be.' To Martha, this sort of thing seemed patronising and annoying, but she was always well aware of her advantages and was prepared to use them when necessary.

By the start of June 1944, the Allied forces were gathering in the south of England for D-Day. More than five hundred journalists, photographers and technicians were assembling with them. Hemingway was one of their number, but Martha, as a woman and as a junior correspondent, was not. She spent the morning of 5 June, the day before D-Day, in London, then decided to head down to the south coast to see if she could find some way of getting to France. There was no doubt in her mind that the accredited journalists would see all the action, but maybe she might just catch sight of a bit of it.

Late that night she was walking along the docks at a port on the coast when a military policeman stopped her. A white-painted ship with red crosses was moored close by, and she pointed to it. She was, she told him, going on board to interview some nurses for her magazine. She had enough identification to prove it, so he let her pass. Martha went on board and, finding a lavatory, locked herself in it without saying anything to anyone. The ship she was stowing away on was a floating hospital, a former civilian North Sea ferry manned by a British Merchant Navy crew. It was carrying a large detachment of American doctors and nurses, and was scheduled to be the very vessel to cross the Channel. No one took any notice of her: they were either too busy or too frightened to worry about a stray civilian. Martha's remarkable luck was holding.

Time passed, and she heard the sound of the anchor being hoisted and felt the ship get under way. After a while she unlocked the lavatory door and stepped out. Night had fallen, and the ship was heading out to sea. Martha's account in *The Face of War* has all the immediacy of notes jotted down soon afterwards: 'Badly spooked... The sweating it out period before leaving then paid off... Was drinking a lot of whisky... I was very scared, drank, got unscared.'

As dawn broke, she stood on deck watching the extraordinary scene, as the biggest armada which had ever been assembled lay spread out before her. She jotted down her disjointed perceptions:

Seascape filled with ships. . . the greatest naval traffic jam in history. . . so enormous, so awesome, that it felt more like an act of nature than anything man made...

Double & triple clap of gunfire. Unseen planes roar. Barrage balloons. Gun flashes. One close shell burst... Explosions jar the ship.

Ernest Hemingway and many of the 557 other accredited journalists from around the world who were covering D-Day found themselves stuck in some way. The correspondent who had the best view of the greatest invasion in human history as it started was Martha Gellhorn.

Like many other foreign correspondents of my generation, I have seen plenty of war crimes committed in front of my eyes; we have lived in ugly times. Yet the worst and longest drawn-out war crime I have seen was unquestionably the siege of Sarajevo by the Bosnian Serbs from 1992 to 1995. An estimated average of thirty shells or mortar shells were fired into the city each day. In the deep cold of every winter the Bosnian Serbs cut off all supplies of electricity and fuel oil, so there was no heating or light; in the heat of every summer they cut off the supply of water. It was an unspeakably brutal attack on a civilised community, and the outside world stood by and did nothing serious to stop it.

The BBC's Martin Bell distinguished himself greatly in Sarajevo, using his considerable personal authority to persuade the rival foreign television teams to set aside their intense rivalry and pool their pictures on a daily basis. This meant that only a couple of teams had to go out and risk their lives each day, rather than ten or twelve. Bell's courage may well have saved the lives of a number of television teams, though plenty of people died.

Jeremy Bowen was another BBC correspondent who did some distinguished reporting in Sarajevo. When the military leader of the Bosnian Serbs, Ratko Mladić, was finally caught and put on trial at the International Criminal Tribunal in The Hague, Bowen was called to give evidence about the Bosnian Serb army's organised shelling and sniping campaign against civilians. 'There wasn't a single place where you couldn't be hit by a shell, and there were a lot of places where you could be shot by a sniper,' he told the court.

Bowen himself witnessed the murder of civilians who were shot in the head on the streets of the city centre by snipers. 'It seems that the Serbs saw civilians not only as a legitimate target, but as their principal enemy,' he said.

In its evidence, the prosecution showed the court a television report filed by Bowen in July 1992 about the funeral of two children who were killed – deliberately, there can be no doubt – by snipers' bullets in July 1992, during an attempt to evacuate them from the city by bus.

His report, which is one of the most memorable of the entire war, showed the moment during the funeral when the cemetery was shelled, just as the family and several children were laying flowers. It was particularly courageous of Bowen and his team to go there to cover it, because the cemetery was a frequent target; and the Bosnian Serbs, whose intelligence from the city was excellent, would have known precisely when the funeral was due to take place. 'There is no doubt in my mind that Serb forces deliberately targeted the cemetery to kill civilians,' he said in his television report.

Plenty of journalists were killed or injured during the siege of Sarajevo. Martin Bell himself was hit in the groin by a piece of shrapnel from a mortar while he was recording a piece to camera. The Catalan photographer Jordi Pujol Puente, charming and jolly, insisted on taking pictures of people doing the 'Sarajevo shuffle' as they dodged across open ground where snipers operated, and was himself killed by a single shot. Allan Little, one of the BBC's finest foreign correspondents, watched and even talked at length to a sniper. The American David Kaplan of ABC News was killed in August 1992 when one of their number placed a bullet with contemptuous precision between the letters 'T' and 'V' marked out on his car with grey masking tape. Walking back at night from the TV station to the Holiday Inn, I was pinned down for half an hour by a sniper who put a bullet into the wall just above my head each time I looked up. At last, I couldn't take any more and got to my feet. The sniper fired at the wall again, a few inches higher than my head, but didn't kill me. It was clearly a matter of choice for him. I raised my hand in gratitude, and walked on.

It was one of the curiosities of the siege that we as journalists could easily drive out of the city where so many people were held prisoner and go up into the surrounding hills where the Bosnian Serb gunners and snipers operated; and when their daily intake of *slivovic* briefly reached the point where they were moderately friendly, they might be persuaded to show you through their telescopic sights the window of your room at the Holiday Inn, a building which stood out horribly thanks to its bilious yellow cladding. Twice the gunners asked me to tell them where in the city they should put a shell, and laughed at my horrified response.

Often we would head to the Bosnian Serbs' headquarters at the former skiing resort of Pale to see the leadership: Radovan Karadžić, Ratko Mladić and Nikola Koljević. Mladić was a bullying thug, who in July 1995 captured the UN 'safe area' of Srebrenica and ordered the murder of 8,000 Muslim males, including many old men and young boys.

Koljević, though wholly unimportant, was in some ways the most intriguing of the three: a mild-mannered English literature scholar from Sarajevo University who specialised in Shakespearian studies: 'How can you possibly read the works of the most humane writer ever, and preside over this siege?' I once asked him. You could put questions like this to him and not risk a beating. He shuffled around and could produce no answer which I could understand. Less than a year later he shot himself.

Karadžić was a weird character whom I found hard to take seriously. He was absurdly vain of his long, greying Donald Trump-like hair, and as a result hated doing interviews outside in the fierce Pale wind. Yet his keenness to appear on television – he always seemed to think he could persuade his audience of the logic of his crackpot views – was so great that I rarely had any difficulty in getting him to speak to me. As he did so, strands of his overlong hair would blow around in the sharp breeze. The Western press called him 'the butcher of Sarajevo', but although he oversaw the brutal siege and helped to plan it, he seemed to have none of Ratko Mladić's thirst for blood. He was a psychiatrist by training, yet there seemed to be nothing scientific about his mind. He was a misty thinker at best, who always used to ramble on about 'geopolitics': often a sign of opinionated ignorance. He also wrote interminable poetry, much of it in the style of the old Serbian bards. One of his books was called *From the Crazy Spear to the Black Fairytale*, and was as hard to understand as its title.

The *Guardian* foreign correspondent and filmmaker Maggie O'Kane, gutsy and gentle in equal measure, with a strong hint of her native Dublin in her voice, made the not particularly safe journey to eastern Bosnia after Karadžić vanished, to see if she could find him. She didn't, but in a BBC1 documentary she found out a great deal of beautifully judged detail about him and the people who supported him:

> 'Kick them out,' Bishop Radovic Amfilohije of Cetinje monastery tells his aides when we attempt to ask him why he's on our intelligence list as one of three bishops offering support and shelter to Karadžić. When we visit he is conducting a three-hour service around the town of Cetinje to mark the first day of Orthodox Lent. He says he is too tired to be interviewed about his monastery being listed as a refuge for Karadžić. 'This

is a place of God and God offers refuge to any man who needs it,' he says, describing Karadžić as a poet and politician. In the church's shrine they still keep the pickled head of Mahmut Pana, the Turkish commander who dared to defy the might of the Serb army.

In Karadžić's home village of Petnijica, Maggie found he was still a local hero:

> His cousin Vusko is one of the few members of the family who have stayed in the village in the Durmitor mountains. 'What did he do that is different from his ancestors? His ancestors were warriors and they fought against and killed the Turks. Today the Muslims are the new Turks, so why should we be ashamed of him?'

Maggie finds a man called Kapor. On the sideboard in his house he has a photograph of himself and his beautiful wife with Ratko Mladić. Mladić has his arm round her waist: 'Aren't you worried about having a photo of yourself with a mass murderer?' Maggie asks in her forthright way:

> 'No,' says Kapor, passing around the brandy again. He then explains to the group around the table: 'What you don't see in the picture is that it is taken with us standing on the bodies of dead Muslims.'
>
> He laughs. There is a barely discernible intake of breath around the table from the other members of the Committee to Defend Radovan Karadžić – still mostly sober. Then the breath is released. It is a joke. He is drunk. Poetic licence. Kapor keeps laughing. The other members of the committee laugh. 'Oh Momo,' says his beautiful wife adoringly.

Maggie O'Kane produced a fine film, but she didn't find Radovan Karadžić. Nor did anyone else till 2008, when the Serbian police arrested him in Belgrade. He had been working for some time at a private clinic under the ludicrous name of Dr Dragan David Dabić. He specialised in alternative medicine, and disguised himself behind a flowing white beard. It was as hard as ever to take him seriously;

yet this was the man who had instigated and overseen a vicious
siege which went on for 11,825 days – longer than the Siege of
Leningrad in the Second World War – and whose orders had killed
an average of almost exactly one person per day during that time:
11,541. Many hundreds of them were children.

Of all the violent places from which journalists have reported in the
quarter-century since the fall of Marxism-Leninism in Europe and
beyond, Chechnya was one of the very worst. There was a frightening degree of political and religious extremism, and the Russian
forces cared nothing for human life or the niceties of journalism.
Above all, as in Syria at the time of writing, they bombed with an
almost total lack of discrimination from the air, which ensured heavy
civilian casualties. Even in Bosnia at its worst, being a Westerner
and working for a newspaper or broadcasting organisation provided
you with a certain limited protection; in Chechnya, as in Syria now,
it gave you none at all.

In the midst of this appeared a crisp, tall, handsome American
woman in her early forties: as attractive in her way as Martha Gellhorn,
but quieter and less inclined to lay down the law. Marie Colvin's easy
New York accent, modified by several decades of writing for the
London *Sunday Times* (she had started with them in 1985 and stayed)
gave her a calming drawl which somehow meant that everyone went
quiet and listened to what she had to say. She was remarkably beautiful, and continued to be, even after she lost her left eye to a piece of
shrapnel in Sri Lanka and wore a startling black eyepatch to cover it.

Above all, Marie was a stayer. I first met her in Baghdad in 1991
when she and a small group of others, of whom I was privileged
to be one, decided to ignore the demands of our organisations
back home to leave, or the warnings of the American forces, or the
threats from Saddam Hussein's government, and hung on to report
the horrors of the first Gulf War. We had no water or electricity,
and not much to eat; but Marie always managed to look good, and
stayed calm and funny. It was great for our morale. For my money

Good Newes to Christendome.

Sent to a Venetian in Ligorne, from a Merchant in ALEXANDRIA.

Discouering a wonderfull and strange Apparition, visibly seene for many dayes together in Arabia, ouer the place, where the supposed Tombe of MAHOMET (the Turkish Prophet) is inclosed: By which the learned Arabians prognosticate the Reducing & Calling of the great Turke to Christianitie. With many other notable Accidents: But the most remarkable is the miraculous rayning of Bloud about ROME.

Done out of the Italian.

LONDON,
Printed for NATHANIEL BUTTER. 1630.

A typical Nathaniel Butter front page, from 1630. Although the story is ludicrous, Butter pioneered features like headlines, illustrations and attention-grabbing language which newspapers to this day regard as standard.

William Howard Russell, correspondent for *The Times*, wearing a uniform specially designed for him. Highly sociable and at ease with everyone from private soldiers to generals, he obtained his best stories by talking to the people involved.

Sab'ring the gunners in the Valley of Death. The dramatic immediacy of Russell's report on the Charge of the Light Brigade on 25 October 1854 electrified Britain. Tennyson based his famous poem closely on it.

Archibald Forbes in his war correspondent outfit. His ride from Ulundi carrying the news of the British victory over the Zulus was one of the great achievements of nineteenth-century journalism, but it effectively brought his career to an end.

Melton Prior's eye-witness sketch of the Battle of Ulundi, knocked up fast so that Archibald Forbes could take it with him on his ride through Zululand. It reached *The Illustrated London News* an entire week before the work of Prior's rivals.

The moment in 1871 when H. M. Stanley probably didn't say 'Dr Livingston, I presume?' He may well have invented the words afterwards. Still, this was arguably the greatest scoop of all time.

George Ward Price of the *Daily Mail*, obeying Lord Rothermere's instructions to stick closely to Hitler. Though the Führer looks distinctly bored, he believed that by talking to Price he was speaking to Britain.

Tom Sefton Delmer of the *Express*, possibly at the very BBC microphone from which he furiously cast Hitler's 1940 peace offer back 'in your lying stinking teeth'. Goebbels assumed this was Britain's official response.

Above: Ernest Hemingway (*right*) on his way to the liberation of Paris with the magnificent photographer Robert Capa (*left*) and Hemingway's French driver, who later told Capa outside the Paris Ritz 'Papa took good hotel'. It wasn't true, but Hemingway had a lot of fun along the way.

Right: Martha Gellhorn with Indian soldiers of the British Army on the 5th Army's Cassino front, Italy 1944.

she was, and remains, one of the finest foreign correspondents I have ever worked alongside.

If she had reported for television, she would have been a major international star: her accent, her coolness, her sheer guts would have attracted enormous attention. But, probably rightly, she didn't like television very much. Although she was never rude or aggressive to people like me, she called it 'show-business', and maybe by her standards she was right. She was a journalist of an older and different type: not the flashy 'special' who descends on a place for a week or so, appears on the screen in front of millions and goes home to collect the awards, but someone who spent months there, understanding the people and the country and writing articles 1,200 words long about them, once a week. William Howard Russell, Henry Morton Stanley and Clare Hollingworth would have recognised her as one of their own; and so she was.

Marie had endless adventures. 'My job is to bear witness,' she once told an audience. 'I have never been interested in knowing what make of plane had just bombed a village or whether the artillery that fired at it was 120mm or 155mm.' Some of her most dangerous times were spent in Chechnya. In December 1999, pinned down by the devastating bombardment of the Russians, she had to escape across the mountains from Chechnya to Georgia. This hair-raising journey is described in *On the Front Line*. It took eight days:

> I looked down to the spectacular depths below us and the snow-covered slopes across the gorge, then thought better of this and kept my eyes on the path. I regretted every cigarette I had ever smoked – and I had smoked a lot in the past few days: cheap Russian tobacco that gave some respite from the bombs and the decisions.

She suffered abominably from thirst, and scooped up handfuls of snow to quench it – not very satisfactorily. At one stop on the mountainside she slept briefly on a pile of damp sheepskins, too tired and sick to eat anything. When it was light, a pair of Russian fighter planes flew overhead and her group had to throw themselves down in the snow. At the next river Marie fell through the ice and plunged into the fast-moving water underneath it. They had now been walking for twenty-four hours, and some of the party decided to turn back; but Marie wasn't a turner any more than she was a leaver. The air was so thin by now that it was hard to breathe, and the wind was ferocious. Someone fired at them. Her guide shouted something in Chechen and the shooting stopped.

Now they were over the border, and the guide found a shepherd's hut which had been abandoned. Since it was Christmas Day, it seemed to her like a good omen. Somewhere in the hut they found some flour which, when boiled up with melted snow, made what she called 'a gluey porridge'. Marie got out her satellite phone and called the *Sunday Times*. Such calls can be extraordinarily comforting, even though the external conditions are just as bad as ever once you hang up. She also managed to get through to someone in Tbilisi who promised to send them a helicopter; since there no roads here, it would be the only way out. But the promises came to nothing, and the battery of her phone was fading fast. At another deserted village, where they found a bit more flour and a tin of peas, she made her last call: to Sean Ryan, the foreign editor of the *Sunday Times*. He had already been in touch with a Georgian general, who had soothed his anxieties by promising that Marie was being cared for in a Georgian village, eating stew and sleeping in sheepskins. She put Ryan right about that.

On 28 December a storm blew up, and their flour was almost finished. They decided to make a run for it: there was a town twenty miles away where they might indeed get stew and sheepskins. But food and rest came a little earlier. At dawn, with the snow a foot deep, they stumbled across a village where just one old couple were still living, too poor to leave for the winter. In their tiny stone house, decorated with a portrait of the great Georgian Stalin, the couple gave them fried potatoes, preserved cabbage and vodka.

As they left the village, they heard the sound of a helicopter. It was only an hour before dark, but the pilot managed to spot them and landed. Although the Georgian general had been useless, Marie's colleague, the journalist Jon Swain (of whom more later), had gone round to the US embassy in Tbilisi and told them that an American citizen was missing on the Chechen frontier: 'I was never happier to have an American passport,' said Marie. 'I walked down the slope to be greeted by an Ernest Hemingway figure with a white beard and blue snow jacket, who said: "Jack Hariman, American embassy. Are we glad to find you..."'

If I'm frank, I loved Marie as much as I admired her; and I'm glad to say that, only six weeks before her death in 2012, at a gathering at the Chelsea Arts Club in London, I told her so.

———

Robert Fisk of the London *Independent* is one of the world's best-known foreign correspondents, with a large and immensely faithful body of readers. He is completely fearless, openly and regularly attacking Israel and the Assad dynasty of Syria, *père et fils*, not from the safety of London or Paris or New York but from his flat in Beirut where he stayed throughout the civil war of the 1970s and '80s, at times when very few Western journalists would venture there. He condemned the attacks of 11 September 2001 in New York and Washington in the strongest terms, and was also loudly right about the foolishness of the invasion of Iraq in 2003 – plus a dozen other American and British policies.

He has his detractors, but then don't we all? They accuse him of exaggeration, of invention, of a wide variety of crimes. I have known Fisk for forty-five years, since the days when he was one of the main correspondents of *The Times* in Northern Ireland, and I was merely a junior reporter trying to understand what it was all about. He has been personally kind about me in his writings, but he seems to harbour a particular dislike of the BBC and has often accused its broadcasters – and that must include me – of cowardice, partisanship and ignorance in their coverage of the Middle East. Once, when I wrote an article defending the BBC against his attacks, no fewer than three of his colleagues on the *Independent* contacted me quietly to thank me.

What no one can deny is that, as well as being brave, Fisk has a remarkable ability to dig out stories; and some of the most extraordinary of them have been his three interviews with Osama bin Laden, in 1993, 1996 and 1997, published in *The Great War for Civilisation*:

> [T]he first time I met Osama bin Laden, the way could not have been easier. Back in December 1993, I had been covering an Islamic summit in the Sudanese capital of Khartoum when a Saudi journalist friend of mine, Jamil Kashoggi, walked up to me in the lobby of my hotel. Kashoggi, a tall, slightly portly man in a long white *dishdash* robe, led me by the shoulder outside the hotel. 'There is someone I think you should meet,' he said... I guessed at once to whom he was referring. Kashoggi had visited bin Laden in Afghanistan during his war against the Russian army. 'He has never met a Western reporter before,' he announced. 'This will be interesting.'

Bin Laden was hugely rich; his family, well placed in Saudi Arabia, had made its money in the construction industry. It is something of a shock, even now, to go into a big hotel or a government ministry in Riyadh or Jeddah and see a metal plaque in the lobby announcing that the building had been put up by the bin Ladens. Osama had broken away from all this and headed off to Afghanistan to fight the Russians; in 1989 I had a brief encounter with him myself, outside the town of Jalalabad in the east of the country, where he tried to persuade the mujaheddin force which my colleagues and I were filming that they should murder us; they had a vote on it, and turned him down. Soon, sickened by the savage in-fighting which followed the withdrawal of the Russian forces, Osama bin Laden went home. But when Saddam Hussein invaded Kuwait and American troops were stationed in Saudi Arabia to help reclaim it, bin Laden left his country in disgust and went to Sudan.

Fisk's driver headed north out of Khartoum on their way to meet him. Kashoggi explained that bin Laden was popular with the people of the area because he had used his own money and equipment to construct a road from Khartoum to the tiny village of

Almatig, out in the desert. That was where Fisk found him. He was sitting under the canopy of a tent in front of a crowd of appreciative villagers, guarded by his Arab bodyguards from Afghanistan. The villagers were thanking him for building the road:

> My first impression was of a shy man. With his high cheekbones, narrow eyes and long brown robe, he would avert his eyes whenever the village leaders addressed him. He seemed ill-at-ease with gratitude, incapable of responding with a full smile when children in miniature chadors danced in front of him and preachers admired his wisdom...
>
> 'Robert, I want to introduce you to Sheikh Osama,' Kashoggi half-shouted through children's songs. Bin Laden was a tall man and he realised that this was an advantage when he shook hands with the English reporter. *Salaam aleikum.* His hands were firm, not strong, but, yes, he looked like a mountain man. The eyes searched your face. He was lean and had long fingers and a smile which – while it could never be described as kind – did not suggest villainy.

Bin Laden's talk was general and unremarkable. There were strands of anti-Americanism in it, but no hint of what the following years would bring:

> [H]is former fellow combatants looked on. Was it not a little bit anti-climactic for them, I asked, to fight the Russians and end up road-building in Sudan? 'They like this work and so do I. This is a great plan which we are achieving for the people here, it helps the Muslims and improves their lives.'

The second time Fisk met Osama bin Laden, it all came about like the start of a late nineteenth-century detective story: something by Max Pemberton, perhaps, or Guy Boothby.

> [O]ne hot evening in late June 1996, the telephone on my desk in Beirut rang with one of the more extraordinary messages I was to receive as a foreign correspondent. 'Mr Robert, a friend you met in Sudan wants to see you,' said a voice in English but with an Arabic accent...

And where could I meet this man? 'The place where he is now,' came the reply. I knew that bin Laden was rumoured to have returned to Afghanistan but there was no confirmation of this. So how do I reach him?' I asked. 'Go to Jalalabad – you will be contacted.'

When he reached the Sheraton Belgravia in London, on his way to Afghanistan, Fisk spotted a likely looking character in the lobby: 'He was trying to look insignificant, but he wore a huge beard, a long white Arab robe and plastic sandals over naked feet.' Fisk told him he would head to Jalalabad and stay at the Spin-Ghar Hotel on the outskirts of the town. The Spin-Ghar is a pleasant place, surrounded by gardens, but in the summer – it was July 1996 – it can be roastingly hot:

> 'CLACK-CLACK-CLACK-CLACK-CLACK-CLACK-CLACK.' I sat up. Someone was banging a set of car keys against my bedroom window. 'Missssster Robert', a voice whispered urgently. 'Missssster Robert'. He hissed the word 'Mister'. Yes, yes, I'm here. 'Please come downstairs, there is someone to see you.'

Only then did Fisk realise that the voice was coming from the fire escape outside. Downstairs, in front of the hotel, an Arab in Afghan robes was waiting for him. Nervously, because he was worried about the possibility of a trap, Fisk followed him out of the hotel grounds and into the town. In the ruins of a Soviet army base, a pick-up truck was waiting for him with three men in the back of it. One had a Kalashnikov, another had a machine gun, and the third had a rocket-launcher with several rockets taped to it: by no means an unusual sight in Afghanistan. His guides paused to pray, then started up the vehicle and they drove off with him.

They drove for hours, and finally stopped as it was getting dark. Fisk got out, and found himself surrounded by al-Qaeda volunteers from all over the Arab world:

> [W]e skirted a small river and jumped across a stream until, in the insect-filled darkness ahead, we could see a sputtering paraffin

lamp. Beside it sat a tall, bearded man in Saudi robes. Osama bin Laden stood up, his two teenage sons, Omar and Saad, beside him. 'Welcome to Afghanistan,' he said.

He was forty, but looked a lot older now than he had less than three years before. There were new wrinkles around his eyes and he was leaner, his beard was flecked with grey, and he looked tired. He sat down with Fisk on a straw mat, and someone brought them tea. This time bin Laden had something interesting to tell him. There had been terrorist attacks against American targets in Saudi Arabia:

> Not long ago, I gave advice to the Americans to withdraw their troops from Saudi Arabia. Now let us give some advice to the governments of Britain and France to take their troops out. . .
> This doesn't mean declaring war against the West and Western people – but against the American regime which is against every American.

Fisk asked bin Laden if he could take his photograph, and he agreed. A man who'd been taking notes of the conversation held a paraffin lamp close to bin Laden's face – Fisk didn't like using flash – and Fisk guided his arm to get the light exactly right on bin Laden's face:

> Then without warning, bin Laden moved his head back and the faintest smile moved over his face, along with that self-conviction and that ghost of vanity which I found so disturbing. He called his sons Omar and Saad and they sat beside him as I took more pictures and bin Laden turned into the proud father, the family man, the Arab at home.

The third and last time Fisk met Osama bin Laden was a few months later, on 26 March 1997. It was in a different part of Afghanistan, and it took him several hours to climb a mountainside by a road which bin Laden had built with his own construction equipment during the Russian occupation. The purpose of the road was to enable the mujaheddin to get high enough to use their British-supplied Blowpipe missiles against the Russian MiGs which flew overhead. After about an hour, bin Laden walked in, dressed in ordinary white Saudi robes. He was limping:

> I still have my notes, scribbled in the frozen darkness with an oil lamp sputtering between us. I've got the quotes which I thought were most frightening. He started off with the old cliché: 'I'm not against the American people, only their government.' Decades of dictatorship out here, of course, have persuaded many Muslims of the region that governments don't represent their people. And I tried to explain to bin Laden that this was not so in the West, that the American people, against whom he supposedly had no argument, regarded their government as their elected representatives. He didn't say much to this, merely the observation that 'We are still at the beginning of our military action against the American forces.'

He went on:

> 'We believe that God used our holy war in Afghanistan to destroy the Russian army and the Soviet Union. We did this from the top of the very mountain on which you are sitting, Mr. Robert. And now we ask God to use us one more time to do the same to America, to make it a shadow of itself.'

Four years later, bin Laden gave the order to launch the attacks of 11 September, which did indeed seem to diminish America for a decade and more, and perhaps permanently. The 9/11 attacks certainly led America to set aside some of the strongest principles which had long made it the champion of freedom – its opposition to torture and to imprisonment without trial, and its open welcome to immigrants, for instance. For Osama bin Laden that alone would have been a major victory.

SIX

M. O.

The only qualities essential for real success in journalism
are ratlike cunning, a plausible manner, and a little literary ability. If you look at the jewels of the profession, you
will see that this must be so.

Nicholas Tomalin, *Sunday Times Magazine*,
26 October 1969

SO MUCH HAS CHANGED for the foreign correspondent over
the years; and yet, as you'll have seen, it's the thesis of this
book that the entire business has in essence remained the same
throughout.

Here, for instance, is a foreign editor sending off his correspondent (a tough, raw-boned character called René Cutforth, as it
happens) to cover the Korean War in 1950:

'Well, I think that's all I have to say,' the editor said. 'But the
main thing to remember is stories in your head are no good to
me. I want them here in the office and I want plenty of them. I
don't care how good your story is, it will be no good to me. And
no heroics, please. You're no good to me dead, and as a prisoner you're a positive liability. . . Right? Have some more sherry.
Passport, visas, press card, cable card, inoculations, money, air
tickets; Miss Crow will look after all that and you'll meet Forbes
in Tokyo on Tuesday night. Good luck.'

That, apparently, was how foreign editors spoke to their correspondents back in 1950 at the BBC, for whom Cutforth worked; they're
more emollient nowadays. Twenty years after that episode, when I

went on my first foreign trip, the BBC gave me precisely the same list of requirements. I never used my cable card, though: cabling despatches instead of voicing them over a broadcasting line was completely *démodé* by the time I was let loose on the airwaves. But the major difference is that by 1970 the editor would never have dreamt of offering me a sherry, because I was much too insignificant. Nowadays it'd probably be illegal.

For the most part, the foreign correspondent's M.O. (which for broadcasters stands for *modus operandi*) remains pretty much what it always has been. You travel to a place by one means or another. You get accredited by the government there, or by the army you want to be attached to – if, that is, you haven't slipped in across the border without being checked. Assuming you're there legitimately, you try to meet up with senior politicians and drop in at your embassy in the hope of getting a bit of local information and a gin and tonic. If, like me, you have another nationality, there are two chances of a gin and tonic; unless of course your other nationality is derived from a Muslim country. Mine being Irish, there are no religious problems about alcohol: rather the contrary, if anything.

Let's suppose you are in Baghdad. You have flown in and probably been picked up by a couple of the local security people who are hired to look after the bureau where you will be working and staying: a villa close to the centre of town. When you've said your hellos and perhaps rung up a couple of friends and contacts to let them know you're in town, and even unpacked if there's time, your thoughts will turn to finding out what's happening. That day, or the next, you'll be driven in an armoured four-by-four, with a security man riding shotgun (not literally, since they aren't allowed to carry weapons), heading for what was once called the Green Zone. At one of the entrances, which used to be among the most dangerous places on earth, you are searched and checked assiduously by Iraqi security men; then you head perhaps to the parliament building to see a politician or two. One advantage of growing old in the job – possibly the sole advantage – is that people you first knew as young activists or maybe political exiles, decades ago, have grown up in the job and become ministers; or even prime ministers.

And then there are the diplomats. They, as much as the politicos and the newspaper editors, will have a line to push; but in a place like Baghdad the foreign ministries of the main countries tend to send their good people, because it's a complicated and important capital. The British ambassador in Baghdad may not have the clout of the American ambassador, but often the Iraqi government will give as much weight to the British view, or even more, because they believe the quality of the British analysis is likely to be good.

At the British embassy you are checked again by several polite Gurkhas with Union Jacks on their shoulder flashes. Now you find yourself in the utilitarian surroundings of the new British embassy, sheltered behind the concrete blast walls which the US army imported in their tens of thousands and left behind when they pulled out. The delightful, sprawling old embassy overlooking the river has been abandoned as far too dangerous. It dates back well over a century, and is the place that Gertrude Bell and the other colonial makers of the new Iraq knew. It's a dangerous pleasure to visit it now, since it is in a moderately hostile area. And anyway it's falling apart, the stairs close to collapse and the offices thick with the dust of decades. I was there the day the diplomats abandoned it, just as the coalition bombing of January 1991 was about to begin. At some point, the British hope to occupy it again, but that won't happen until there's peace in Iraq; so maybe it'll just stay empty and abandoned.

In the ambassador's residence, part of the new complex, you settle down in a comfortable armchair with the ambassador and his senior staff. The gins and tonics appear, accompanied perhaps by magical biscuits cooked and served by the ambassador's very British gentleman's gentleman. The pleasant landscapes on the wall, the portraits, the heavy curtains, the good Persian carpets, the grand piano, all seem to belong in an embassy somewhere pleasant and civilised. Only, outside the blast walls, Baghdad is a dangerous place, and these things merely camouflage that fact.

Hundreds of foreign correspondents like me must have come to visit dozens of British ambassadors in Baghdad over the decades, enjoyed a decent glass of something, and had a chance to discuss the situation. The correspondent gets the ambassador's feel for what the Iraqi government is thinking and doing, and what the Foreign Office thinks about it back in London; the ambassador gets the relatively fresh views of the foreign correspondent, and perhaps a whiff of the atmosphere in the streets where a journalist can wander and a diplomat rarely can. To an ambassador bottled up for weeks on end in a claustrophobic place like the Baghdad Green Zone, the correspondent can provide a welcome link with the world outside the blast walls.

And then you go back to that world, and get down to work, thinking through the different viewpoints and trying to fit what you have heard into your own framework, work out for yourself what is going on, building up your own view. And if you are fortunate enough to have well-informed local colleagues – producers, translators, fixers, drivers even – their understanding of the situation will be particularly valuable, because they are likely to have less of a political axe to grind.

I can't imagine that any of this has changed a great deal since the days of Henry Crabb Robinson, two hundred years ago, except in the finer details. The means of transportation and transmission of information are different, obviously, but the way everybody goes about things is surely pretty much the same. And when, at the height of the civil war in Iraq which followed the American-led invasion of 2003, there was no electricity and you had to read by torchlight or even candlelight, and lie all but naked on your bed because of the throbbing heat, it felt as though nothing had changed at all.

'How do you get your news?' people always ask. By keeping your eyes and ears open, I suppose, and consulting people you can trust. Time and advancing technology have given the people in London a much better opportunity to micro-manage the coverage, given that they are only a phone call away. It took a letter from John Delane weeks to get from Printing House Square to William Howard Russell in the Crimea; and since it would usually be out of date by the time it arrived, Delane would have to accept whatever Russell sent him back by the same slow means. Those, the modern foreign correspondent is often tempted to think, were the days.

Still, correspondents who aren't expected to fill the unforgiving minute with sixty seconds' worth of news and surmise, are free to find their own stories, and travel round as they please, as long as they feed the beast with despatches once or maybe twice a week. My method of working may have some basic similarities with those of Russell and Forbes, but the practical differences are huge. For people like Marie Colvin, and for other foreign correspondents whose work I particularly admire, such as Kim Sengupta and Patrick Cockburn of the *Independent*, I suspect that Russell and Forbes could slip into their seats after a quick half-hour fill-in about how the world has changed since the 1870s, and would find it quite congenial.

———

Sue Lloyd-Roberts worked very differently from most of us. The entire world was her area of operations. In her time she reported from North Korea, Tibet, Syria and Brazil, and everywhere in between. She specialised in uncovering stories of greed and cruelty, environmental crimes, and the mistreatment of children; it was she, inevitably, who reported from China on the execution of prisoners to order so that their internal organs could be harvested. She received a seven-year prison sentence *in absentia* – but of course, being Sue, she went back to China in disguise to do some more reporting in the years that followed. In 1997 she went to Burma, pretending to be a clothes manufacturer, and uncovered shocking abuses in the garment trade. She reported from a Romanian orphanage which sold its children to anyone who wanted them, whatever their motive.

More than anyone else at the time, Sue revealed the cruelty of female genital mutilation, and kept on pressing the subject until governments started doing something about it. Hers was a magnificent record of courage and selflessness and adventure, yet she didn't just restrict herself to investigative work – she also did the fearless, straightforward foreign correspondent stuff: in 2011, for instance, she became the first journalist to get into the besieged Syrian city of Homs. She was driven through the endless roadblocks, sitting in the back of a car and pretending to be the driver's sister. She had a fake ID to back that up, and covered over the slight problem that she couldn't speak fluent Arabic by pretending to be deaf and dumb: an ancient and rather obvious trick for infiltrators, you might think, but she carried it off successfully.

Years before, Sue had tired of going round with a television crew and the big camera which declares your presence and function to everyone. The smaller the camera, the more likely Sue was to use it. Sometimes the pictures were shakier and less sharp and the sound more muffled than if she had brought a camera crew with her; but a camera crew would have been stopped at the border. And the interest of her pictures was such that you never minded their inferior quality. In fact, the inferior quality added to the excitement of watching them.

Sue's companion for many of her great exclusives was a charming young Irishman, Ian O'Reilly. They first met in 1994, when Sue had just won an award from the Royal Television Society for her prisoner organs report from China, and Ian was working as a part-time temp on *Breakfast News*. They hit it off immediately. Ian had done a course in television after leaving school, and had just finished a master's degree in acting and drama. He was to get plenty of real-life drama in the years that followed, and found himself doing a good deal of acting. And he discovered how exciting it was to work like this, and to get your report broadcast.

They were lucky. When they started working together, Sony had recently introduced its DV camera, a great improvement on the Hi8. It was perfect for their requirements: unobtrusive, and easily available to Western tourists. There was nothing that attracted attention about someone who wielded a camera like that.

Sue and Ian talked endlessly about stories, rejecting some ideas and trying to develop others. Often their biggest problem wasn't so much to get into a closed, hostile country as to persuade some BBC editor to allow them to do it. Editors come in all forms and standards: some are worriers, while others are open-minded and adventurous. And there's always the question of money. As the years went on and Sue and Ian's reputations grew, their ideas became easier and easier to sell; yet the money was always difficult. Still, the BBC always has little pots of cash secreted around the place, and Sue had the backing of people like Helen Boaden, the head of news and a strong advocate of good exclusives and of getting more women on the air. It helped greatly, too, that Sue had worked closely on the magazine *Isis* with the BBC's director-general, Tony Hall, when they were at Oxford together. In a big, bureaucratic organisation like the BBC, the more friends in high places that you have, and the more that other people know that, the easier will be your path through the system.

Sue's way of working was completely different from anyone else's. She was a member of the foreign affairs unit, of which I was the titular head, but no one asked her in the middle of the afternoon to go into the studio and answer questions about a bomb explosion in Nigeria. Her one function was to produce exclusive stories, usually undercover. Better still, she wasn't expected to fulfil any kind of quota; the management knew that she could be trusted to do her work without being fussed over. In the years while her children were at school she would only travel abroad during term time, and she would do one trip in the summer, when they went to stay with her ex-husband.

Sue and Ian spent about half their time in the office on pre-production – that is, the organising of everything that could be organised for their next trip – a quarter of their time actually travelling and gathering their material, and the remaining quarter in post-production and editing. Sue wasn't always the easiest person to work with: she was short on patience and highly intelligent, so that – as Ian now says – she found that the world moved achingly slowly. Still, she had the support of her second husband, Nick Guthrie, a television current affairs editor who could also be impatient, but who suited her remarkably well and made her very happy.

Ian O'Reilly's background in drama meant that he taught Sue a good deal about the importance of developing the characters and back-story they assumed when they were working undercover. Ian was usually her nephew, the son of her much, *much* older sister, Sue would say. Since he was Irish and she often travelled on an Irish passport, that made sense. If for some reason she was travelling on a British passport they had a story for that too: this older sister of hers had eloped to Dublin with a rogue of an Irishman named O'Reilly. It explained just about everything. Sue had an academic turn of mind, so her pose as a north London housewife with an interest in history, archaeology, botany or ornithology was pretty close to reality. She would often consult academics, particularly at Oxford, to help her explain to the local police or government officials why she might want to be in some particular part of Burma or Sri Lanka: it was in order, she would explain, to look for a special set of ruins, or some bird or animal, or because a battle had been fought there.

Both of them did the filming, and it didn't matter who picked up the camera and videoed a particular sequence. Naturally, Ian shot the pieces to camera and the interviews, and as time went on he did more of the filming than Sue. Still, she always made sure she knew how each of their cameras worked, and she used to keep a very small palmcorder in her bag, which they knew as the 'Suecam', in case she and Ian became separated.

Before I interviewed Ian about the way he and Sue had worked together, he prepared a list of dos and don'ts for anyone who might want to follow in their footsteps. I've adapted it slightly:

Back story – Keep it simple, plausible and as close to the truth as possible.

Current story – Always have a worked-out reason why you are at any given place at a given time, doing whatever you are doing. It can be good fun to work out on long drives.

Costume – Dress for holiday, not work. (Sue generally wore flowery cotton dresses and a hat, Ian generally wore shorts, tee-shirt and a hat.)

Accoutrements – They usually had a holdall or rucksack with towel, swimming costumes, holiday reading, etc. Sue also had her work costume (blue shirt and white linen trousers) in this bag, 'in case it turned cold'; it was the outfit she would wear on camera. In Sue's personal bags they also had guide books, maps, etc. In Ian's personal bag they usually had the main camera, mini-tripod, batteries, tapes, etc. On display they always had the small camcorder. They used it often to film each other saying silly things or commenting on their recently arrived lunch, in order to defuse any suspicions. No one expects an undercover reporting team to have fun.

Movements – Stick to the tourist trail as much as possible. Always weave in a quick visit or two to something vaguely touristy during your day. If possible have lunch somewhere touristy or at least public. Walk slowly. Move slowly.

Hotels – Never stay in an expensive downtown business hotel. Get advice, and try to stay somewhere a bit more touristy with a pool or a garden, even in a city. If you have any free time, don't stay in your room. Sit out by the pool, be visible, be casual, be slow, film each other jumping in and out of the pool. Live the character of a tourist.

Travel – If possible try to move around by taxi; it looks more touristy. If at all possible, ask the local people you are working with to organise a regular-looking English-speaking taxi driver loyal to the group to work with you as a driver-link man and a bit of a fixer as well. The taxi can bring you where you want to go without consulting anyone. If he is challenged, the driver can say he just picked you up that morning and that you are a bit crazy. A regular taxi driver has greater credibility and deniability, and more miles on his clock, than an ordinary driver who the authorities may think knows more than he is saying.

I met Ian in a small hotel in central London, just round the corner from the BBC, which he and Sue had often used for editing; it was cheaper, in internal accounting terms, to hire a room there and work in it than it was to use an edit suite in the BBC headquarters. It was also more secure: no one could look over their shoulder here, so there was no danger that their story might leak out. The hotel was close to All Souls church, where Sue's memorial service had been held, not long before. I'd last seen him there.

We asked the waiter for coffee, and I made notes as Ian talked over the details of his twenty-year partnership with Sue. Then he passed me the printed document – the main points of which I've listed above.

'Here are the details of our M.O.,' he said, with a touch of pride in his voice.

'Aren't you just handing over the tools of the trade for all the cops and secret policemen to see?' I asked.

Tears came to his eyes.

'It doesn't matter now,' he said. 'It's all over. Finished.'

Not long ago, a British national newspaper carried an article by a lively young journalist who had started doing some interesting war reporting for television. Perhaps because of his inexperience, though, it is all rather self-revealing. This is his account of what he had done:

> I was in – – for less than ten days before war broke out. My knee-jerk reaction was to use my experience of online streaming to set up my own channel to relay a soundscape of – – and to present breaking news with my humble webcam.

Well, at least his webcam is humble. He goes on:

> I did this for between 12 to 16 hours each day: an intense experience and my first real taste of war corresponding. The stream

went viral and was viewed by people from all over the world, including major figures like Professor Noam Chomsky.

It's important to let your character compliment [*sic*] your career. Something which suits me well in my role as a war reporter: the ability to perform under intense stress.

And here are his tips for success:

1) Discipline and self-control
One minute I'm covering peace talks, and the next it's the – – plane crash. You need to have the stamina of a soldier to exercise self-care and manage yourself both psychologically and intellectually.

Self-control is essential for making good decisions. People who respond with panic become frenzied and make illogical decisions. You must be calm but maintain the ability to act quickly while under pressure. It's important to go with your gut, feel the situation, and engage your brain.

2) Risk management
This is important for survival. Take a healthy amount of risk, but also exercise caution at the same time. The more risks you take, the stronger work you can produce. You need to make surgical decisions under intense time constraints to manage your safety but, at the same time, being objective journalistically.

3) Willingness to learn
This will increase your skills and versatility. You never know when you may need a particular skill. When I started broadcasting the – – war, I never knew I would call upon my skillset in operating a live stream.

4) Be comfortable with the uncomfortable
I normally run on eight hours' sleep, but you need to be able to produce a report that has to be made rapidly so, sometimes, you have to forgo sleep. There's a continuous momentum driving you to work as quickly as possible, so you're always looking to literally [*sic*] cut corners. It's important to have a mindset of absolute efficiency to operate like a machine.

A healthy ego is, I suspect, an important part of every good journalist's tool-kit; I certainly can't think of a successful foreign correspondent who is notably lacking in this department. But if it is all that he or she possesses, then true success is likely to be elusive. The correspondents who show themselves to best advantage in this book have one essential thing in common: the most important thing for them is to grab their readers and listeners and viewers by the lapels and say, 'This is really important: you've got to listen while I tell you about this particular story or person or cause.'

Thomas Gibson Bowles, known to everyone as 'Tommy', was only twenty-nine when he arrived in Paris for the siege in September 1870. He had a sizeable ego, but he also had a tremendous, overriding interest in other people. His M.O. was to get as close as he possibly could and discover what was happening to them, then pass on the information to his readers. He was naïve, certainly, and a bit excitable, but that only makes his writing more charming. He has a passion to tell us what life is like for the people of Paris under siege.

He wasn't the only foreign correspondent to get into the city; the slow approach of the Prussians after the battle of Sedan meant that many of the big British and American newspapers, and those from one or two other countries, had time to get into Paris before the siege began. Tommy Bowles, though, was the best of them, because he was fresher and more enthusiastic.

His main competitor was a man ten years his senior, a florid, self-publicising character, Henry Labouchère of the *Daily News*, who used his position as a quarter-shareholder in the newspaper to get himself appointed correspondent in Paris for the siege. Calling himself 'The Besieged Resident', Labouchère was to write despatches which made him a household name and trebled his newspaper's circulation. He was clever and unconventional, and a great many of his judgements turned out to be a lot more accurate than those of Tommy Bowles. But Bowles emerges from the reporting of the siege of Paris as a far more attractive character.

Labouchère, whose French grandparents had settled in London in 1816, had a conventional upper-middle-class background, going to Eton and Trinity College, Cambridge. Yet his behaviour was often the reverse of conventional; once he ran off to join a Mexican circus after falling in love with a lady acrobat. The Foreign Office gave him a series of junior postings abroad, but sacked him when he told them he was too busy to take up a job in Buenos Aires. He stood for Parliament in 1865 as a Liberal and was elected; but the result was overturned. In 1867 he won another seat, but at the general election a year later he lost it. As a politician he became a radical and a republican; Queen Victoria once called him 'That viper!' Now he turned to theatre management and to journalism, where his loud, often angry opinions attracted great attention.

By the standards of the twenty-first century, Labouchère was an unappealing figure: he had a loathing for feminists, gays and Jews, though he supported measures to curb cruelty to animals. Later in life, when he managed to get back into Parliament, he introduced what became known as the Labouchère Amendment. Sodomy had always been a crime, but Labouchère managed to widen the homosexuality law to criminalise any form of sexual activity between men. It was under this amendment that Oscar Wilde was prosecuted, and received the maximum penalty: two years' imprisonment with hard labour. Characteristically, Labouchère argued that Wilde deserved a much longer sentence.

Directly Tommy Bowles arrived in Paris, he discovered two things. The first was that everyone he knew seemed to have fled; and the second was that rents had fallen to remarkably low levels: 'I have got a splendid suite of apartments over Giroux's shop, some ten white-and-gold rooms, with a long range of balcony looking on the boulevard, for *six francs a-day!*'

Bowles settled into his inexpensive flat, full of a young man's enthusiasm for Paris and its people. He was certain that they would fight, and fight well, and his early articles for the *Morning Post* contained several pointed criticisms of the general British assumption that the Parisians would quickly cave in. *The Times*, for instance, was particularly scathing about 'the city of luxury and pleasure', and forecast a quick end to the siege.

Labouchère, who was universally known as 'Labby', agreed with *The Times*. He was particularly annoyed by the self-regarding, bombastic things he read in the Paris newspapers; *Le Figaro*, for instance, wrote:

> In order that Paris, in which there is a genius which has given her the empire of the world, should fall into the hands of the barbarians, there must cease to be a God in heaven. God would have to cease to exist in heaven. Like God, she exists, and like God she is immortal. Paris will never surrender.

Labby disliked the French press on principle, and wrote scathingly but accurately in the *Daily News* of its general attitude: 'France is the world, Paris is France. The boulevards, the theatres, some fifty writers on the Press, and the *bourgeoisie* of the fashionable quarters of the city, are Paris.' He also developed – correctly, as it turned out – a deep scepticism about the fighting abilities of General Louis Trochu, the governor of Paris and commander-in-chief of its forces: 'I was looking at him the other day, and I never saw calm, serene self-complacency more clearly depicted upon the human countenance.'

Labby's own self-complacency was pretty serene too. His opinions were habitually loud, and despite his French extraction he had a certain amount of contempt for the French. Perhaps, too, the act of writing for a distant readership, from whom he rarely received any comeback, encouraged him to speak out more openly than he might have if he had been writing for the people around him. The Parisians, he wrote, 'hope against hope that what they call their "sublime attitude" will prevent the Prussians from attacking them, and that they may pass to history as heroes, without having done anything heroic'. When a couple of photocopies of his articles in the *Daily News* were smuggled into Paris by pigeon post there was a big fuss, and Labby had to keep his head down for a week or two.

Tommy Bowles used to wander round the streets, talking to as many people as he could, and when there was fighting he liked to be on hand to witness it. Henry Labouchère, by contrast, wrote about the fighting from the safety of his suite at the Grand Hotel, relying on the information he received from his contacts, which was usually good. There are plenty of journalists who still do this: it's safer, naturally, and you are closer to your best sources of information. Yet with a huge international story such as the siege of Paris it is usually the detail that counts, at least as much as the overall picture; and when you compare the reporting of Tommy Bowles and Henry Labouchère, there's a far better and more interesting texture to Bowles's writing, even though Labby is a more reliable guide to the general situation.

On 29 November, the day of the Great Sortie when the defenders of the city burst out to attack the Prussians, Bowles noted that things went well at first. He got as close to the fighting as possible, and took up his position on a hill at Créteil, only 500 yards from the Prussian lines. The Parisian forces captured several of the Prussian positions 'at the point of the bayonet', as Bowles put it. Half an hour later, though, he could see that the French skirmishers were falling back, even though they were still in good order. He was particularly interested to see how the Belleville Brigade, volunteers from one of the biggest working-class areas of the city, were behaving. This was one of the key moments of the entire siege, and a good showing by the men of Belleville might well have driven the Prussians back. But it wasn't going to happen:

> '*Nous sommes battus*, ['we've been beaten']' they muttered, looking with pale faces at one another, while some of them silently left the ranks, and walked with a careless air towards the rear.
>
> Advancing again, I found that the skirmishers were huddled up rather than rallied behind their wall, while the road, which before had been perfectly deserted, was covered with stragglers making for the village in a weary, downcast way.

Neither Bowles nor Labouchère, nor the rest of the small number of foreign correspondents in Paris, were under the same competitive pressure that they would normally have experienced. It should have been possible for them to use the telegraph to send their despatches, but the Prussians discovered the telegraph cable which had been secretly laid along the bed of the River Seine, and cut it. After that the alternatives were limited. Almost every courier who took messages out was captured, and canisters and even dogs floating in buckets down the Seine were all intercepted.

The only way in which a correspondent's report could find its way from the encircled city of Paris to the outside world was by balloon. Félix Nadar, who had taken some spectacular pioneering photographs from balloons and been celebrated by the great cartoonist Honoré Daumier, wrote to the Council for the Defence of Paris on 17 September proposing that balloons should be used to send letters to the outside world. The council agreed, and the first flight took place only a week later, with bags containing 276 pounds (125 kilograms) of mail. It was a great success, coming down to earth fifty-two miles away, near the village of Craconville in Haute-Normandie.

The balloon should have been carrying despatches from the British and American correspondents in Paris. Tommy Bowles, for instance, had written a letter to his editor at the *Morning Post*, discussing the previous day's fighting at Pierrefitte and Villejuif, and reporting that the streets near the Porte d'Italie had been thronged with people who received the victorious General Trochu with frenzied applause. They 'offered cigars and sympathy to the wounded, many of whom were Prussians – fair-haired, innocent-looking boys, most of them, and by no means the ferocious warriors that they have been painted by the Parisians.'

But the main item of news which Bowles reported was the manner in which his despatch had been sent out of Paris:

If anybody had told me three months ago that on this day [Saturday 24 September 1870] I should be walking along the boulevards seriously considering of sending letters to England by means of a balloon, I should have avoided the prophet as a dangerous lunatic; yet that is precisely what I have just been doing...

Tonight there was a meeting outside a café of all the correspondents of English newspapers, who, finding outdoor conversation inconvenient, did me the honour to adjourn to my rooms, sinking, like the Parisians, all our home differences for a common object.

So eight highly competitive journalists, the correspondents of *The Times*, the *New York Tribune*, the *Pall Mall Gazette*, the *Daily Telegraph*, the *Standard* (nowadays the *London Evening Standard*) and the *Morning Post*, plus Henry Labouchère of the *Daily News*, sat round in Bowles's spacious flat over a friendly bottle or two and talked it over: 'It was arranged that we should secure the balloonist, and to him is committed this letter, which, if any Prussian gets and reads it, I hope may induce him to desert.' They also settled on a price: they would pay five pounds a letter.

But there was a problem. The despatches were supposed to leave on a balloon at three o'clock the following morning, Sunday 25 September. At the last moment the pilot demanded £100 before he would leave, while the correspondents were only prepared to give him £40. Bowles had just reached agreement on a price when someone burst into the room and announced breathlessly that the balloon had already left. General Trochu had apparently gone down to the place where the balloon was being got ready, cut the guy ropes, and sent it off on a military mission. Depressed, Tommy Bowles wrote in his despatch that day: 'I am left with all that able correspondence on my hands which, it was hoped, would so fully enlighten the world as to the situation and aspect of Paris.'

No doubt the other correspondents interrogated him pretty closely, and demanded to see that his letter was there with the others; not all foreign correspondents are entirely trustworthy when it comes to sending off the material of their competitors. But Bowles was a decent, reliable young man, which is presumably why he had been given the job of looking after it in the first place. The experience taught him a lesson that foreign correspondents to this day can understand and sympathise over: 'The chief business of a correspondent just now is not so much to write, as to run about after the means of sending his writings. . .'

After the teething problems, though, the system began to work well. In total, sixty-five manned balloon flights were made during the siege, and all but eight were successful. Three disappeared, presumably crashing into the sea, and the Prussians, watching frustrated as the balloons flew over their heads, managed to capture only five of them. In all, an estimated 2.5 million letters were carried out of Paris.

As the siege conditions tightened, Bowles described each turn in the story. His despatches make pleasanter reading than Labouchère's because he doesn't look down on the Parisians. He is an eyewitness, not a judge:

> Paris as yet hardly feels the siege. There is hardly anything run out in the way of food except fresh fish and fresh butter. We shall, however, be put on rations very shortly. . . Another sign of the times is a decree fixing a *taxe*, or maximum price, for horse meat, which has hitherto been exempt from official interference. The best portions of a horse are to be charged 1fr.40c. the kilogramme (or about 61/2d a lb.)

But Tommy Bowles has the over-optimism of youth, and at this early stage in the siege he is inclined to give plenty of hostages to fortune:

> Fresh meat is the only article of food likely to come to an early end, for there are ample supplies of everything else, and besides the enormous public stores of bread, wine, and reserved provisions, most people have laid in a private supply of them to meet the last eventualities.

Labby was much more cynical, and as times grew harder he enjoyed shocking his complacent English readers with accounts of the meat he was eating. He liked both horsemeat and cat, he wrote.

Horse was a little sweeter than beef but rather similar to it, while cat was:

> something between rabbit and squirrel, with a flavour all its own. It is delicious. I recommend those who have cats with philopro-genitive proclivities, instead of drowning the kittens, to eat them. Whether smothered in onions or in a ragout they are excellent. When I return to London I shall frequently treat myself to one of these domestic animals. . . [C]at served up for dinner is the right animal in the right place.

And later: 'This morning I had a salmi of rats – it was excellent – something between frog and rabbit.'

Yet even Labby, with his delight in shocking the people back home, felt he had gone too far when it came to dogs:

> I own for my part I have a guilty feeling when I eat dog, the friend of man. I had a slice of spaniel the other day; it was by no means bad, something like lamb, but I felt like a cannibal. Epicures in dog flesh tell me that poodle is by far the best, and recommend me to avoid bull-dog, which is coarse and tasteless.

He maintained that dogs could sense that the hungry people of Paris wanted to eat them: 'The humblest of street curs growls when anyone looks at him.'

As things got worse, ordinary house rats were sold for a franc, but a fat sewer rat fetched 1 franc, 50 centimes. By the first week of the New Year Labby was eating elephant from the zoo: 'It was tough, coarse and oily, and I do not recommend English families to eat elephant as long as they can get beef or mutton.'

The readers back home were appalled, naturally, but they loved it all the same. Henry Labouchère guessed this, and dished it up to his readers with a cynical glee.

Tommy Bowles had started off rather liking horsemeat, but he soon changed: 'I have now dined off camel, antelope, dog, donkey, mule and elephant, which I approve in the order in which I have written... [H]orse is really too disgusting, and it has a peculiar taste never to be forgotten.'

As the winter continued, conditions grew worse and worse. Hunger and disease killed increasing numbers of people. The despatches of correspondents like Bowles, Labouchère and John Augustus O'Shea of the *Standard* played a big part in swaying the feelings of people in Britain. Many, like Queen Victoria herself, had supported the Prussians because they thought the Emperor Napoleon III was essentially a military dictator who ruled over a corrupt and immoral society. Gradually, though, their sympathy for the sufferings of the people of Paris grew, and the Prussians began to seem like brutal invaders. Queen Victoria started writing to her Prussian relatives begging them to show magnanimity to the Parisians; that turned Prussian opinion against Britain.

'Two days ago,' wrote Tommy Bowles in a shocked report on 17 January:

> I saw a terrible spectacle. A little child, who could scarcely have been more than five years old, had been killed by a shell while playing in the street. His arm was entirely taken off, and one side of his face was carried away, while his fair curly locks were dabbled with blood and brains, and his blue pinafore was saturated with gore. They had just picked him up when I arrived, and were carrying him tenderly in, his little feet hanging piteously down. 'Grand Dieu! What will become of his poor mother?' said a woman close by.

The dividing line between France and Britain on the one hand, and Germany on the other, which would dominate the first half of the following century, was laid down in the winter of 1870–71 as a result of reports like that.

For more than three weeks in January 1871 the Prussians fired around 12,000 shells into the city, killing or wounding around four hundred people. When this didn't bring the city to its knees, Bismarck took over operational control of the siege, and ordered heavy-calibre siege guns to be used. After a hammering of a kind which no European city had experienced at that time, Paris surrendered on 28 January. Its food stocks were starting to run out, though there had been no actual starvation, and its will to continue fighting had simply evaporated. The German Empire, as it had now become, demanded control of Alsace and Lorraine. The Prussian army staged a victory parade through Paris.

Bowles, Labouchère and O'Shea were depressed, hungry and exhausted, and desperate to go home. Their last despatches contain no trace of the humour of earlier weeks, and they convinced themselves, and their editors, that the story was over. Tommy Bowles rode out of the shattered city and made it through the Prussian lines to Versailles. There he had his first decent meal for four months: 'It may perhaps not greatly interest readers to know that I revelled in an omelette, a *sole au vin blanc*, and a *Chateaubriand*.'

Henry Labouchère, for his part, never lost his superior attitude: 'I really am sorry for these vain, silly, gulled humbugs. . .' Yet his essential judgement was a very different one: 'Laugh at the French, abuse them as one may, it is impossible to help liking them. Admire, respect the Prussians as one may, it is impossible to help disliking them.' That was to become the British approach for more than seventy years, and perhaps longer.

Labby still seemed young when he arrived in Paris at the start of the siege. After just a few months he looked quite old, and his beard was streaked with grey. But his letters from Paris had greatly added to his reputation. He was re-elected to Parliament not long afterwards, and added jingoism to the list of things he hated. Tommy Bowles, too, aged during the siege, and his lightness of mood seemed to leave him. He followed Labouchère into the House of Commons, and many years later was the elder statesman who encouraged the young Winston Churchill to get on his feet and make his maiden speech.

But both of them, like the other foreign correspondents, made the journalist's greatest mistake: they left Paris too soon. The end of the siege was quickly followed by the Commune, and the fierce bloodshed associated with it. If anything, this story was better than that of the siege; yet there was scarcely any professional reporting of it in the British or American press. People abroad found the

Commune bewildering and senseless, and were disinclined to read about it. If Labouchère and Bowles had stayed on, they might have changed that.

———————

It was only at the start of October 2010 that I knew finally that I would be going to Burma to report on the release from house arrest of Aung San Suu Kyi, the opposition leader who had been a prisoner for seven years. I had never been to Burma, and although several BBC correspondents had met Daw Suu, ('Mother Suu', or 'The Lady', as she was known to her followers) I never had. In the BBC, with its variety of departments and levels of management, you have to compete with a range of other people; and the only way to succeed is to make sure you have the support of some key figure in the system. I was lucky: I had an excellent working relationship with the foreign editor, Jon Williams, who wasn't necessarily very popular with other people in the News Department (he was capable of tremendous, titanic rages), but was one of the best and most imaginative foreign editors I've ever worked with. He was later offered a similar job by ABC News in New York, and took it. But for now he was in charge of deploying people to foreign stories, and he agreed to let me cover The Lady's release.

There was, however, a serious problem. The Burmese dictatorship, fierce and pretty effective, didn't allow foreign journalists into the country without permission, and that permission was very rarely given. At the airports, I was told, the immigration officials were equipped with laptops, and they googled foreigners who arrived in Rangoon to see if they were listed as journalists. Directly Google showed who you were, you were politely led off to a small room and kept there until it was time for the next plane back to the place you had come from. My name, alas, is all over the internet; that's what happens when you've spent a lifetime reporting on other people's business. Could I be certain that I would be allowed in, Jon Williams asked? There was no point in lying to him; but, I said, I had a plan.

It wasn't much of one. I am a British citizen, but during the Falklands War, when the Argentines refused to accept anyone with a British passport, I discovered that I was entitled to an Irish one, since my grandmother had been born in Cashel, County Tipperary. The fact that she was the daughter of a British army officer who was based there in order to make sure that Ireland would never issue its own passports didn't matter; the Irish citizenship law specifies that the children and grandchildren of people born on the island of Ireland are eligible. I use my Irish passport whenever I travel to countries which Britain has some major dispute with (there have been surprisingly many of these over the years) or where there is a greater than usual chance that I might be kidnapped. The British won't pay ransoms to terrorist groups; I have a suspicion the Irish might, if only to be different from the Brits.

My plan for getting into Burma rested on the traditional Irish willingness to regard rules and regulations as something to be got round, not worshipped. I went to see a senior and very charming Irish official, taking my Irish passport with me, and explained my reasons for wanting to go to Burma. She was immediately positive and sympathetic, as I'd hoped; imagine the reaction of a British government official if you asked one of them for help like this. I have four names altogether, I said: John Cody Fidler Simpson. How about issuing me a passport in, say, just two of them? Well, she answered cautiously, by law I could call myself pretty much anything I liked; but for a passport I would have to keep my surname as it was. That was a disappointment, since I'd hoped she'd give it to me in the name 'John Cody'. Unfortunately that wouldn't be possible, she said. The best she could do was 'Cody Simpson'. Better than nothing, I thought. But as I drove home in a cab afterwards with my brand new Irish passport, I realised that it was useless. When you google someone's name, Cody Simpson for instance, the rest of the name comes up too, just in lighter type. At the immigration desk in Rangoon airport, it would be immediately obvious that I was a journalist, and all my efforts would be in vain. I got home and chucked the passport across the kitchen table.

'Waste of bloody time,' I told my wife.

After a while, though, it occurred to me to find out what would happen if I googled 'Cody Simpson'; and it was then that I discovered that there was a celebrated Cody Simpson, a (to me) rather awful Australian teenaged boy singer, much adored by pubescent girls, and perhaps their mothers, around the globe. Twenty-eight pages on Google were taken up with Cody Simpson and his doings; the first mention of me came on page twenty-nine, and surely no immigration official would be conscientious enough to power through twenty-eight pages of grinding, smirking Australian testosterone.

And so it proved. I flew to Bangkok, then caught a flight to Rangoon. I got off the plane in a state of real nervousness; if the plan didn't work and I was sent back to Bangkok there would be much derision among the various people who wanted to be here instead of me. The Burmese didn't worry me; the derision did. A pleasant-looking young woman in a dark green uniform which seemed to be a half-size too small for her smiled at me, took my passport, tapped 'Cody Simpson' into her laptop, gazed for a moment at the ghastly teenaged images, then stamped the empty page of my passport and handed it back. I was through.

Just before noon the next day, feeling like someone out of *Greenmantle*, I walked into a teahouse, after making elaborately sure that I wasn't being followed, and saw my friends and colleagues, Nick Springate and Adam Mynott, sitting at the other end of the garden at the back. Nick was the producer in charge of the entire operation, and Adam was the correspondent who was based in Asia and covered Burma when he could. Did he object to my presence? Well, it's never much fun to have someone coming in and taking the main part of the coverage away from you, but he was as pleasant and good company as ever, and his reports were much praised afterwards, back in London.

After we had discussed our tactics they took me to join up with Tony Fallshaw, our cameraman and a good friend of mine over the years, at our hotel. We moved around Rangoon, often followed by secret policemen on the little red mopeds which only they were permitted to import: something of a giveaway. Jumping out of a taxi, we would hop across the low concrete walls which divided the highway and catch a taxi travelling in the opposite direction. The secret policemen, not being able to lift their mopeds over the walls, couldn't follow. Springate, an incomparable organiser, had arranged things so I was staying at a public guesthouse which was actually inside the compound of the British embassy, and the embassy staff were protective and very supportive. I knew that directly I got through the gates of the compound the secret police would be powerless. All I had to do was get there.

In the end, one fiercely hot night, we forced our way through a huge, excitable crowd outside Aung San Suu Kyi's house, with Fallshaw holding his heavy camera way above his head and getting some remarkable shots. The heaving mass of people suddenly went quiet, as someone on the other side of the high gate put a chair in place, and the woman who had been invisible for seven years hopped onto it lightly and looked over the top of the gate at us. It was a wonderful, exhilarating moment, and many people wept.

'BBC!' I screamed through the noise, and The Lady, who had relied on the BBC's broadcasts throughout that time to tell her what was happening in the world, smiled back and gave us her first reaction to being a free woman again. We were only a foot away from her, but it was really hard to hear her gentle voice over the racket all around us. She really is remarkably beautiful, I thought, in spite of the crushing heat and the excitable crowds and the pressure of trying to get things done in this noise and sweat and near-hysteria.

The following day it was just as hot but a little calmer. We waited for hours, and in the end got the formal sit-down interview Nick Springate had arranged. We were all drenched with sweat; but not The Lady. She was as cool and collected as ever.

'You've been cut off from the world for so long,' I said. 'Is there anything about life today that surprises you?'

'It's these little phones,' she said, laughing and holding one up. 'When I was locked away the phones seemed so big. And now...'

It was a delightful moment. And as my colleagues and I stood beside her and had our photographs taken, I remember reflecting that I owed it all to the kindness of an unstuffy Irish official, and the fame of a teenaged Australian heart-throb called Cody Simpson.

SEVEN

Scoops

[T]he reporter's quest for facts brings rewards of its own,
which only partly have to do with being proved right in
the end. The truly addicted reporter (and most of the
other kind drop out of the game sooner or later) will
never tire of joining in the chase, watching the adren-
aline flow, and bringing all available ingenuity to bear
on a situation which, like life itself, is never tidy, finite,
or simple.

Edward Behr, *Anyone Here Been Raped and
Speaks English?*, 1978

JOURNALISTS PLACE A VALUE on exclusive stories which most
normal people find difficult to comprehend. They struggle and
deceive and spend large amounts of money to get them, and
congratulate themselves inordinately when they appear in print
or on the air; yet all too often other news organisations ignore
them, unwilling to give a rival any kind of acknowledgement,
and anyway perhaps uncertain whether the originators of the
scoop have got the details of the story entirely right. Sometimes,
the very idea that one journalist has got a story ahead of all the
others can create a frenzy of personal criticism and hostility in
rival sections of the press, which most people outside journalism
find either bewildering or distasteful. Still, news reporting is a
deeply competitive business, and if you take the competition out
of it you are in danger of extracting the spirit and style from it
as well.

The grander news outlets prefer the word 'exclusive' to 'scoop'; yet 'scoop' is how most journalists think of it privately, no matter how elevated their organisation might be. The word has the connotation of reaching out at the end of a game of poker and gathering in the chips you've won. Most reporters have had an exclusive at some time or another, and a very good feeling it is. But there are a handful of stories which have transcended the ordinary nature of journalism and gone round the world. Some of these have changed history; others have imposed themselves on us by their dramatic quality, or more especially because they have imprinted an idea or an image in minds. We might hope that one day we will be remembered for some overriding scoop like this, but it happens to very, very few journalists indeed. Henry Morton Stanley was one of them; yet his great moment of fame was to turn a little sour afterwards.

We left him standing outside the village of Ujiji, having ordered Livingstone's servant Susi to tell him he was coming. He was only a couple of hundred yards outside the village, but the crowds were growing thick around him. Susi came running back: the Doctor hadn't believed him, and wanted to know the name of the man who had arrived to see him. In the meantime, though, Livingstone had been told that the explorer was definitely a white man. Perhaps he had even seen the Stars and Stripes which Stanley's man was holding aloft and waving. Now the Arabic grandees of the place had gathered in the open area outside Livingstone's hut, and the Doctor had come out himself to wait for Stanley to arrive.

'I see the Doctor, sir!' said Stanley's servant Selim excitedly. 'Oh, what an old man! He has got a white beard!'

Stanley himself was full of violent emotion:

[W]hat would I not have given for a bit of friendly wilderness, where, unseen, I might vent my joy in some mad freak, such as idiotically biting my hand; turning a somersault, or slashing at trees, in order to allay those exciting feelings that were well-nigh uncontrollable. My heart beats fast, but I must not let my face betray my emotions, lest it should detract from the dignity of a white man appearing under such extraordinary circumstances.

Poor Stanley: at this critical moment in his life and career the workhouse boy has to force himself to behave like the kind of English gentleman he admires so much yet can never fully emulate. In his book he describes Livingstone's appearance in detail; though he packs his account with the kind of detail he would surely only have had the leisure to observe after the first excitement of the meeting was over:

> As I advanced slowly towards him I noticed he was pale, that he looked wearied and wan, that he had grey whiskers and moustache, that he wore a bluish cap with a faded gold band on a red ground round it, and that he had on a red-sleeved waistcoat, and a pair of grey tweed trousers.

Stanley's instinct was to run towards him and embrace him, but he didn't know how Livingstone would react. So, he says, he did what 'moral cowardice and false pride suggested was the best thing' and walked deliberately up to him, raised his hat, and said the four words which no one would ever forget:

'DR. LIVINGSTONE, I PRESUME?'

In his book he puts them in capital letters and a bold typeface, so significant were they in his own mind.

'Yes,' said Livingstone with a kindly smile, raising his cap slightly.

They shook hands, and Stanley, allowing himself a little more emotion, said, 'I thank God, Doctor, I have been permitted to see you.'

'I feel thankful that I am here to welcome you,' Livingstone replied.

He insisted that Stanley should sit in his special seat on the verandah of his hut, and asked him what the news was. By this stage, of course, Stanley himself had been travelling in the wilderness of Africa for months, but he knew about the opening of the Suez Canal and told Stanley about it.

'You have brought me new life. You have brought me new life,' Livingstone kept repeating.

Suddenly Stanley remembered something: the bottle of champagne and the silver goblets he'd brought all this way in order to celebrate the moment of meeting. His servant ran off and fetched them, and the two drank each other's health before settling down to a big meal prepared by the Doctor's cook.

It was a splendid occasion, and the entire world would remember Stanley's words of greeting. 'Dr Livingstone, I presume?' is probably the most familiar phrase ever written by a journalist – and yet there is a strong likelihood that Stanley never said it. Certainly Livingstone didn't record the words in his own journal, nor in the accounts of the meeting which he wrote within days to James Gordon Bennett of the *New York Herald* and to his daughter Agnes on 18 November. Maybe, of course, Livingstone simply failed to hear the words spoken, or maybe he forgot them. All the same, he quoted everything Susi told him about Stanley's arrival, and his account of the meeting was otherwise detailed and sharp. And there is one other deeply significant, if mute, piece of evidence: Stanley tore out and destroyed the page of his notebook which described the actual moment of meeting.

Why should he have done such a thing? The likelihood must surely be that the notes he took at the time didn't support the claim that he'd said 'Dr Livingstone, I presume?', and he wanted to get rid of the clearest evidence for what he actually did say: whatever that was. The phrase certainly appears in Stanley's published journal, but that seems to have been put together more than a year later in London, after he had written up and published his book *How I Found Livingstone*. The first mention of 'Dr Livingstone, I presume?' is found in Stanley's despatch to the *New York Herald* of 2 July 1872, eight months after the meeting took place. The date on this despatch is 23 November 1871, but the original manuscript of it has disappeared, so it could have been written weeks, even months later, before Stanley sent it off to New York. He could have brooded for a long time over the way he wanted to present the great moment of meeting to the world.

He was well aware that people thought of him as brash, ill-bred and poorly educated. Perhaps he reflected on the undemonstrative way the British, whom he admired so much, would behave in circumstances like this, and wanted his readers to think he had shown a calm, stiff-upper-lip British manner. His description of his feelings of nervousness sounds entirely plausible, but it's possible he wanted to embellish the actual moment with something that sounded more dignified. If so, he would have had to destroy the page of the notebook where he'd recorded what really happened: the only page in any of his Livingstone notebooks which has disappeared.

Does it matter? Not really. What counted was the long and immensely dangerous journey he had made across Africa, and the fact that he had genuinely found Livingstone. If he falsified his account of the meeting, it was a bit of attempted self-improvement. The trouble was, it did him absolutely no good; in fact it became a real burden to him. People started making fun of his famous words almost immediately, and both in London and New York people who recognised him in the streets would yell it out, often mockingly. It was as if they sensed that there was something not quite right about the whole episode, and homed in on it; or perhaps, in that class-sensitive age, they knew that Stanley, the triumphantly self-made man, wasn't quite what he made himself out to be. He was responsible for other great stories during the rest of his life – in particular the expedition to find Emin Pasha in the dark heart of Africa, and his efforts to explore the Congo and support King Leopold's colonisation of it – and to some extent these took the attention away from his magnificent exploit in finding Livingstone. But 'Dr Livingstone, I presume?' is the one thing everyone knows about him to this day.

Sometimes, with no careful preparatory work, no expenditure of money or effort and no expectation, scoops simply drop from the sky and land at the feet of whichever journalist happens to be in the right place at the right moment. These may not be the most noble of exclusives, but they are always deeply satisfying.

The Astoria is a massive, seven-storey hotel in St Petersburg. It opened in 1912, and within five years it was the centre of journalistic activity during the revolutions of February and October 1917, when the city was called Petrograd. Three weeks after the Bolsheviks had seized power, a gentle, serious-minded thirty-two-year-old foreign correspondent from the *Manchester Guardian*, Morgan Philips Price, slipped out, alone and unnoticed, through the grand revolving doors into the freezing cold of a Petrograd November night. Neither he nor the other correspondents based in the hotel knew it, but he was on his way to one of the twentieth century's great scoops.

His plan was to go to the office of Leon Trotsky in the Smolny Institute, a former school for wealthy girls which the Bolsheviks had taken over as their seat of government. Trotsky often made himself available to speak to foreign journalists, and Price thought he might be able to pick up a story that evening. As it turned out, he picked up rather more than that.

Trotsky's secretary was a tall, attractive, jolly woman in her early twenties called Yevgeniya Petrovna Shelepina. She had only started working at the Smolny a fortnight earlier, when the initial stages of the Revolution were scarcely over. Most of the small number of Western correspondents still left in Petrograd would drop in occasionally, and it was around this time that she met the *Daily News* correspondent, Arthur Ransome, who was later to marry her and write the *Swallows and Amazons* books. She soon started an affair with him. Ransome was secretly working for MI6, and he told them about his involvement with Shelepina and his Bolshevik sympathies. As long as he kept on sending back high-grade information, MI6 didn't seem to mind.

Trotsky told Shelepina that he was too busy to see Morgan Philips Price, but he suggested to her that he might like to glance at a particular set of papers which were piled up untidily on her desk. Price flicked through the ones on top, and realised their importance immediately; they were the texts of the secret treaties which Tsarist Russia had entered into with its wartime allies, Britain, France, Romania and Japan. Shelepina needed a little persuading, but finally she agreed to let him take the documents away, as long as he promised to bring them back the next day. He gave her his word, and headed back to the Astoria with a packet of international dynamite under his arm.

All that night Price stayed up, copying out the documents, and so was able to keep his promise to take them back in the morning. They contained full details of the deals Britain and France had done with Russia, and also with Italy, to keep them in the war with Germany. Britain had secretly agreed to allow Russia to annex Constantinople (something the British had gone to war to prevent in 1854, and came close to fighting over in the late 1870s). Parts of Persia were also to be handed over to Russia. Britain and France together agreed to allow Russia to take over large parts of Turkey and what was called 'Southern Kurdistan'; nowadays part of Iraq. France agreed to give Russia a completely free hand in fixing its western borders, which meant extending them through parts of what is now Poland, Germany and the Baltic states.

The *Guardian* published the secret treaties piecemeal, from November 1917 to February 1918. They had a sensational effect on European and international politics, and showed how badly Britain and France had been behaving in private. Woodrow Wilson, the American president, was regarded as justified in calling for 'open covenants of peace openly arrived at' and his hand was greatly strengthened in the discussions on peace treaties with Germany and its allies. Some of Britain's promises to Russia cut completely across its undertakings to the leaders of the Arab Revolt, and T. E. Lawrence was enraged when he read the details. The British prime minister, Lloyd George, who had been privy to most of the secret deals, declared emolliently that circumstances had changed now that Russia had dropped out of the war, and that Britain was willing to reconsider the relationships with her allies.

Morgan Philips Price had scored a magnificent scoop, which uncovered the sweetest of secrets: those which governments want to keep hidden. If Arthur Ransome was annoyed that the woman who would soon be his girlfriend, Yevgeniya Shelepina, had handed a world exclusive to one of his rivals, he didn't say anything about it publicly. Later he was successful in persuading MI5 that he and Yevgeniya had lost her enthusiasm for Marxism-Leninism and should be allowed to come to Britain. In 1919, Ransome started working for the *Guardian*, taking over from Price, who was transferred to Berlin. Ransome got permission to get Yevgeniya out of the country by agreeing to carry two million roubles' worth of diamonds and pearls abroad; they were used to set up the international Soviet-controlled network, Comintern. Back in England he married Yevgeniya in 1924, after divorcing his first wife. They lived happily together for more than forty years, and were buried side by side in the Lake District which inspired some of his best-known children's books. It must have seemed impossibly far from the Smolny Institute.

In *Scoop*, Evelyn Waugh managed to make fun of a range of foreign correspondents. Most of them thoroughly deserved it; even William Deedes, who didn't, was nevertheless distinctly vulnerable to mockery. But Waugh was grossly unfair to one man who plays a walk-on part in the book:

> Mr Pappenhacker of The Twopence was playing with a toy train – a relic of College at Winchester, with which he invariably travelled. In his youth he had delighted to address it in Latin Alcaics and to derive Greek names for each part of the mechanism.

There was no doubt which newspaper Waugh meant: only *The Times* cost twopence, and the name Waugh gave its correspondent in his version of Abyssinia was dipped in poison too. 'Mr Pappenhacker' was based on George Lowther Steer, an English-speaking South African who had indeed been educated at Winchester and had gone on to Christ Church, Oxford. Both the school and the college were regarded at the time as being greatly superior to Waugh's school, Lancing, and his Oxford college, Hertford. These were things Waugh was inclined to take to heart.

He revenged himself on Steer by calling him, in some of his other writings, 'a zealous young colonial reporter', or simply 'the colonial', and giving him the absurd name 'Pappenhacker' in *Scoop*. Writing to Diana Cooper, Waugh called Steer 'a very gay South African dwarf'; 'gay' presumably doesn't have its modern connotation here. Steer's biographer, Nicholas Rankin, quotes an American diplomat's description of him: 'boyish, small-bodied, fox-faced with a mischievous glint in his eyes'.

He was also tough and brave, as he later demonstrated. Oddly enough, Steer's second wife, Esmé Barton, who fell in love with him at the funeral of his first wife, had also been a victim of Waugh's savage wit. In his earlier novel, *Black Mischief*, she is Prudence Courtenay, the daughter of the British ambassador to Abyssinia (as Esmé was in real life) and Waugh made her out to be empty-headed and promiscuous. Reading the book and recognising the attack on herself, Esmé Barton threw a glass of champagne at Waugh when she came across him at a nightclub in Addis Ababa.

Waugh had intended to write a serious book about the fighting in Abyssinia, but Steer got in first with an account which received much praise and good reviews. That made Waugh his enemy, and in his review of Steer's book he was at his most vicious: 'Mr Steer. . . had great sympathy, I think it is not unfair to say affinity, for those nimble-witted upstarts who formed the [Emperor's] entourage, like himself African born, who had memorised so many of the facts of European education without ever participating in European culture.'

Steer tried to ignore all this. He was a lively, sociable man, but he had a strong moral sense, and felt that journalism should be more than just the retailing of facts. He believed strongly in the journalism of advocacy, and it wasn't difficult to detect in his writings that he supported the cause of Haile Selassie against the Italians. In the same way, when he moved on to cover the Spanish Civil War for *The Times*, he gave his clear backing to the Basques in their fight against Franco. Nevertheless he wasn't interested in writing propaganda, and his reporting for *The Times* was invariably calm and balanced.

On 27 April 1937 he and a Reuters correspondent, Christopher Holme, were in the village of Ambacegui, near Guernica, when it was attacked by six German fighter-bombers. They took shelter in a bomb crater while the planes returned again and again, machine-gunning the village. Directly it was safe to leave they headed back to Bilbao, where they had dinner with several other correspondents. While they were still sitting round the table a Basque official came rushing in and told them that the town of Guernica was on fire. The attack on Ambacegui had just been a sideshow; Guernica had been the real target. Steer, Holme and two others decided to make the fifteen-mile drive to Guernica right away. The others decided to wait till it was light.

The four correspondents arrived at eleven o'clock. The night sky was lit up by burning buildings, and frenzied efforts were still going to dig out the dead and injured. Steer discovered from the survivors what had happened, and found the remains of three incendiary bombs bearing German markings. Then the correspondents headed back to Bilbao. The Reuters man, Christopher Holme, filed his story immediately, but it came too late for any but the last editions of the British press. Anyway, it was impossible for a brief, tightly written news agency despatch to convey the reality of something like the deliberate destruction of a town. The horror lies in the kind of detail an agency correspondent doesn't have the scope to provide. Steer had had an immensely tiring and frightening day, and he was physically and emotionally drained. His deadline had long since passed, so he decided to get his head down for a few hours, then write his despatch when he was feeling fresher.

We have long become used to the deliberate targeting of civilians, so it has lost its ability to shock us. The Prussians had attacked Paris in the war of 1870, and the Kaiser's army had done the same in Belgium and France during the First World War. In each case, civilians had died in considerable numbers. Somehow, though, these seemed to be exceptions to the way in which wars were waged, and in the post-war mood of cynicism many people thought they had been greatly exaggerated by the Allied propaganda machine. The Italians used similar tactics in Abyssinia and Libya, but these were colonial wars, in which different rules were thought to apply. Spain, however, was in Europe. The deliberate decision to wipe a European city off the map as an act of war was deeply shocking. In the despatch he sent from Bilbao on 28 April 1937 (though he dated it 27 April), Steer set out to describe in his despatch to *The Times* the methods of warfare which much of Europe would soon be facing:

> Guernica, the most ancient town of the Basques and the centre of their cultural tradition, was completely destroyed yesterday by insurgent air raiders. The bombardment of this open town far behind the lines occupied precisely three hours and a quarter, during which a powerful fleet of aeroplanes consisting of three German types, Junkers and Heinkel bombers and Heinkel fighters, did not cease unloading on the town bombs weighing from 1,000lb downwards and, it is calculated, more than 3,000 two-pounder aluminium incendiary projectiles. The fighters, meanwhile, plunged low from above the centre of the town to machine-gun those of the civilian population who had taken refuge in the fields...
>
> At 2 a.m. today when I visited the town the whole of it was a horrible sight, flaming from end to end.

The strength of Steer's report lies in its coldly factual quality. The first emotive adjective, 'horrible', comes more than a hundred words into the report, by which time the readers will have decided for themselves how bad the attack on Guernica had been. The rest of Steer's piece goes into detail about the brutal damage and the savage injuries which the German high explosive and incendiary bombs had wrought; but the effect that it had on British and European sensibilities came primarily from Steer's apparently cool and dispassionate opening.

It caused a Europe-wide clamour. The head of the Nationalist press bureau, attached to General Franco's headquarters, announced that Basque activists had blown up their own town, in order to get international sympathy. In Britain, several right-wing intellectuals immediately attacked Steer for his report, and this alarmed *The*

Times to such an extent that it cabled him to ask for a further 'judicious' statement. The fact that Christopher Holme of Reuters had seen precisely the same things that Steer had, and had reported them in full, seemed to make no difference.

At this point, no doubt, Steer should have maintained a dignified silence. Instead he lost his temper, and the statement he wrote showed (not least by spelling the name of the town 'Gernika', Basque-fashion) whose side he was on. Nevertheless *The Times* published it. A couple of weeks later Steer was able to settle the question of responsibility for the bombing of the town conclusively by quoting from the log book of a German pilot who had been involved in the Guernica raid and was shot down near Bilbao.

Steer left *The Times*, and settled in Paris to write a book about the war against the Basques, which he called *The Tree of Gernika*. In it he no longer felt the necessity for balance; he even talked about 'we' and 'us' when he mentioned the Basque forces. Martha Gellhorn approved of the book, and recommended it to her friend Eleanor Roosevelt.

The despatch which made Steer's name wasn't quite a scoop in the strictest sense because Reuters' Christopher Holme was with him in Guernica and actually filed his account first. Holme was generous enough to say afterwards that Steer's report had been much better than his. Still, the bombing of Guernica can genuinely be called Steer's exclusive because the intensely powerful yet restrained fashion in which he wrote it attracted such attention nationally and internationally.

There was another reason for the primacy of Steer's story: it was reprinted in *L'Humanité*, the French Communist Party newspaper, where Pablo Picasso came across it. At the time, Picasso was working on a mural for the Spanish government's exhibit at the 1937 World's Fair in Paris. After reading Steer's article he scrapped his original plans and painted *Guernica* for the Spanish exhibit instead: probably his single best-known work.

Clare Hollingworth quickly realised that the Polish officials she met in Warsaw had no real idea of the threat they faced from the Germans. The Poles had accepted the completely wrong-headed assessment that Poland's military strength was greater than that of Germany, and they believed far too implicitly in the promise of support which the British and French had made to them. The Poles tended to believe that if Germany made the mistake of invading Poland, they would occupy Berlin by Christmas. It was true that the Polish army was being built up to two million strong, with reservists joining the regulars, but the government seemed to have no aware-ness of the strength of Germany's tank divisions or its aircraft. All the talk was of the unstoppable Polish cavalry – mounted on horses.

Clare headed for Katowice, close to the German border. As usual, she went to see the British diplomats based there; here, as every-where else Clare went in the world, it was an important part of her M.O. The consul-general, a man called John Thwaites, offered to let her stay in his apartment; his wife and children had been evac-uated to Britain. Long years later, when Thwaites was dead, Clare revealed that they started an affair the day she arrived. This may have explained why, the following morning, Thwaites agreed to let Clare use his official car. When he asked her where she was going, she told him, 'Across the border.'

'You're a funny old girl,' Thwaites replied, clearly thinking she was joking. He let her go.

With the Union Jack fluttering, Clare drove off in the diplomatic car in the direction of Nazi Germany. The border guards on both sides, Polish and German, saluted and let her through. She said later that she assumed they were thinking: 'A young girl – she's perfectly harmless.' This supposed harmlessness was an important part of the way she operated, and she continued to use it and develop it into middle age and then old age. It worked almost every time.

At the German town of Beuthen she stocked up with wine, film for her camera and electric torches. Then she headed on to Gleiwitz, which is nowadays in Poland and called Gliwice. On the road she passed detachments of motorcycle despatch riders, going fast: at one point there were sixty-five of them in the same group. She carried on driving past a long hessian screen which prevented anyone on the road from looking down into the valley; but with Clare's luck a gust of wind whipped the hessian from its moorings as she passed, and she saw the sight the German army was trying to hide: scores, perhaps hundreds, of tanks. It was von Rundstedt's Army Group South, which had linked up with Reichenau's Tenth Army.

When Clare told Thwaites, he couldn't believe that she'd got into Germany; she had to show him the supplies she'd bought to prove it. He hurried into his office and sent a long cable to London. Clare, meanwhile, rang Hugh Carleton Greene in Warsaw, and he contacted the *Telegraph* foreign desk. On Tuesday 29 August 1939, after only three days as a journalist, Clare got her first Page One lead:

1,000 TANKS MASSED ON POLISH BORDER.

TEN DIVISIONS REPORTED READY FOR SWIFT STROKE.

Her name wasn't on the story; the *Telegraph* didn't use bylines.

Three mornings later, at 5 a.m. on Friday 1 September, Clare was awakened by a noise like the banging of a door. It was Polish anti-aircraft fire. When she looked out of the window she could see planes flying high overhead. She rang Greene and woke him. Later he described it as the most dramatic moment of his life.

'It's begun!' Clare shouted excitedly.

Greene in turn rang a senior official in the Polish foreign ministry and told him.

'Nonsense,' he said. 'Negotiations are still going on.'

He was just about to ring off when the air-raid sirens began sounding in Warsaw.

A matter of seconds earlier, Clare got through to a second secretary at the British embassy in Warsaw. His reaction was precisely the same: 'Rubbish. The Germans and the Poles are still negotiating.' She held the telephone out of the window so he could hear the sound of war for himself.

Still, when her chauffeur arrived for work, he dismissed the firing as merely air-raid practice, and Clare began to wonder if she'd got it wrong: 'My own reaction, for the moment, was actual fear: fear that I had made the gaffe of my life by reporting a non-existent war.'

Confirmation soon arrived that the war had indeed started. So far, though, the tanks which Clare had spotted had not yet crossed into Poland. Characteristically, Clare drove back to the border to investigate, but found that the Polish front line was still holding. She returned to Katowice. The following day Britain still hadn't declared war, and the Polish government ordered the British consulate there to close down. Clare and Thwaites set off for Krakow, but Thwaites had forgotten something so they had to turn round. As they did, an anti-aircraft gun opened up from a rooftop and suddenly German planes were diving down and firing into the streets. The two of them leaped out of their car and took cover, but drove off again when the raid was over, and finally reached Krakow.

On Sunday 3 September, Britain declared war. By now, Clare and Thwaites had been joined by four others. A middle-aged Englishwoman delayed them by insisting on buying 'toothpaste or hairpins or face-cream' (Clare's disdain for this kind of frivolity was always strong). She returned, 'hung thick as a Christmas tree with little bags. Then she summoned up holdalls, carpet-bags, suitcases, handbags and a typewriter, all of which she insisted on bringing with her.' Their car was a four-seater, but six of them were now jammed in it, including a Jewish-Czech refugee who had worked for the anti-Nazi underground in Katowice. Clare told the others that he must come with them.

The Polish government had abandoned Warsaw, and was now briefly based in Krzemieniec. Clare linked up with the British diplomats there. The meeting is described in Patrick Garrett's *Of Fortunes and War: Clare Hollingworth, First of the Female War Correspondents*. The ambassador, Sir Howard Kennard, was amusing and generous, but unusually blunt for a diplomat. He also shared the habitual male chauvinism of his generation:

'Hmmm, you're a peculiar woman, Miss Hollingworth,' he greeted me. 'What are you doing, running about in the middle of all this? Love of excitement, I suppose.'

'I'm a journalist, Sir Howard. This is how I earn my living.'

'Pfff, journalist! What's the trouble? No family?'

Clare wasn't offended; she realised that he was a man whose help she could rely on. Simply being here provided her with another exclusive story: all the other British journalists in Poland had left.

Travelling around Poland, often on her own, she was exposed to all sorts of dangers; she was shot at and bombed several times. Much later in life, she told me that these things had never frightened her. Having seen her in some life-threatening situations, I could believe it. She always insisted that she enjoyed being in the middle of a battle. Being in danger, she wrote, gave her 'a serene glow', like the sensation you get from a cold bath. Her Polish experiences also taught her two other important things: firstly, if there are bombs going off around you, you are better off outdoors; and secondly, you should never allow air raids to deprive you of a good night's sleep. I took her advice right from the start, and have never regretted it.

Hugh Greene had left for Romania with the rest of the British press corps from Warsaw, but had come back to Krzemieniec to meet up with the Polish government again. When he bumped into her, they were both delighted, and Clare opened a bottle of champagne from a crate which the French consulate in Katowice had given her; they couldn't fit it into their own vehicles.

'We drank it out of tin mugs,' she said.

The two of them had plenty to celebrate. Clare's independence of mind and gutsy reporting meant that the *Daily Telegraph* had been the first newspaper on earth to announce the start of the Second World War, and she had kept it ahead of every other news organisation in covering the war in these early stages. The *Telegraph*'s success was entirely the work of a young woman in her twenties who had been a journalist for just a matter of days.

The BBC, never knowingly undermanned, sent forty-eight corre-spondents to cover the D-Day landings. It has been estimated that the accredited press corps produced almost a quarter of a million words on that day alone. Most of the accredited journalists wallowed on transport ships offshore, throwing up and demand-ing unsuccessfully to be allowed ashore. Ernest Hemingway, who had suffered concussion and an injured knee in a car crash in the London blackout not long before, was on board a transport ship off the Normandy coast. He wrote a despatch for *Collier's* which was clearly intended to give the reader the false impression that he had landed on the beaches.

Hemingway was in a difficult position. He had built up his own legend relentlessly as the hard-living, hard-drinking hero of the First World War and the Spanish Civil War, and even though alco-hol, injury and advancing age were all taking their toll, he knew he had to continue living up to the legend. Martha Gellhorn, who had come to Britain to report on the war, wrote to him with increas-ing scorn when he insisted on staying in Cuba. In November 1943 she wrote to tell him he must put an end to his 'shaming and silly life', but encouraged him to head for London by saying that he was a hero to everyone there. At last he obeyed, and joined her in the Dorchester Hotel. By this stage, though, their marriage was pretty much over and they had ceased to share a room. Much later she told me that he insisted on taking over the hotel room of a permanent resident, a nervous elderly lady, because it offered better shelter from falling bombs; the hotel moved the old lady out because it was so keen to have someone as celebrated as Hemingway staying there.

He got his revenge on Martha by insisting on working as a war correspondent for her magazine, *Collier's*. With a remarkable lack of loyalty to her, *Collier's* accepted him at once. Since news maga-zines were allowed to have only one correspondent in any particular war zone, this meant that Martha lost her official accreditation. It didn't matter. She still managed to cover the D-Day landings as a stowaway.

Her ship dropped anchor off Omaha Beach, in the American sector, on the morning of 6 June. The very first phase of the invasion was over. Bulldozers were at work on the beach, getting rid of the remaining mines. In the water around the ship floated the bodies of American GIs who had been drowned, dragged down by their heavy packs and equipment when they had jumped into water that was too deep for them. The injured were starting to be brought from the beaches to the ship in landing craft and in the ship's own boats – floating ambulances. Martha did what she could, handing out drinking water and organising food for the injured, and interpreting for the French and Germans among them. The German prisoners, probably relieved to be still alive, started talking and laughing too loudly, and Martha was told to shut them up: 'When they giggled too much I said *"Ruhig"* [quiet] on d[octo]r's orders and they were all instantly silent.'

Finally, when night fell, her moment came. With the ship's medical staff, she jumped into the water as the invading troops had done some twelve hours earlier, and waded to shore with the waves waist-high. Her job, like that of the other nurses, was to find the wounded and get them ready to be picked up directly it got light. She crossed the beach and climbed a path which was marked as being clear of mines, noticing the 'sweet smell of summer grass, a smell of cattle and peace and the sun that had warmed the earth some other time, when summer was real'. Red flares hung in the sky, lighting the smashed tanks and abandoned trucks. The gunfire was deafening. 'Village really smashed', she noted; 'church like collapsed paper bag'.

Eventually, though, the nurses were recalled to the ship. The doctors on board had been operating all night, and there was no room on board for any more cases. The ship's engines started up, and she headed off to England: 'Great speed & efficiency of loading. Special tenderness towards coloured wounded... Burn cases. Blood soaked bandages. Everyone watching in silence. Mass of German prisoners marching to POW cage... terrible seedy bunch.'

As Martha watched the prisoners disembarking, she noted how small and unhealthy they looked: not at all the blond giants of Nazi mythology. She wasn't allowed to question them, because the Geneva Convention forbade it. Then she went back to London to write up her remarkable experiences. She turned them into two articles, one about the hospital ship and how efficient and caring its American staff had been, and the other about the way the German prisoners had looked and behaved.

Soon, though, the military police came for her. She had broken the law by sailing to France without permission, and was sent as a prisoner to an American nurses' training camp outside London. There was no question of charging her with any crime; it was just a way of demonstrating official disapproval. She was told she'd only be able to go back to Normandy when the nurses had finished their training. Being Martha, she slipped out under the perimeter fence and went back to London that night.

Ernest Hemingway had a less successful time on D-Day. He crossed the Channel on an attack transport called the *Dorothea M. Dix*, but didn't make it to the beach. Perhaps his injured head and leg forced him to stay on board. When the next edition of *Collier's* came out, Martha's two stories about her exploits were a lot less prominent than Hemingway's account, which led the magazine. His photograph dominated the front cover, and his swashbuckling exploits filled the opening pages. If you read his article without knowing what had really happened on the *Dorothea M. Dix*, you would imagine he was the dominant figure in the entire exploit: it was called 'How we took Fox Green Beach'. Lieutenant Robert Anderson commanded the vessel, but according to the article, Hemingway had studied the maps of the coastline so well that it was he who spotted the key landmarks such as the church tower of Colleville, and guided the transport inshore. The text contains no hint that Hemingway might not have landed with the other men, and there are descriptive passages which deliberately give the reader the strong impression he did: 'I saw a piece of German about three-foot long with an arm on it sail high up into the air in the fountaining of one shellburst.'

It's possible, of course, that Hemingway saw this through binoculars, or even with the naked eye, from the transport ship;

if so, perhaps he reassured himself he wasn't necessarily telling an outright lie. More probably, he didn't care. He gives the reader the clearest impression that he landed on the beach, and the magazine's editors certainly thought he had. Shortly after he had sent over his story to them, he followed it up with a cable to say that a German division had been sent in 'just where *Collier's* correspondent landed'.

In the years that followed, the story of Hemingway's D-Day heroism grew. In the early 1960s, after his suicide, a magazine called *True* published a long account called 'Hemingway's Longest Day'. A veteran of the landing, who isn't named, is quoted as saying 'this Hemingway guy' had taken command of a combat team which was pinned down by German fire, and led the men to safety in the shelter of a hill. Then he crawled back to report to the beach commander. The writer was a friend of Hemingway's, William van Dusen, and the unnamed veteran who supplied him with the details turned out later to have been Hemingway himself.

Yet even though he didn't go ashore on D-Day, it wasn't because he had lost his nerve. Given the injuries to his head and leg it was brave of him to go out on the transport at all. His injuries took six weeks to heal, but after that he was soon racing around the liberated part of Normandy in the sidecar of a captured German motorcycle. This episode ended badly when he and his driver nearly ran into a German anti-tank gun and had to jump into a ditch. The Germans kept on firing at them for two hours. Hemingway injured his kidneys and hurt his head again.

The legitimate correspondents hated the way Hemingway and his followers carried weapons and acted as self-appointed intelligence-gatherers for the Americans; such things, they felt, were against the journalists' code of conduct. But Hemingway was Hemingway – he wasn't just another reporter. And he needed to feed the legend. General Jacques Leclerc of the 2nd French Armoured Division told him to 'buzz off' when he tried to join up with the leading French tanks, so Hemingway went to a nearby bar and had a drink or two: 'Paris was going to be taken. . . I had a funny choke in my throat, and I had to clean my glasses, because there, below us, gray and always beautiful, was spread the city I love best in all the world.'

Together with his ragtag group of friends, he claimed, he drove off down a sidestreet and joined up with the first of Leclerc's tanks. 'I took cover in all the street fighting,' he wrote in *Collier's*, though the meaning of this isn't clear, and he later boasted that he entered Paris 'with the very first troops'. But if this is true, he didn't provide any detail about it. Various legends sprang up: according to one, 'Task Force Hemingway' was fighting at the Arc de Triomphe while the main forces of General Leclerc were still held up down along the Seine. And when Leclerc finally reached the centre of town he supposedly found a sign on a church door that read: 'Property of Ernest Hemingway'. That sounds like a joke rather than a genuine anecdote.

Did he liberate the Ritz Hotel? The great photographer Robert Capa, whom Martha Gellhorn dearly loved, maintained that when he arrived at the Ritz that evening Hemingway's French driver met him and told him 'Papa took good hotel'. But in reality Hemingway stopped off to clear out some German soldiers from a building near the Bois de Boulogne, then looked in at the Travellers' Club on the Champs-Elysées for a glass of champagne. He only reached the Ritz later, and it already been taken over when he got there. None of this matters too much, of course: Hemingway was certainly on hand when Paris fell, and he had a huge amount of fun while it happened. And anyway he wasn't a journalist in the sense that Martha was: he was a world-renowned writer of fiction with a huge ego to support.

As for Martha, after being arrested and escaping, she was left with no identification or travel documents except her passport, and Hemingway had made sure she couldn't be re-accredited to *Collier's*. She thought things over carefully, and decided that the easiest war front to travel to would be Italy. Everyone was concentrating on the fighting in France now, but there was still plenty of fighting to be covered on the way north from Rome. She went to an RAF station, where she found a sympathetic pilot who was under orders to fly to

Naples. She spun him a story about needing to meet up there with her fiancé, and he obligingly got her onto his plane.

Once there, she hitched a series of rides and ended up with the Eighth Army, which had fought its way across North Africa and was now working its way northwards from Rome. The city had fallen two days before D-Day. The Eighth Army was exactly the kind of force Martha liked: an irrepressible collection of nationalities, British, South Africans, Canadians, Indians and New Zealanders, and a sizeable collection of Poles. It was the Poles whose company she enjoyed the most, and she linked up with the Carpathian Lancers, a cavalry regiment. She went racing round with them in their jeeps, her chiffon scarf blowing in the wind. After all the problems with Hemingway and with military officialdom, she felt free at last.

EIGHT

Facing the Dictators

Previously he had been badly wounded, but after he recovered from the gas attack he stated that he had seen a vision and received a message. He had been summoned as the saviour of Germany. . . Hitler, the tub-thumping patriot, may be heard from again some day.

Daily Express report from Hitler's trial in Munich, 27 February 1924

HAROLD HARMSWORTH, 1ST VISCOUNT Rothermere, co-founder with his brother, Lord Northcliffe, of the *Daily Mail* and the *Daily Mirror* and one of Britain's most powerful press lords, is a difficult man to love. In January 1937, when Rothermere was invited by Hitler to the Berghof, Joseph Goebbels noted in his diary: 'Rothermere pays me great compliments. . . Strongly anti-Jewish. . . He is a strong supporter of the Führer.'

The following year, on 1 October 1938, he sent Hitler a telegram congratulating him on invading the Sudetenland, and calling him 'Alfred the Great'. Papers released by MI5 in 2005 revealed that he sent further congratulations in 1939 to Hitler on invading Czechoslovakia, and encouraged him to do the same to Romania. Hitler's work, Rothermere said, was 'great and superhuman'.

One of the minor pleasures of researching this book has been to read Rothermere's long-forgotten *Warnings and Predictions*, published in August 1939, just as Britain was declaring war on Hitler's Germany. It was ghost-written at very short notice by one of his newspaper editors, William Collin Brooks, who had an awkward threefold task: presenting everything Rothermere had said and done as a purely patriotic endeavour, eradicating the memory of the grovelling the great man had done to Hitler, and keeping Rothermere himself sweet. In *Scoop* terms, Collin Brooks was Mr Salter to Rothermere's Lord Copper, forever assuring him 'Up to a point, Lord Copper'. This leads Brooks to some lovely touches in writing *Warnings and Predictions* in his boss's voice:

> If the new Germany chose to rearm vigorously, as any man of sense knew she would and must arm... Britain, by her geographical position and her economic circumstances, would be the most endangered. So impressed was I by this conviction that on November 14th 1933 I published the following article, which is as fresh and vital today as the day it was written.

The fresh and vital article (which Rothermere probably didn't write either) was about the need for Britain to build up its air force. That had indeed been one of Rothermere's key concerns during the 1930s. His idea seemed to be that Britain should make itself militarily strong, while Nazi Germany did the dirty work of sorting out Soviet Russia. The problem was that by the time *Warnings and Predictions* came out, Nazi Germany and Soviet Russia had just signed the Ribbentrop Pact; not something that Rothermere had warned about or, presumably, expected.

The book contains nothing about the embarrassing hero-worship Rothermere had displayed towards Hitler, naturally; but it can't always hide his feelings about him:

> In the afternoon of January 31st 1933 the evening papers of London were displaying the news that Herr Adolf Hitler had become Chancellor of the German Reich.
>
> George Ward Price [the chief special correspondent of the *Daily Mail* and Rothermere's private emissary] happened to come into my room. I said to him:–
>
> 'Ward Price, I want you particularly to remember what I am about to say. This will prove to be one of the most historic days, if not *the* most historic day, in the latter day history of Europe.'

The book then goes into a discourse about how foolish Western newspapers and statesmen had been to regard Hitler as a ludicrous, Charlie Chaplin figure, a mere clown. With the Second World War just starting, it doesn't of course mention that Rothermere had regarded him as 'great' and 'superhuman'.

George Ward Price needed no great prompting about how to report the doings of Adolf Hitler. Price was an unattractive character, cold, solitary and largely humourless, though he certainly had an extraordinary career and was a great adventurer. He was taken on by the *Daily Mail* in 1906, while still a student at Cambridge, and in 1909 made his first reporting trip to Berlin, where he learned to speak excellent German.

After Rothermere's first meeting with Hitler, at the end of 1934, Price was appointed the *Mail*'s Berlin correspondent, with instructions to get as close to Hitler as possible. He was to follow Rothermere's wishes faithfully over the next few years. The result is still discernible: in press photographs and newsreel pictures Price can often be seen, grinning away, while Hitler is talking.

In his memoirs, published in 1957 and entitled, with distinct self-congratulation, *Extra-Special Correspondent*, he describes how Hitler invited him to join his motorcade to Vienna when the *Anschluss*, or union between Germany and Austria, was announced:

> I was in the third of the long convoy of cars, and could see him bombarded with flowers in every township on the route...
>
> The heading given next day by the London *Times* to the news of the Anschluss was 'Rape of Austria'. That afternoon Hitler addressed a vast crowd in the big parade-ground of the Burg, which had been the palace of the Habsburg dynasty. By chance I met him as he came down the staircase from delivering this oration. His face glittered with tears. 'Is that a "rape"?' he asked scornfully, waving a hand at the tight-packed, cheering multitude below.

A few months earlier, in 1937, he had written a rather different book, called *I Know These Dictators*. He certainly did. Hitler liked to have Price around because he was silent and appreciative, and provided him with a direct link to British public opinion through Rothermere and the *Mail*. Mussolini liked Price because he found his presence flattering. Price knew his place: he never asked difficult questions of either of them. He wasn't a Nazi or a Fascist, and may not even have been a thoroughgoing sympathiser; but he allowed their thinking to influence the tone of some of his writing. He certainly doesn't show the faintest hint of moral disapproval: 'The world is confronted by a new technique of government. A great development in political history is going on before our eyes. We should study it with an open mind. The Fascist and Nazi Revolutions are too momentous to be judged with personal bias...'

Talking to Hitler:

rather resembles the Socratic form of dialogue; the inquirer propounds a theme, and Hitler enlarges upon it. When more than two people are present, even though they are of his intimate circle, there is no general discourse. Either Hitler talks and they all listen, or else they talk among themselves and Hitler sits silent.

Mussolini, a former journalist, seems to be more to Ward Price's personal taste.

He is too good-humouredly cynical to be a victim of *folie de grandeur*. Businesslike, quick-witted, instantaneous and apt in his replies, he conveys the impression of a successful man of the world who is an expert at his job and enjoys doing it...

Whereas Mussolini is objective and practical, Hitler is subjective and mystical. Mussolini delights in complicated reports and official memoranda. Hitler detests them and shuns discussion of administrative detail. The one is a realist, the other a visionary. Mussolini's mental processes are dominated by facts; Hitler's are governed by ideals.

These judgements are scarcely deep, but they have the attraction of direct, personal observation.

Price interviewed both Hitler and Mussolini on various occasions. He never challenged Hitler in any way; an interview with the Führer was merely a question of turning the rhetorical tap on and off every now and then. With Mussolini, he knew he could get away with raising one or two of the tougher questions – the murder by Fascists of the Italian Socialist Party deputy Giacomo Matteotti in 1924, for instance. But he accepted Mussolini's answer in every case; there were no challenging follow-up questions.

By 1937 those Jews who remained in Germany were being made to suffer heavily. George Ward Price had no interest whatever in what was happening to them. On the contrary, he clearly sympathised with Hitler's views, and allowed them to permeate his writing. 'From the native German standpoint,' he writes, Jewish immigration into Germany from Eastern Europe 'was a danger to national culture, for foreign Jews brought with them no standards but those of cosmopolitan materialism. And while these meaner elements of the Jewish race were exploiting German depression, the intelligentsia of the same stock was getting a stranglehold on the learned professions.' This passage is interesting because of its shift in voice. The first sentence is sourced to 'the German standpoint'; by the second sentence we are hearing Ward Price's own opinions – complete with characteristic Nazisms like 'exploiting' and 'stranglehold'.

At times he becomes an outright apologist for Hitler's Reich. There have been 'gross and reckless exaggerations' about the concentration camps, for instance:

> To blacken the whole Nazi régime because a few of its subordinates may have abused their powers is as unfair as it would be to condemn the Government of the United States for the brutalities of some warder in charge of a chain-gang in the mountains of West Virginia.

Rothermere must have liked all this when he read it; Price would never have written such things otherwise. He stuck close to Hitler and Mussolini, and avoided asking them any awkward questions whatever, because those were his instructions.

If he had applied some touch of moral discrimination, it might have helped him to gauge the two dictators more accurately. But that wasn't the point, as far as he was concerned. His sole concern was to keep his access to them. Any challenge to their character or their political approach, any awkward question in an interview, any hint of criticism in one of his articles, and that access would be gone. So, quite probably, would his close relationship with Lord Rothermere.

Journalists of any worth are in the job because they want to tell people what is happening. George Ward Price was in the job so that he could continue to stay in the job. For him, the access he had obtained to Hitler and Mussolini was an end in itself, not a useful way in which he could tell his readers more accurately what their use of power portended. Price is a perfect example of the journalist as moral eunuch. There have always been plenty of them.

———

By contrast Denis Sefton Delmer, known as Tom, was a much more engaging rogue. His first book of memoirs, *Trail Sinister*, published in 1961, is frank in a Falstaffian way: 'I am in my late fifties now. I am bald. My navel has long given way to the insubordinate pressure of my enormous paunch. And long ago, too, I have given up trying to be a dandy or caring overmuch how odd and ridiculous I may appear.'

His parents were Australian, and because his father had a job as a university professor in Berlin before the First World War, Sefton Delmer was born there. His father was interned at the start of hostilities, and the family was trapped in Germany, often taunted and ill-treated, until in 1917 they managed to get official permission to leave the country. Tom spoke excellent German, therefore, without having any great affection for the country.

After leaving Oxford in 1927, he went back to Berlin and bumped into Lord Beaverbrook, the owner of the *Daily Express*. Beaverbrook was in many ways as right-wing as Lord Rothermere, and if anything more nationalistic; but he was never taken in by Hitler and the Nazis, and (as we have seen) encouraged Philip Pembroke Stephens to write his series of anti-Nazi articles in 1933.

Now, Beaverbrook took a liking to Sefton Delmer and hired him. He remained with the *Daily Express* for most of his career.

In September 1928 Delmer became the paper's Berlin correspondent. It was the following February when he set eyes on Hitler for the first time. He was appearing at a Nazi rally, and wasn't speaking into the microphone properly. For a long time Delmer couldn't make out what he was saying. Finally he understood: Hitler was talking about fruit. '"We Germans must not eat oranges," he was saying. "We must consume no fruit, no food which we have not grown ourselves." That was enough for me. A crackpot, I decided.'

He watched the perspiration drip down Hitler's face, and make his starched collar go limp. At the end, Delmer was the only person there who didn't raise his arm in the Nazi salute, and he was threatened with a beating as a result.

Yet he started to realise that there might be more to Hitler than he'd thought, and he decided to get closer to him. First he cultivated the chief of staff of Hitler's SA, Ernst Röhm; and Röhm took him to meet Hitler at the Brown House in Munich. It was the first time the Führer had been interviewed by a British journalist. Delmer's assessment of him was both snobbish (Hitler said 'Pleased to meet you' when they met, which set him down as lower middle class) and insightful: 'He reminded me of the many ex-soldier travelling salesmen I had met in railway carriages on my journeys across Germany. He talked like one, too.'

Like George Ward Price, Sefton Delmer wrote his memoirs after the war, when only a crank would have defended Hitler. But whereas Price was silent about his true attitude to Hitler, Delmer was openly scornful – as he certainly had been at the time.

Röhm was sure that Sefton Delmer was a British agent, and persuaded the rest of the Nazi hierarchy of that. In fact, it's clear now that he wasn't formally working for MI6, but it is not impossible that, like other journalists of the time and later, he passed occasional bits of information to them. He found the idea that he was a British agent rather flattering, and it certainly pleased the Germans; with George Ward Price they felt they were speaking to

British public opinion, but with Sefton Delmer they thought they were in direct contact with the true decision-makers of the British government.

Delmer's contacts with the top Nazis became so good that the British Foreign Office in turn suspected him of being a German agent. In 1932 he travelled round Germany in Hitler's personal aeroplane during his election campaign, and in February the following year he secured a great scoop when he walked through the smoking ruins of the Reichstag with Hitler in the immediate aftermath of the fire. He said afterwards that when he phoned through his story to the foreign desk at the *Express*, the sub-editor was more interested in the fire than anything he had to say about being with Hitler. Beaverbrook, however, was overjoyed with Delmer's story. The *Express* was fighting a fierce duel with the *Mail*, and Delmer had beaten Price in a critical head-to-head battle. Neither man mentions the other, or indeed the other's newspaper, in his memoirs.

A number of people criticised Delmer at the time for seeming to be so friendly with the top Nazis. For some reason Price received less criticism. Delmer maintained he had simply been doing his duty as a journalist; and the comparison between the two men is certainly in his favour. Nazism had no private attraction for him whatever; and although he gave Hitler an easy time when he interviewed him, and may well have grovelled to him as much as Price did, he didn't sell his soul to Nazism.

During the war Rothermere pushed George Ward Price to one side; he represented a part of the *Mail*'s history which Rothermere wanted to forget. Delmer, by contrast, did good work in Poland and France during the early days of the war, and remained one of Beaverbrook's favourites. He left the *Express* in 1940 and joined the BBC's German Service as a broadcaster. Later he went to the Special Operations Executive and organised German-language black propaganda stations which were successful in undermining enemy morale. He was given an OBE for his work after the war, which showed that the British government had no anxieties about his pre-war sympathies.

One of the great moments of Sefton Delmer's career – and there were plenty of them – was his first formal BBC broadcast to Germany in 1940. He was sitting in the studio, waiting for his turn to start speaking, when the announcer read out a news item about a peace offer which Hitler had made to Britain an hour or so before. It proposed terms which were completely unacceptable to British public opinion. Delmer, without any authorisation whatever from his bosses or the British government, spoke live and unscripted into the microphone in German:

> Herr Hitler, you have in the past consulted me as to the mood of the British public, so permit me to render your Excellency this little service once again tonight. Let me tell you what we here in Britain think of this appeal of yours to what you are pleased to call our reason and common sense. Herr Führer, we hurl it right back at you. Right back in your lying, stinking teeth.

Predictably, it caused consternation at the BBC, though Churchill was highly amused. In Berlin, Goebbels assumed that this must be the British government's considered response to Hitler's offer.

Especially since it came from someone he still believed was a top British agent.

Dictators, it goes without saying, do not relish being challenged. And since the essence of an interview should be to challenge, it follows that most dictators prefer not to be interviewed. George Ward Price and Tom Sefton Delmer didn't interview Hitler in the sense that a modern journalist is expected to interview a political leader, putting alternative points of view and bringing up instances where the facts run counter to political rhetoric. Instead, they simply steered him towards a particular subject, then recorded his answers. Getting in to speak to the great man in the first place was the hard part: the actual business of interviewing him was relatively easy.

Joseph Stalin rarely spoke to foreign correspondents. He was prepared to open up to someone like Milovan Djilas, the Yugoslav writer and politician, who got on well with him, but these were private conversations which were published only after Stalin's death. Stalin did, nevertheless, speak to the British writer H. G. Wells, who visited Moscow in 1934. The resulting article was printed in the *New Statesman*.

Stalin showed himself immediately to be a very different character from Hitler or Mussolini. He was even more deadly, in terms of the number of people who died as a direct result of his policies, than either of them; yet although he turned into one of the worst dictators the world has seen, he managed to give the impression that he was just an ordinary citizen who happened to have been singled out to head the Communist Party of the Soviet Union. The Emperor Augustus followed something of this approach in early imperial Rome. When Wells came to see him on 23 July 1934, Stalin spoke as though they were on a level, two open-minded men talking over a set of political questions. Wells, who was pretty full of himself, knew he didn't have to be cautious in the questions he put; there was no question that he would be taken prisoner or beaten up afterwards if he were disrespectful. As a famous international writer and thinker, he was entirely safe.

It's easy, with hindsight, to criticise Wells for being too soft on Stalin. The dreadful outburst of state terror that was to follow the murder of Kirov in Leningrad was still five months in the future. He could, perhaps should, have pressed him on the key issue of Stalin's entire leadership: whether radical political change was possible without savage cruelty, expropriation and state-sponsored terror. But Wells wasn't a journalist or a politician, he was a writer and thinker who was as keen to present his own views as he was to hear about Stalin's; and anyway hard-hitting interviews were a great deal more rare in the 1930s, even in Britain, France and the United States.

Stalin had a cynical, deflating wit which completely set him apart from Hitler or Mussolini, and he showed it at the very start of his interview with Wells:

WELLS: I am very much obliged to you, Mr Stalin, for agreeing to see me. I was in the United States recently. I had a long conversation with President Roosevelt and tried to ascertain what his leading ideas were. Now I have come to ask you what you are doing to change the world?

STALIN: Not so very much.

From that point on, the meeting between them was less of an interview than two lines of argument which simply rolled past each other without any inter-reaction:

WELLS: Propaganda in favour of the violent overthrow of the social system was all very well when it was directed against tyranny. But under modern conditions, when the system is collapsing anyhow, stress should be laid on efficiency, on competence, on productiveness, and not on insurrection.

STALIN: Capitalism is decaying, but it must not be compared simply with a tree which has decayed to such an extent that it must fall to the ground of its own accord. No, revolution, the substitution of one social system for another, has always been a struggle, a painful and a cruel struggle, a life-and-death struggle. . . [T]he Communists say to the working class: answer violence with violence; do all you can to prevent the old dying order from crushing you, do not permit it to put manacles on your hands, on the hands with which you will overthrow the old system.

It has its interest, certainly, but it is scarcely very enlightening. Stalin told Wells nothing he hadn't said many times before. He met a certain number of Western visitors over the years that followed, but he scarcely ever laid himself open to questioning again in this way: he saw no reason for it.

––––––––

There is always a temptation for foreign correspondents to champion a cause. Often it starts with the realisation that a political movement or a government isn't as radical as it's made out to be; or perhaps that its radicalism is the result of unreasonable pressures or opposition. In the first half of the twentieth century, plenty of journalists followed John Reed, the American chronicler of the October Revolution, by finding a cause in Soviet Russia. In the second half, plenty of others found it in Cuba. One or two have found their cause in countries like Nicaragua, Angola or Venezuela: often because of the damage done there by the United States, rather than because of the attractive qualities of their respective revolutionary governments.

The American Edgar Snow is one of the earliest and best examples of a foreign correspondent who is attracted in the first place by a culture, and then by a revolutionary movement; finds himself granted excellent access because of his sympathy and interest; and ends up becoming an apologist for an ideology.

In his late twenties, Snow and his wife Helen Foster moved to China. They taught at a university in Beijing, and came into contact with student activists who supported the resistance to Japanese aggression in China. From there Snow was invited to visit the revolutionary headquarters of the Central Committee of the Chinese Communist Party in the town of Bao'an, which is nowadays known as Zhidan County. He reached it in the summer of 1936, as recalled in *Red Star Over China*:

> Remains of its fortifications, flame-struck in that afternoon sun, could be seen flanking the narrow pass through which once emptied into this valley the conquering legions of the Mongols. There was an inner city, still, where the garrisons were once quartered; and a high defensive masonry, lately improved by the Reds, embraced about a square mile in which the present town was located.

He was greeted by crowds of soldiers shouting a welcome. 'The effect pronounced upon me was highly emotional,' Snow admitted later. Many journalists, who are often by nature solitary and anonymous, have discovered the attraction of being treated as heroes; but it is rarely good for their intrinsic sense of objectivity. So it proved in

Snow's case. He found Mao Zedong, in particular, interesting and likeable, and his interviews with him and the other leaders over the next few weeks introduced an important new force in world politics; his revelations have been described as 'a world-class scoop'.

In some ways Mao's strategic thinking was a revelation. 'The pivotal strategy must be a war of manoeuvre,' he told Snow, 'and important reliance must be placed on guerrilla and partisan tactics. Fortified [i.e. fixed-position] warfare must be utilised, but it will be of auxiliary and even secondary importance.' At other times Mao was hopelessly wide of the mark:

> SNOW: In the event of a Sino-Japanese war, do you think there will be a revolution in Japan?
> MAO: The Japanese revolution is not only a possibility but a certainty. It is inevitable, and will begin to occur promptly after the first severe defeats suffered by the Japanese Army.

In his interviews with Snow, Mao always seemed to be holding back, realising no doubt that his remarks would be read around the world. Sometimes Mao or his faithful lieutenant Zhou Enlai would come back to Snow afterwards and ask him to change something. Nowadays Western journalists frown on that kind of thing, but since Snow was more interested in presenting Mao's ideas to the outside world than in challenging them, he always seems to have agreed. For him, reporting and propaganda had become inseparable.

There is a close – it's tempting to call it a causal – link between dictatorship and madness. By no means all dictators are mad; Mussolini wasn't, and neither were Stalin or Saddam Hussein, but there has been a long line of others who were either insane when they took power or were pushed into insanity by the heady experience of ruling without any real checks or control. Idi Amin of Uganda became seriously unhinged as a result of unbridled power, and it became dangerous merely to be in his presence. The Emperor Bokassa of the Central

African Republic (which he renamed the Central African Empire) may not have been guilty of cannibalism as the French government alleged, but he was certainly delusionary. In exile he decorated his throne room with portraits and busts of Napoleon; not a good sign. Finally, when he was released from prison in the CAR at the end of his life, he was said to howl at the full moon.

Colonel Gaddafi was, I believe, insane rather than merely eccentric. On the various occasions I met and interviewed him over the years, his behaviour grew stranger and stranger. When I first encountered him in 1978, sitting in his tent in the desert, he threw his head back and laughed loudly at every question I asked. Then, instantly, he would face me again and answer without any hint of humour. In the 1980s and '90s he became noticeably odder, and so did his dress sense. Once when, together with a hundred other journalists from leading international organisations, I was invited to Tripoli to meet him, he kept us waiting for nearly a week at a hugely expensive hotel. Finally, we were gathered together in an audience room at his palace, and he made an appearance in a long coat, an 'ulster', of the kind Sherlock Holmes wore in the late Victorian illustrations to his adventures; it was made from cloth with a glaring coloured check.

He stalked through the room, smiling and even speaking to one or two of us, then wandered out of the door at the far end. In the sudden silence we heard the door being locked behind him. That was it: time to leave Libya.

It wasn't dangerous to interview him; you could ask fierce questions and be fairly certain that there would be no unpleasant consequences. Another time when I met him he broke wind energetically and with relish throughout the entire forty minutes of our meeting. I thought long and hard before reporting this; it seemed likely that I wouldn't be allowed back to see him if I did. Yet it was so characteristic of his weirdness that I felt it would be a form of *suppressio veri* if I kept quiet about it. In the end I allowed the pictures and sound in my television report to show what was going on, without actually referring to it: a bit feeble, I suppose. But I mentioned it specifically in an article for a British Sunday newspaper, which the edited headlined as 'Warm Wind of Compromise Blows from Gaddafi'. The office of the then British prime minister, Tony Blair, complained privately to the BBC that I had made fun of a serious world statesman; but when the revolution broke out against Gaddafi in 2011, I managed to get a visa to return to Tripoli, and even succeeded, with the help of a well-placed friend, in getting an interview with Gaddafi's dangerous son Saif-al-Islam.

Other dictators have proved much more dangerous to cross. In December 1978 two American journalists, Elizabeth Becker of the *New York Times* and Richard Dudman of the *St Louis Post-Despatch*, and a British academic, Malcolm Caldwell, were invited to Cambodia by the Khmer Rouge government which had taken power in April 1975. Caldwell was an open supporter of the Khmer Rouge, and often defended it against the allegations of mass killing and torture for which irrefutable evidence had built up. Elizabeth Becker wrote afterwards that they travelled in a bubble and no one was allowed to speak freely to them during their tour of the country. The communist cadres wore black pyjamas, and the few peasants she saw were dressed in rags. People answered her questions through the official translators 'with blank faces or occasional expressions of fear'.

'Now, as I walked up the semi-circular driveway into the former palace of the French colonial governor, I too was shaking,' she wrote. They were met by a group of officials and led into an immense audience chamber. Pol Pot sat like a king in front of the huge windows at the far end. 'Here was the man who had committed some of the worst crimes in modern history and he was not what I had expected.' He was, she later recalled, elegant, with a pleasant smile and 'delicate, alert eyes'. He was much more polished than the photographs she had seen of him, and was dressed impeccably in a tailored Mao-style grey suit. 'His hands were especially refined, his gestures nearly dainty.'

He didn't stand up to greet them. His foreign minister Ieng Sary walked to and fro behind him. It quickly became clear that this was not to be an interview, but an audience. In a soft voice, speaking without notes, Pol Pot went on and on about the threatened Vietnamese invasion of 'Democratic Kampuchea', as the Khmer Rouge had renamed the country. He was convinced that if the Vietnamese invaded, the West would intervene on his side. 'Except for the occasional flickering of a wrist,' wrote Becker, 'Pol Pot remained motionless as he laid out his worst-case scenario, bragging that he would convince the US, Europe and most of Asia to support him. I left convinced he was insane.'

Malcolm Caldwell, the British academic, had a separate meeting with Pol Pot. Afterwards he came back in a euphoric mood to the guesthouse where the three of them were staying.

About eleven o'clock Becker was awakened by the sound of gunfire. She ran out into the corridor to see a heavily armed Cambodian man pointing a handgun at her. She stepped back into her room and heard more gunshots. An hour later a Cambodian came to her door and told her that Caldwell was dead. She and Dudman went to his room, and found that he had been shot in the chest. The body of a Cambodian was also lying in the room. Elizabeth Becker thought it possible that he was the man who had pointed the gun at her. 'There are no words to describe the fear and horror of that single night,' she wrote later. Three days later the Vietnamese invaded, and the Khmer Rouge government was quickly overthrown.

Who killed Malcolm Caldwell, and why? There have been various suggestions. Four of the guards at the house were arrested, and after being tortured at the terrifying S-21 prison two of them made confessions. They said that Caldwell had been killed by subversives who wanted to prevent the Khmer Rouge from making friendly contacts with the outside world. The distinguished pro-Vietnamese writer and journalist Wilfred Burchett maintained that Pol Pot had had some disagreement with Malcolm Caldwell, and had ordered him to be shot. Elizabeth Becker believed that he had died because of the general anarchy which existed under the Khmer Rouge. 'Malcolm Caldwell's death,' she said, 'was caused by the madness of the regime he openly admired.' She and Richard Dudman left the following morning for Beijing, taking Caldwell's coffin with them.

The most detailed analysis suggests that the number of people who died or were murdered in Cambodia as a direct result of the policies of the Pol Pot regime numbered between 1.8 and 3.42 million. The US bombing which precipitated the Khmer Rouge takeover of power killed around 40,000 people.

Pol Pot carried on a guerrilla war inside Cambodia against the Vietnamese, though he was being treated for cancer in China. When the Vietnamese withdrew from Cambodia, he refused to join in the peace negotiations. The Khmer Rouge army started falling apart in 1996, after he had suffered a major stroke. He ordered the execution of his faithful, lifelong supporter Son Sen, who had tried to do a deal with the government in Phnom Penh. After that, Pol Pot was arrested by the Khmer Rouge military chief and tried for Son Sen's murder.

The American correspondent Nate Thayer (who had met Pol Pot after Elizabeth Becker and Richard Dudman) and a cameraman, David McKaige, managed to get to the Khmer Rouge camp at Anlong Veng where the trial was to take place. It was an extraordinary achievement. Thayer said afterwards, interviewed on C-Span in 2001, that Pol Pot had maintained complete silence during the proceedings.

> They made it clear, and I believed them, that I was to interview Pol Pot after the trial. Pol Pot literally had to be carried away from the trial – he was unable to walk – and I was not able to talk to him. I did try to talk to him. He did not answer any questions, and he did not speak during the trial.
>
> Every ounce of his being was struggling to maintain some last vestige of dignity.*

On 15 April 1998 the Voice of America, which Pol Pot always listened to, announced that the Khmer Rouge had agreed to hand him over to an international tribunal. He died during the night, supposedly of heart failure. Thayer arrived the next day and photographed the body. He was then asked to drive it to the place where it was cremated. Thayer said afterwards that he believed Pol Pot had committed suicide rather than allow himself to be handed over to the Americans. He had, Thayer believed, taken a lethal dose of Valium and chloroquine, two medicines which he had been prescribed. The body was quickly disposed of, in spite of requests from the government that it should be medically examined.

The video of Pol Pot's trial appeared on ABC News in the United States, and ABC made it available around the world. Thayer claimed that he had an agreement with ABC News that it would only appear on the ABC programme *Nightline*, and that its distribution was done without his agreement. 'The story won a British Press Award for "Scoop of the Year" for a British paper I didn't even know had published it,' he said. 'I even won a Peabody Award as a correspondent for *Nightline*. But I turned it down.'

It was the first time anyone had rejected a Peabody Award in its fifty-seven-year history.

The tradition of the highly experienced foreign correspondent has been strong in American network television; if there is a problem with the range and depth of US television coverage, it lies less with the quality of the reporting, than with the parochial nature of much of the editorial process. The foreign news items which are commissioned tend to be short, lacking in any kind of context, and pitched at a pretty low level. The less you tell people about the world, the less they will want to know about it, and the less demand there will be for it: American newspaper, online and television coverage of the world is (with some honourable exceptions) already quite far down this disturbing downward spiral.

The Canadian-born Peter Jennings, one of the three top network anchors from the 1980s into the first decade of the new century, was a highly experienced foreign correspondent with a knowledge and understanding of the Middle East which put ABC first in terms of the quality of its broadcasting. Time and again Jennings forced the programme producers to broadcast reports on issues they would much rather have avoided. I knew him well; and it's one of my great regrets that I should have failed to recognise him six months before his death from lung cancer.

We were standing outside the Iraqi parliament in Baghdad in February 2005, and Jennings was wrapped up heavily against the sharp cold.

'Don't you talk to your old friends any more?' said the familiar voice, now unusually husky. He looked thin and grey and small.

It was typical of him to have made the difficult journey to Iraq at such a time. He chatted away, and I could see that he was as well informed about Iraqi politics as ever.

'Make sure you keep in touch,' were his last, ironic words as I said goodbye.

An entire television era came to an end with his death. Once Jennings was gone, the two long-serving anchors of NBC and CBS, Tom Brokaw and Dan Rather, both made their plans to step down.

Rather was born in 1931, seven years earlier than Jennings, and his reporting career was longer; though his foreign experience was more limited than Jennings's. His drive, and his willingness to take risks, led him to report from Afghanistan during the Soviet occupation. When he was shown wearing Afghan mujaheddin clothes he was nicknamed 'Gunga Dan' by the bitchier elements of the American press, even though his local guides must have insisted that he dressed like them. But Rather's decision to put his safety on the line in spite of the very real dangers meant that when CBS wanted a replacement for Walter Cronkite as chief anchor, he got the job instead of the more experienced Roger Mudd.

Rather interviewed Saddam Hussein twice, once before the first Gulf War and once in 2003, shortly before the Americans and British invaded Iraq. Saddam was another dictator who used interviews as a megaphone to bray forth his views; there was no question of a discussion, and Saddam rarely listened to the questions. He had various techniques for making himself one up. When the interviewer was ushered into the vast, elaborately decorated room in the presidential palace which was used for this purpose, Saddam invariably held out his hand at a low angle, which meant that the interviewer had to bend slightly to take it. It was at this precise point that the official photographer took the key picture, which seemed to show the interviewer bowing to Saddam. The throne-like chair Saddam sat in was a little higher and larger than the interviewer's, which also gave a sense of superiority.

Rather, having interviewed Saddam before, was harder to trap, and Saddam treated him with a certain respect, which wasn't how he usually behaved towards foreign journalists. The transcript of the complete interview shows that there was a good deal of inter-reaction between them. Still, Saddam said nothing of great interest: he never seemed to, on these big set-piece occasions. He challenged President George W. Bush to a televised debate on the issues, which he invited Dan Rather to moderate, but he must have known perfectly well that no such thing would ever happen.

Saddam was a dangerous man to cross, and during his years in power he had hundreds of thousands of people murdered in one way or another. Yet in private he could be pleasant and jovial, and he wasn't without a certain sense of humour. An American newspaper correspondent who went to see him in the early 1980s decided beforehand that he would have to raise the question of Saddam's human rights abuses. To the American's horror, Saddam jumped up, and, grabbing him by the jacket, pulled him out of the room and out into the courtyard where the official cars were parked. Saddam jumped into his Range Rover, waving the American into the passenger seat, and roared off out through the gates. His security guards, wrong-footed, flung themselves into the escort cars behind him.

Saddam drove to the centre of Baghdad, and when he saw an elderly man in a white dishdasha walking along the street he stamped on the brake, jumped out and jabbed his swagger stick under the poor old man's chin.

'You know who I am?'

The man nodded: he was too terrified to speak.

'This American reporter thinks I'm unpopular in Iraq. What do you say?'

The old man started babbling about how he and everyone else in the entire country adored him. Saddam let him go, and laughed in his characteristically harsh way.

'So now you know. They all love me.'

And, still laughing, he drove the correspondent back to the palace.

Saddam was an appalling man in many ways. But those of us who sat through his trial and had to watch him being hanged on camera, the howls of his executioners ringing in his ears, retained a certain respect for him. And I personally shall never forget meeting his gaze in the courtroom, and watching the anger in his eyes turn to a certain humorous warmth.

President Robert Mugabe of Zimbabwe is ninety-two at the time of writing. He still seems to have remarkable energy, and if the stories a few years ago that he was losing his mental alertness were true, the process seems to have slowed down now. I met and interviewed him seven times over the years, and always found it an unpleasant experience. Mugabe was accustomed to being the cleverest person in any group he found himself in, whether the others were his own ministers, or senior British officials, or journalists like me. He always turned everything round in a mocking, spiteful way to make you seem clumsy and slow-witted.

'Ah,' he said when a BBC colleague of mine once asked him how long he was going to stay in office, 'the regime-change question.'

In 2015, though, he got his comeuppance from a young and attractive Nigerian journalist who, from a studio in New York City, hosts a satirical programme for Nigerian television called *Keep It Real*. Adeola Fayehun has a charming but sharply edged style, and no political leader in Africa is entirely safe from her ridicule and her cutting comments. More than seventy million in Nigeria and around Africa follow her each week via the internet. It's not surprising: Adeola is utterly fearless.

In May 2015 the newly elected President of Nigeria, Muhammadu Buhari, was inaugurated, and leaders from across the African Union came for the ceremony. Among them was Robert Mugabe, the current head of the AU. There was chaos as long lines of official cars jammed together outside the Eagle Square Conference Centre in Nigeria's capital, Abuja. Mugabe's official limousine was among them.

Adeola's colleague on *Keep It Real*, Omoyele Sowore, was on hand, and saw Mugabe slumped in the back of it. The video of the incident is a delight to watch. Sowore sticks his head through the open window: 'Mr Mugabe, how are you?'

Mugabe is a man from a very different generation, and three and a half decades of official protection have kept him away from this kind of intrusion. 'I am well, thanks,' he replies. He smiles, but looks uncomfortable:

SOWORE: Are you happy to come to Nigeria?
MUGABE: Very happy.
SOWORE: Well, you know they also want elections in your country. When is it happening next in your country?
MUGABE: In my country? Well, we had our elections...

At that point an aide hurries round to open the door for Mugabe, who goes into the conference centre to hear President Buhari's inaugural speech. Afterwards, his security team allow him to go back to his car on foot; not a good decision. Adeola sees her opportunity: 'When I saw him walking I was like, wait a minute, I can ask my questions.' She had been annoyed earlier, when he arrived, to see how many of the journalists simply said: 'Mr President, give us a smile.' Asked about the incident on television later, she said: 'That did something in me. Of all the questions that you could ask Mugabe – "Give us a smile"! What do we do with his smile? I was a bit irritated by that. I wasn't looking for a smile.'

Adeola's instincts showed that she was a real journalist: someone sparky and courageous, someone on the lookout for a story, someone who had paid attention to the old cliché about speaking truth to power. There was a big crowd around them, and plenty of security men to elbow her out of the way. But over it all Adeola's sharp voice was impossible to ignore:

> Mr President, don't you think it's time to step down, sir? When will there be change in Zimbabwe just like we are having in Nigeria? When are you stepping down? How is your health? How do you feel, now that you are in Abuja to witness a democratic handover of power when there is no such in your own country? Is there democracy in Zimbabwe? There is no democracy in Zimbabwe. It's about time to step down. It's enough. We want to come to Zimbabwe for inauguration as well. Invite us. . .

Mugabe's bodyguards were clueless and shambolic, pushing and shoving her but not daring, away from their own patch in the new Nigeria, to do anything worse. 'I can't understand what you're saying,' Adeola said grandly when a couple of the bodyguards yelled at her in Shona. On the soundtrack you can hear at least two other reporters, both Nigerians, taking their cue from her and starting to call out tough questions.

The whole time, Mugabe walked through the crowd with Adeola's voice ringing in his ears, his lips pursed in displeasure, trying to look as though he was somewhere else altogether, and not making a success of it. The man who throughout his life had relied on his sharp tongue to silence and humiliate his questioners, was himself being silenced and humiliated. These were precisely the questions that needed to be put to him, and never were; and it happened because a young Nigerian journalist had the bounce and self-confidence to ask the right things of this representative of an older, more corrupt and abusive Africa.

Dictators rely on their henchmen to silence questions like these, but they also rely on the fear that usually prevents journalists from asking them; not just fear for their lives, but fear for their careers. Dictatorships come and go, and people who are banned today are sometimes the honoured guests tomorrow. Adeola Fayehun may one day be an honoured guest in Zimbabwe.

'There are so many questions to be asked,' she said on television later when she was asked to describe what had happened.

There are indeed.

NINE

Taking Risks

The sense of danger must not disappear:
The way is certainly both short and steep,
However gradual it may look from here;
Look if you like, but you will have to leap.
                   W. H. Auden, 'Leap Before You Look', 1940

IN 1988 THE INTENSE debates in Moscow at the top levels of the Soviet Communist Party provided some of the most interesting stories I have ever covered as a foreign correspondent. Day by day important new details were emerging from the political debates which Mikhail Gorbachev, as secretary-general of the party, encouraged. Nikolai Bukharin, the liberal-minded former head of the Comintern, was suddenly rehabilitated. He had been a general favourite within the party, and Stalin's close ally in the battle against Trotsky, but arrested as a traitor and executed in 1938. Now, at the bookshop in the Kremlin conference centre, you could buy postcards with his picture on.

Matryoshka dolls, with caricatured figures of Lenin, Stalin, Khrushchev, Brezhnev and the rest nestling one inside the other, were first on sale in the street markets, then withdrawn in case the delegates from the more conservative outer regions might be scandalised by them, then allowed on sale again. New approaches to the economy were being proposed. It looked as though the Soviet government might apologise formally for the invasions of Hungary in 1956 and Czechoslovakia in 1968. Might the communists even allow non-communist parties to take part in elections? Anything seemed possible. The police no longer intervened to stop my colleagues and me from door-stepping the delegates in the corridors and finding out what was being discussed; and the delegates no longer refused to talk to us.

One morning I found myself standing in Red Square in the early summer sunshine, talking to a former colleague from the BBC World Service. With his pleasant face and smiling, open manner, he looked out over the delegates as they poured out of the Kremlin in a jovial, almost paternal fashion. John Rettie, who was sixty-two, had been asked by the *Guardian* to come to Moscow to cover the extraordinary changes which were taking place in Soviet politics. And although he was too modest to point it out, the things that were happening in front of our eyes were due in part to a scoop of his when he'd been a Reuters correspondent in Moscow in the mid-1950s.

By now Rettie was best known for his reporting from Latin America, where his 'anarcho-liberal' views, as he described them, had turned him into a passionate supporter of countries such as Mexico, Nicaragua, Guatemala and El Salvador, which had to live in the shadow of the United States – or, in the case of Argentina, of Britain. But the memory of his Russian days was still strong.

The year 1956 had been one of those which, like 1968, 1989 and 2001, proved to be an important milestone. Stalin had been dead for three years, but the memory of what had happened during the quarter-century of his ferocious personal rule still haunted the lives of his political successors; and because Stalin's domination had been so devastating, two soviet politicians, Nikita Khrushchev and Anastas Mikoyan, in particular, came to believe that it wasn't enough simply to move on to the next stage of Soviet political development. The myth of Stalin had to be confronted.

In the pleasant sunshine, John Rettie and I were walking slowly across Red Square, away from the Spassky Gate. He pointed in the direction of the Central Committee building of the Soviet Communist Party. He told me that in February 1956 he had heard that the lights were still burning there, late into the night. This seemed strange, given that the party's 20th Congress had been formally closed that afternoon; Rettie and Sidney Weiland, his bureau chief, had written their stories about it and sent them to London hours before. Within a few days a rumour started to go the rounds, to the effect that Khrushchev had made a sensational speech at the end of the congress attacking Stalin and accusing him of a sustained campaign of torture and murder, going back decades.

For months now there had been criticisms of what was known as 'the cult of personality', and although Stalin's name hadn't been mentioned, everyone knew whose the personality was. At the congress, Mikoyan, as Khrushchev's chief supporter, had even made some relatively mild criticisms of Stalin by name in a speech which was cleared for publication. Yet it didn't seem altogether abnormal for the new regime to start distancing itself a little from its predecessor; the political atmosphere in Moscow was clearly several degrees milder than it had been three years earlier, in Stalin's last days. Both Rettie and Weiland had been invited more than once to drinks parties at foreign embassies where the top Kremlin figures were guests. Once, at a Norwegian reception, Khrushchev had even thrust a glass of Norwegian akvavit at Rettie and said: 'This is a lot better than that whisky we had at your embassy last week. Here – try it!'

Soon, well-informed people were starting to suggest that Khrushchev himself had denounced Stalin in the most sensational fashion. Sidney Weiland wrote a despatch about the rumours, but when he presented it to what was effectively the censors' office at the Central Telegraph building, it wasn't passed for transmission, even in mutilated form: it was simply suppressed.

A few days later, at the start of March, Rettie was preparing to go on holiday to Sweden. The evening before he left, the phone rang in his flat. It was a Russian, Kostya Orlov, whom he'd met a number of times and suspected of working for the KGB, the successor to Stalin's MGB.

'You're going on holiday tomorrow,' Orlov said, though Rettie hadn't told him about this. 'I must see you before you go.'

Rettie invited him to come straight round. Orlov was a sleazy character, inclined to drink too much, but he had given Rettie some good, if not particularly important, stories in the past. He was precisely the kind of person Soviet intelligence often used to make contact with Westerners. He turned up soon afterwards; and brought with him information which would give John Rettie one of the great scoops of the twentieth century.

Rettie assumed that the entire apartment block where he and other foreign journalists were living was bugged. He put on one of his Sibelius records and turned the sound up high in order to cover their voices. Without using any notes, Orlov launched into an extraordinarily detailed account of the secret speech Khrushchev had made at the 20th Congress just over a week before. It was sensational. Khrushchev had gone into great detail about the crimes committed under Stalin – the widespread arrests, the savage torture, the mass executions, the death camps where old Bolsheviks, intellectuals and military officers were murdered by the million. These things were speculated about, but there had never been any public acknowledgement of them in Stalin's brutally controlled police state. People in the Communist Party itself preferred not to think about what had happened, and lavished their affection and praise on Stalin still. And now the man who had taken his place was revealing his crimes.

Orlov quoted two anecdotes from the speech, both of which sounded like off-the-cuff comments by Khrushchev. In one, he revealed how Stalin used to humiliate the people around him, and called them by the familiar 'thou', as if they were children or servants.

'Once he turned to me and said, "Hey, *khokhol*, come on, dance the *gopak*."'

Khokhol is a crudely abusive term for someone from the Ukraine, as Khrushchev was, and the *gopak* is a fast, complicated Ukrainian dance involving a great deal of twirling round and kneeling in it. For Khrushchev, short, fat and completely out of condition, to be forced to dance it in front of all Stalin's courtiers was a deliberate humiliation.

The second of Orlov's anecdotes was also revealing. One of the delegates, infuriated by the things Khrushchev was saying about Stalin, yelled out, 'So why didn't you get rid of him?'

Khrushchev paused and looked round. 'Who said that?'

The delegate, in the body of the hall, kept his head down. Khrushchev repeated the question. Still no answer.

'Now,' said Khrushchev, 'you can understand why we didn't try anything against him.'

Orlov told Rettie something else. When the secret speech was read out to party organisations in Georgia, Stalin's homeland, the response had been angry and violent. There were riots in which people had been killed. It would have been impossible for Rettie or any other Western journalist to check this sort of thing out. In 1956 the Soviet Union was still a deeply secretive country, in which every source of information was controlled.

John Rettie's problem was that the sole source for all of this was Orlov himself; there were no documents and no recordings to back up what he had said. Orlov might have made the whole thing up, in order to discredit the Western media and distract attention from the confusion the international Communist movement found itself in. There was a certain amount of danger to Rettie himself. He would probably be thrown out of Moscow, and it might be difficult for him to get a posting to any other pro-Soviet country, at a time when Moscow's influence in Eastern Europe, Africa and Asia was growing.

More immediately, there was a threat to Reuters itself: Orlov's story might be a malicious plant. News agencies depend on their ability to break stories faster than anyone else, but they are also dependent on their reputation for accuracy – Reuters above all. If it put out Orlov's version of the story, and the real text of the secret speech was published later and shown to be completely different from the version Orlov had given Rettie, Reuters' reputation would suffer badly.

Who was Orlov, anyway? If, as Rettie had always assumed, he was a KGB hanger-on, that didn't mean he spoke with any kind of authority, or that his employers, if they were indeed from the KGB, had authorised him to divulge information. The entire business seemed thoroughly suspicious, and highly questionable. And yet John Rettie's instinct was that Orlov was telling the truth.

It was nearly midnight by the time Orlov left. Rettie, deeply uncertain what he should do, called Sidney Weiland, who lived in an apartment block in a different part of Moscow. They met in the street outside the Central Telegraph Office in the centre of town, where they couldn't be overheard. They trudged up and down the snow-covered streets while Rettie read out his notes, pausing sometimes under the street lamps. Weiland was as shocked and fascinated by it all as Rettie had been, and he felt, as Rettie did, that the entire story was essentially correct. It was therefore important to get it out as soon as possible.

They knew that a *New York Times* correspondent was leaving Moscow on holiday the next day, and they assumed that directly he was out of the country he would report the rumours about the speech. At present the outside world knew nothing whatever about it, but Rettie and Weiland both realised that if their much fuller story came out after the *New York Times* one, its effect would be greatly weakened. In the end, standing in the snow, they shook hands on it: when Rettie reached Stockholm he would break the story as Orlov had told it to him.

Rettie and his wife had been due to stay in Stockholm with a Finnish diplomat who had served in Moscow, but in the 1950s Finland was still struggling to be independent from Russia, so Rettie thought it might be awkward for them if he put the story out from their apartment. Instead, the Retties spent their first night in a Stockholm hotel. He typed out his story and dictated it to Reuters over the phone in an American accent which he put on for the occasion. When he told me the story in Red Square, years later, he demonstrated the accent he'd used. It was laughably unconvincing, and the Reuters copy-taker in London, who knew him well, said 'Thank you, John', when he finished dictating.

The agency gave the story maximum priority. At that period, every Reuters subscriber around the world had a telex machine linked exclusively to its wire, and when an important story came up it carried a signal, in the form of printed stars, which rang a bell on the machine. Rettie's story came with all the available stars, so that bells rang in every newsroom around the world. Reuters tried to safeguard Rettie's position by putting a Bonn dateline on his first story, about the speech, while his second story, about the riots in Georgia, was datelined 'Vienna'. Both were ascribed simply to 'Communist sources'. They caused a sensation.

After a few days, when he thought the dust had started to settle, Rettie flew back to Moscow. He felt distinctly nervous, but he wasn't stopped at the airport and went back to his work as usual. Maybe the dodge of pretending that the two stories came from West Germany and Austria worked, though if the KGB had indeed been responsible for the leak it would have known perfectly well what had really happened. But there were no complaints, no threats of expulsion, and no worsening of East–West relations; instead, these continued to improve. Some months later the *New York Times* got hold of a full copy of Khrushchev's speech from sources in the Polish Communist Party, and this showed that Orlov's account had been remarkably accurate. There was, however, no mention of the *gopak* incident, nor of Khrushchev's comeback to the heckler in the hall. This reinforced the assumption that Khrushchev had sometimes extemporised while he was making the speech.

By October, though, the delayed effect of the speech was starting to take hold. There were political crises in both Poland and Hungary, followed by open warfare in the streets of Budapest. In order to bring Hungary to heel, Khrushchev had to order Russian tanks into the city. In Moscow the atmosphere returned to freezing-point. No top officials turned up at the diplomatic receptions now, and ordinary Russians shrank away when foreigners tried to speak to them in the streets. The policy of de-Stalinisation was greatly toned down, especially after there had been trouble in other parts of the Soviet Union when the secret speech was read out at party meetings.

Rettie noticed that when he went out in the street he was followed ostentatiously. He felt that this was a sign that the KGB were trying to intimidate him. Perhaps they wanted to recruit him, or to make him denounce the West. He decided he had to get out. Sidney Weiland agreed, and Reuters recalled him to London.

Did the KGB instruct Orlov to give Rettie the details of the speech, and, if so, from how far up in the Soviet system did the order come? When the *Guardian* sent Rettie back to Moscow in 1988 to cover the crumbling of the Soviet Communist Party, he went to see Sergo Mikoyan, Anastas's son.

'It was quite likely to have been Khrushchev,' Sergo told him, 'possibly with my father's support. My father was the only colleague of Khrushchev to urge the exposure of Stalin from the first, and his strongest supporter in this throughout. But any decision to use you to tell the world about the speech would have left no trace.'

Khrushchev had warned the party not to wash its dirty linen in public, yet it must have been part of his strategy to allow the details of his speech to leak out to the Soviet population at large. It couldn't have been done through the Soviet press, so the only way to do it was through the Western media. And the one thoroughly respected organisation whose reports were taken just about everywhere was Reuters.

In 1990 John Rettie gave an interview to *Moscow News*, which was now increasingly free of any official control, about the way the secret speech had been leaked to him. Shortly afterwards he had a call from Kostya Orlov himself; it was the first contact they had had since 1956. Orlov was enraged that Rettie should have described him as an informer, but he agreed to let Rettie come and talk to him. During their long conversation, Orlov still refused to admit that he had been working for the KGB. When Rettie put to him all the things he had said that implied strongly he had indeed been a secret agent, Orlov's answer was that Rettie had made them up. In the end, Rettie told him there was no point in talking any more, and left.

It had been one of the great scoops of the twentieth century, but it was very different from many of the others. John Rettie had to trust everything to his hunch that the slippery Orlov had told him the truth. He did, and he was right; and as a result he received great credit for ever afterwards. But supposing he had been wrong?

It was May 1978, and I was standing at the window of a flat in Moscow admiring the view. The sun shone on a yard with various kids' playground stuff, all imported from Finland or Sweden because Soviet factories didn't turn out the kind of things consumers wanted. Beyond were some pretty dreary buildings, and a lot of overhead wires. The sunshine made the view bearable, but for most of the rest of the year it would have been unutterably depressing.

When I turned away from the window, though, I was in an utterly different world: British home counties, down to the silver-framed photographs on the antique rosewood side-table and the Laura Ashley armchairs and chaises longues. Richmond, I would have said, or maybe South Kensington. It was a large drawing room, and off in the distance I could see the doorways of three, maybe four, bedrooms. There surely weren't many better flats in the whole of Moscow. Even Leonid Brezhnev, whose bristly, jowly, unnaturally dark-haired picture appeared just about every day on television and in the newspapers, couldn't have had a flat that was all that much pleasanter than this one.

I was the first guest to arrive for the drinks party.

'Without wanting to be rude,' I said, as a gin and tonic made its way towards me in my host's hand, 'how on earth does the correspondent of the *Daily Telegraph* get a flat as nice as this?'

The Russians hated the *Daily Telegraph* almost as much as they hated the BBC. In fact, I had just come downstairs from the distinctly poky BBC flat in this Stalin-era building dedicated to foreign journalists and diplomats, and had passed a Soviet satirical poster, framed and hanging in our hallway. It showed a rowing boat with a *Telegraph* man sweating away at the oars and a BBC man shouting orders to him through a loudhailer. They were heading for a weir and certain drowning. The Soviet state may have thought this was highly satirical, but it wasn't exactly prophetic. Within thirteen years it would be *Krokodil*, the unamusing 'funny paper' of the Soviet Union, which went over the weir, and the Soviet Union with it.

So why, I wondered, if the BBC had to live in a rabbit hutch, did the *Daily Telegraph* flat look like something out of *Country Life*? Dick Beeston, the *Telegraph* correspondent, laughed, and at that moment his wife Moyra came into the room, cool and elegant.

'He wants to know why we're living in the lap of luxury, darling.'

Moyra laughed too. 'It comes of having friends in high places,' she said.

And since the other guests (who would have known all about it) still showed no sign of showing up, they told me the story.

They had been sent to Moscow the previous autumn for a six-month trial period. If they could put up with the discomfort, they could stay: it was up to them. Their previous postings had mostly been in warm, pleasant places: Amman, Beirut, Nairobi, Washington. In Moscow the UPDK, the bureau which dictated where and how foreign correspondents should live, decided to make an example of the *Daily Telegraph*. There were no flats available, the UPDK told them: they would have to live in a hotel until one came free.

Nowadays the Ukraina hotel is expensive and rather good: one of those wedding-cake buildings, modelled on American skyscrapers of twenty years before, which Stalin dotted round Moscow. It is owned by the Radisson group. In the Beestons' days it was reserved for foreigners whom the Soviet government didn't care about.

'The whole place stank,' Dick said. 'They used the lift to piss in. Still, the lift didn't usually work anyway, and we were stuck up on the eighth floor.'

'And it was absolutely freezing last winter,' Moyra chipped in. 'The heating broke down in November and never came on again. We had to go to the Bolshoi every night to keep warm.'

Fortunately she was a ballet enthusiast, while Dick liked opera. In those socialist times even good seats at the Bolshoi cost just a few roubles, so it wasn't the drain on their bank account that it would be now, in the unregenerate capitalist present.

One snowy February night in 1978, three months before I visited their flat, they went to see *Otello*. In his book *Looking for Trouble: The Life and Times of a Foreign Correspondent* (Brassey's, 1997), Dick describes the scene. As the lights were going down, four people came in and took the empty seats in front of the Beestons: two bodyguards, a youngish woman, and an older man of around sixty-five. Moyra nudged Dick.

'Look who it is,' she hissed in his ear.

Dick looked. There could be no doubt about it. The shape of the head, the ears, the dark, thinning hair: it was Kim Philby, the Foreign Office traitor who had defected to Moscow in 1963, fifteen years before. No Western journalist had seen him or spoken to him during that entire time.

Directly the curtains went up at the interval, Dick tapped Philby on the shoulder. The minders were appalled; not so Philby.

'As I live and breathe, Dick Beeston!' Kim said in his old familiar voice, with a broad smile. . . 'And Moyra. I heard you were in Moscow. I hope the Soviet authorities are looking after you well.' He then introduced us to his wife Rufina who was smartly dressed in a black top and velvet skirt. . .

He chatted easily to them about the past, and remembered the names of their children, who had been at school with his when Philby, like the Beestons, was based in Beirut. Dick told him that his son, also named Richard (who was to become foreign editor of *The Times*, and die tragically young at the age of fifty) was now at Westminster – Philby's old school.

'"Ah, Westminster. You should be careful, sometimes they produce some, some. . ." He began to stutter. "Bad hats?" I suggested – and he grinned.'

Nevertheless Philby's stutter seemed to have improved, and he was clearly drinking less.

'How are you finding things in Moscow?' Philby asked conversationally.

This was the Beestons' big chance, and Dick knew it. His account in his autobiography, *Looking for Trouble*, is mildly bowdlerised, but in their Moscow flat only three months after the meeting at the Bolshoi he gave me the full, original version.

'Well, actually, Kim, old boy, things are pretty fucking awful. We're stuck in the Ukraina, which is freezing cold and stinks of piss and shit, and we'll have to go back to Washington in a few months if the bloody UPDK can't find us a decent place to live.'

'That sounds pretty bad for someone from the old crowd,' Philby said. 'I'll see what I can do.'

The heavies made Philby and his wife leave while the last bars of *Otello* were still being played, so they couldn't speak to him again. Dick was in a hurry too. He raced round to the United Press International office to send over the story of their meeting with Philby in time for the *Telegraph*'s first edition. It was a big scoop – 'Missing traitor speaks after fifteen years' – and the *Telegraph* splashed it across the front page.

Two days later the UPDK rang. For once, the voice on the other end was polite. Would the Beestons care to go round to the foreigners' compound in Sadovaya-Samotechnaya Avenue and have a look at a flat there?

Dick knew very well which flat it was. Some weeks earlier it had become vacant and he'd asked the UPDK if he could rent it, but they'd decided to give it to the Jamaican ambassador; Jamaica was flirting with a leftward shift towards Moscow at the time.

'What's the point?' Dick barked irritably. 'You've already given it to someone else.'

'No, no. Go and see it, and if you want it, it's yours.'

Dick told me the whole story as he heard it later. Earlier that morning the Jamaican ambassador had been in the bathroom shaving when there was a knock at the front door. A large official was standing in the doorway, and he wasn't polite. 'You must get out by noon,' he said. 'We need this place for someone else.'

Not long afterwards the Beestons received a letter from Philby:

I am glad you got your flat at last, and would like to think it was the result of a few telephone calls I made after our meeting at the Bolshoi. . .

Did I really say 'as I live and breathe'? I have tried it out several times and it sounds unlike me. It was more probably 'Good God' – and you, with your usual tact, altered the phrase for fear that my invocation of the Almighty might get me into trouble with the authorities.

Dick reflected on the affair afterwards: 'It was the everydayness of the encounter which I found so odd. Just two old colleagues meeting by chance after years, as if nothing had happened to a friendship except the passage of time, when in fact so much had happened and nothing could be the same again.'

They wrote to Philby via his post box, suggesting a meeting, but he turned them down. The KGB would have instructed him to do so; maybe it still wasn't absolutely certain about his loyalties.

There is a postscript, however. In 1994 Beeston went to stay with his son Rick, who by that time was *The Times*'s bureau chief in Moscow. The Soviet Union had collapsed, and so had the Russian economy. Rufina, Philby's widow, invited them round to dinner at the flat she had shared with her husband. She was living in poverty, since her KGB pension had dwindled away to almost nothing, thanks to the terrifying inflation Russia was going through. She had had to sell off some of Philby's books, letters and personal belongings in order to keep going, but she'd kept an engraving of Rome which still hung on the wall; a present from his fellow traitor, Anthony Blunt. There was also a framed photograph of the Normandie Hotel in Beirut, where Philby used to meet Beeston for drinks when they were foreign correspondents in Lebanon:

Before leaving, I asked her if she remembered Kim's efforts to find us somewhere to live in Moscow and our allocation of an apartment shortly after our meeting them. 'Oh yes,' she said, 'Kim was so happy. He said it is not often you are able to do things to help old friends.'

More powerful than the deep ideological divide, the shock of Philby's treachery and the passage of time, the old pals' act which had linked the two men as foreign correspondents was still in full working order.

———

One evening in April 1981, David Nicholas, the remarkably success-ful editor of ITN, whose instinct for a news story and skill in dealing with his staff were legendary, sent a telex to his man covering the Iran–Iraq War, Jon Snow. A businessman in London, Peter Melia of Silverline Shipping, had called ITN to say that while Snow was doing a piece to camera from the Iraqi side of the waterway that divided the two warring countries, he'd spotted something in the background over Snow's shoulder: a brand new 40,000-ton bulk carrier called the *Al Tanin*, which Silverline owned. The company had lost all contact with its crew, and neither Iraq nor Iran had given them any help about it. Could ITN do anything?

Jon Snow was that admirable combination, a serious corre-spondent who was also something of an adventurer. Despite his conventional upper-middle class background, he had an instinctively radical approach to the world, though he always maintained a sense of fairness even towards those he disagreed with. Snow made *Channel 4 News* the sharp, watchable entity it has remained for decades. The viewer could always sense that beneath the brilliant-coloured ties, the slick suits and the surpris-ing socks which they saw in the studio, there lay a reporter who was completely at ease out in the field. Many newsreaders feel intensely nervous when they have to leave the protection of the studio and the autocue behind them. Not Jon Snow. As a corre-spondent, he had always been up for stories which involved a bit of excitement.

David Nicholas, who also had an instinct for adventure, informed him that the ship's owner had appointed Snow the *Al Tanin*'s agent. That gave him the legal authority to rescue the fifty-seven men and women, many of them British, on board. With his characteristic openness, which many other people of his stature might well have tried to cover up, Snow wrote later: 'I jumped at the chance. As well as anything else, it meant I'd be able to get into Basra dockyard, a place forbidden to journalists and crawling with war secrets.'

He managed to make contact by phone with the *Al Tanin*'s captain, who told him there were three British wives, fifteen British officers and forty Philippine sailors on board. They were low on food and water, and had to stay out of sight below deck.

Snow decided to swim the filthy waters of the Shatt al-Arab with an Iraqi commando friend of his at midnight, and the captain promised to hang a rope ladder down the ship's side for them. But there were misunderstandings, and Snow and his Iraqi friend left at the wrong time. They were accompanied by Snow's renowned camera crew, Chris Squires and Nigel Thompson, and by Robert Fisk, who was then working for *The Times*. Fisk described in *The Great War for Civilisation* how Snow had invited him to be part of the group:

> 'Now listen, Fisky, old boy, if you can find a decent map, I'll let you come along,' he said. I immediately remembered my grand-father Edward, first mate on the *Cutty Sark*, and all that I had read about the merchant marine. Every ship's master, I knew, was required to carry detailed charts of the harbours and waterways he used. So I hunted down a profusely bearded Baltic sea-captain whose freighter lay alongside in Basra docks, and he agreed to lend me his old British Admiralty survey of the Shatt al-Arab.

Curiously referring to himself in the third person, Robert listed the others involved in the adventure and ended up rather gloomily with himself – 'and Fisk, who would come to regard this as the last journalistic Boy's Own Paper story of his life. The rest of my report-ing would be about tragedy.'

Fisk and the members of the camera team weren't going to swim the Shatt al-Arab with Snow and the Iraqi commando; apart from any other considerations, there were only two wetsuits.

It was a distinctly frightening prospect. There was a strong current in the Shatt, and the danger of being swept across to the Iranian riverbank and captured was a real one. It took them some time to swim across, but finally the Iraqi commando spotted the rope ladder and grabbed it, while Jon hung on to his leg. It was a very long and painful climb up the tanker's side.

'Mr Snow, I presume,' the captain greeted him, echoing Henry Morton Stanley.

They agreed a plan. The next night the captain would order two of the ship's lifeboats to be launched, with the entire crew, plus the British wives, in them. But there was a problem: the gantries hadn't been greased for the seven weeks the ship had been anchored there, and they would make a terrible racket as the lifeboats were lowered. The Iranians would be alerted, and everyone could well be captured.

'Don't worry,' said Ahmed, the Iraqi commando, 'we'll fire some guns.'

Unlike so many plans of this kind, everything worked perfectly. The gantries made an appalling racket, but the Iraqis opened fire almost immediately and drowned it out. The lifeboats were lowered into the water, and crossed the Shatt al-Arab. In *Shooting History: A Personal Journey*, Snow recalls:

> After what seemed an interminable time, the boats puttered into view, fifty-seven pale faces turned towards us. Every one of them had made it, and I had played a minor role in securing their safety. We had a scoop, an incredible scoop. The next day, Fisk's piece dominated *The Times*'s front page.

Fisk himself added some characteristic details:

> . . . an English girl appeared on the slippery deck and asked: 'Will someone help me ashore?' It was one of those quintessential moments so dear to Anglo-Saxons. The British were cheating

danger again, landing on a tropical shore under a quarter moon with the possibility of a shell blowing them all to pieces and three young women to protect.

Jon Snow had been much too modest by talking of his 'minor role'. The rescue couldn't have happened without his fearsome swim in the dark. It was a feat which bore comparison with Archibald Forbes's ride through Zululand a century before.

Max Hastings is journalistic royalty. His father was Macdonald Hastings, who became one of the best-known correspondents during the Second World War, beginning with some beautifully crafted reports for the magazine *Picture Post* from torpedo boats protecting convoys in the English Channel. The photographs accompanying his text showed how dangerous and exciting these outings were. Later he reported on the D-Day landings, and on the fighting which followed. Macdonald Hastings was married to Anne Scott-James, later the editor of *Harper's Bazaar*, a witty and remarkably elegant woman who often appeared on radio and television in the 1950s.

When I first met Max, not understanding how louche and nonconformist this background made him, I disliked him intensely. He was everything I wasn't, or didn't feel myself to be: privileged, upper class, connected and clever. In 1969, having not yet been allowed to go near Northern Ireland, I had to interview him for Radio 4 on the troubles there, which he had been covering for the *Twenty-Four Hours* programme on BBC Television. Max was brave and articulate, and made an excellent interviewee; I didn't like that either. I tried not to sound deferential, and failed. In later years he became a hugely successful war correspondent for television and newspapers, and his books won awards and gained big sales. He loomed over me physically (six foot five to my six foot two) and professionally. Once, when he was editor of the *Daily Telegraph*, he invited me to Brooks's Club in St James's Street, and offered me a job as the paper's Americas editor over a gin and tonic. After I explained that I wasn't very good at working for a hands-on editor and thought we would clash, he grinned and said he was really a pussycat to work for; and we parted on friendly terms.

What I had forgotten all these years was that journalists are instinctive democrats. I've met many autocratic ones, but never in all my fifty years a snobbish one. Max has a delightful frankness about himself and his life which makes him an excellent companion, and he sheds the trappings of grandeur – the awards, the knighthood, the editorships, the stratospheric contacts – like taking off an overcoat on a cold day. Above all, he remains a working journalist who writes daily and still wants to see things for himself.

In April 1982 Max was at home in Northamptonshire, writing a book about the Normandy campaign, when a friend rang to tell him about Argentina's invasion of the Falkland Islands. Max never listened to the radio or watched television while he was writing his books, so he knew nothing about it. He was thirty-six, and felt he was getting too old to be a war reporter. His decision not to stay in Saigon when it fell (he called it 'bottling out') had convinced him never to risk his life in war again. Yet this was different: a unique post-imperial adventure in which he could follow the British army, which he loved, to glory. He describes the moment in *Going to the Wars*:

> I put down the telephone in the kitchen and said to my wife Tricia, 'I feel it's for this moment I was born.' (Promise – I really did say that.) 'I've *got* to go.'
>
> 'You should have grown out of all this by now. You say yourself you don't think there's actually going to be a war. And what about your Normandy book?'
>
> 'I can do that any time. There will never be another Falklands task force...'

The war which no one had expected duly took place, and Max Hastings was on hand for the landing on the Falklands and the fighting at Mount Kent. He hadn't endeared himself to most of the other journalists covering the war because his contacts were much better than theirs, and he was so undeniably grand. Max might not have felt any class consciousness towards the rest of the press group, but they certainly did towards him. They could have put up with that, perhaps, but when Lieutenant-Colonel Michael Rose, the boss of the SAS, offered to take him with him, even the broadsheet journalists with whom he was on good terms were enraged. Soon the only member of the press pack he was really friendly with was Robert Fox of the BBC.

Robert was a friend of mine from the days when I first decided that I wanted to be a foreign correspondent. Brilliant but too wayward and individualistic to fit easily into a big organisation like the BBC, he later went to the *Evening Standard* where he throve. He had many great moments, especially during the Falklands War, but I always felt the most characteristic of them all came in 1991 at the end of the first Gulf War, after the US air strikes at the Mutla Ridge on the column of Iraqi stragglers and looters who fled Kuwait.

With typical carelessness, most journalists were content to report that 'thousands' of Iraqis and their hostages had died in the attacks, often burned alive in their vehicles. Only one journalist cared enough about the precise numbers to go out and count the bodies as they lay decaying in the desert sun: Robert Fox. Inevitably, he found that the numbers were in the hundreds, rather than the thousands most of the correspondents had claimed.

———

At East Falkland, Max Hastings managed to hitch a ride in a helicopter to Mount Harriet, and linked up with the Marines of 42 Commando. Another journalist, Kim Sabido of Independent Radio News, asked if he could go with the lead company in the coming attack. Max Hastings thought it over, but decided not to go with him. With typical honesty he wrote afterwards:

> I knew that I did not possess the bottle. . . Kim got a fine yarn, but won much less kudos than he deserved for his courage in

all the excitements of the days that followed. His decision to go with some of the first men up Harriet was the bravest act by a journalist in the war.

In the bone-chilling cold and darkness, a murmur ran down the column:

'Keep on the track of the man in front. From here on, this is the only swept path through the minefield'. . . I placed my huge boots one by one upon the peat with a care my mother must have wished I had displayed twenty years earlier towards her herbaceous borders.

The attack was a complete success, and 300 prisoners were soon being escorted down the hill. The British had expected this to be the hardest position they would have to attack, and it had fallen quickly with a loss of two men killed and twenty-four wounded. The victory showed how far superior the British soldiers were to the Argentinian conscripts, most of whom were poorly trained and wholly unwilling.

Max found a Wessex helicopter which took him back to the British ships at San Carlos Water. He jotted down his account of the battle as they flew, and eventually managed to get to the communications ship. Once there, he punched out a long telex tape of his story, rolled it up and handed it to the wireless operator to transmit to London. Then he found a place to sleep.

The next day, back with the advancing troops, Max had just lit up a cigar which had been sent to him by a London shop (together with a half-bottle of brandy) when a couple of Argentine Skyhawks dropped several 1,000-pound bombs on them with remarkable accuracy. The nearest fell only thirty-three yards away, yet no one was hurt. Suffering with a heavy cold, Max went trudging off with the others: 'feet soaked and chilled, bergens and web equipment straining on our shoulders, jumping clumsily and vainly to avoid the deeper waterlogged holes. I still clutched the walking stick that had been my faithful support on every hike since the day of the landing.'

The Argentines ran for it, but now the British were being shelled from Port Stanley and couldn't fire back for fear of hitting the civilians there. Max was too tired to worry. He leant against a stone wall and fell asleep.

When he woke, snow lay over everything: bergens, ponchos, sleeping figures. Max got out his typewriter – still the way journalists wrote their despatches in 1982 – and started tapping out a story about 2 Para: 'Their morale is sky-high. Their certainty that they have won and that the enemy is collapsing is absolute. They are very cold, very dirty, but in their mood this morning, they could march to London.'

He was gathering up his equipment when an army captain shouted an invitation to him to jump aboard his armoured vehicle. They ground on up the last part of the hill until they reached the lip, and there below lay the heart of the islands they had come to liberate:

> Two or three miles down a concrete road eastward, white and innocent in the sudden sunshine, stood the little houses and churches of Port Stanley. In a few minutes this place, the climax of months of ambition, as distant as the far side of the moon at breakfast, had been transformed into a prize lying open for the taking.

British soldiers could be seen making their way past the old Royal Marine barracks at Moody Brook, below the ridge, and a company of Paras was ordered to march down the road to Port Stanley, covered by the guns of Scorpions and Scimitar armoured vehicles on the ridge. 'By now, fierce and selfish ambitions were crowding into my mind,' wrote Hastings. 'There was a chance, just a chance, that we could be the first into Stanley. It would be the greatest scoop of my professional life.'

The soldiers received orders to stop. They began to brew up and hand round the cigarettes they'd found in an abandoned Argentine position:

> I wandered down the road. It stretched empty, the cathedral clearly visible perhaps half a mile ahead. It was a peerless

opportunity. I thought, very consciously: if I can walk down that road and live, I can bore everybody to death for the next twenty years talking about it.

He pulled off the military webbing and camouflage he'd been wearing, though there was nothing he could do about the camouflage cream which covered his face:

Then, in a blue civilian anorak and clutching my walking stick with the deliberate notion of appearing as harmless as possible, I set off towards the town. 'And where do you think you're going?' demanded the NCO in charge of the picket on the road, in the traditional voice of NCOs confronted with prospective criminals. 'I am a civilian,' I said firmly, and walked on unhindered.

As he approached the cathedral he saw a group of Argentine soldiers.

'Good morning,' he said, with an enthusiasm he didn't feel. They did nothing to stop him. A hundred yards ahead he saw a group of civilians coming out of an official-looking building.

'Are you British?'

'Yes,' they shouted back. They were Falkland Islanders.

They pointed out an Argentine colonel on the steps, and Max introduced himself as a correspondent of *The Times* because he thought the colonel wouldn't have heard of the *Evening Standard*. They chatted amicably for a few moments, then Max asked if he could go and talk to the British civilians. The colonel agreed.

He was welcomed by the Catholic priest and by the local head of Cable and Wireless, the sinews of the Commonwealth. He bumped into an Argentine TV crew, who filmed him and asked him to take their photo. They in turn took his. It was, he said, the moment when he was sure he would survive, and that he would get his great story. Finally, he reached the true symbol of Britain's presence in the South Atlantic: the Upland Goose pub: 'I walked in. "I'm from the task force," I said. For the first and probably last time in my life, the twenty or so people gathered inside clapped me to the bar in their joy.'

The proprietor asked him if he'd like a drink. 'A whisky would be a work of genius,' Max answered, and downed it in one:

'How about another?'

'Can you spare it?'

'We've got cases and cases in the cellar.'

At that moment, I began to suspect that the Argentines had not been entirely brutal occupiers. British troops in similar circumstances would have emptied the pub in a week.

The *Standard*'s banner headline on 15 June read:

MAX HASTINGS
leads the way. . .

THE FIRST MAN INTO STANLEY

It was, he said afterwards, the happiest moment of his career.

During the half-century I have been a journalist, and leaving aside the Watergate scandal, which was for the most part a regular flow of small and often highly detailed exclusives over a period of years, there have of course been large numbers of major scoops: far too many even to remember. Some were the product of sheer good luck, of being in the right place at precisely the right moment. Others were the result of patient hard work and the cultivation of contacts over a long period of time; one example was Jane Corbin's revelation on the BBC programme *Panorama* of the secret negotiations between Israel and the Palestinians under Yasser Arafat which led to the Oslo Peace Accords in 1993.

In some ways, though, the greatest exclusive of the past fifty years came not from inside information but as a piece of first-class reportage. It made an enormous impact on world opinion not simply because of the story itself, but because of the words in which the story was told.

It happened in 1984, and the foreign correspondent who was responsible was Michael Buerk. As with most television reporters, his writing style was usually cramped by the demands of television news, which tend to favour brief statements of fact and a minimum of adjectives. His reporting was already much admired, and he was a highly effective operator, but even his close colleagues didn't realise how well he could write when he was set free from the everyday constraints.

He first covered the subject of famine in Ethiopia at the urging of the BBC, which wanted a story to counter an ITV special about world hunger. The BBC's motive was scarcely very uplifting, but it worked. Buerk came back with a strong but not overwhelming story.

Six months later, as a follow-up, the foreign desk urged him to go back to Ethiopia to see how the famine was developing. He travelled with a long-serving and perceptive BBC radio correspondent, Mike Wooldridge, and a much-respected freelance cameraman, Mohamed Amin, who did some of his best work for the BBC.

The Marxist government in Addis Ababa, whose gross failings had played an important part in the famine, did its best to stop them travelling to the area that was most badly affected. Buerk later wrote:

> It was Mo who solved that problem. He got a call from the Christian evangelical charity Worldvision. They put a higher priority on publicity than most charities. They were rich enough to lease a Twin-Otter plane to operate in Ethiopia and keen enough on media exposure to be looking for a film cameraman to film television appeals for money in the famine area. Mo stitched up a Faustian deal with its two representatives. . . Mo would film them with the starving babies, if they took us where we wanted to go.

Reluctantly, the relevant government departments in Addis gave them their permissions.

They flew to Makele, the capital of the province of Tigray. Below them vast crowds of people were swarming around a barren stretch of land on the southern edge of the town. It was their first sight of the famine. Since he had been there six months earlier, the situation had become far, far worse:

> In a wide swathe around Makele, 85,000 people lay about without food, without water and without hope. They'd walked there from all over the province and just sank down where they had come to a stop. All were hungry, all were exhausted, some were literally dying on their feet. We watched an old woman who had just arrived as she died, face downward in the dirt. An old man, probably her husband, stood over her body fingering a cross and staring out towards a horizon bare of any kind of hope or consolation.

They found a group of women who were picking over a pile of donkey dung, looking for grains which they might be able to eat.

Buerk and his two colleagues spent the night at a filthy hotel, and left before dawn:

> The night was peopled by mortal ghosts. The road was full of them. Wispy figures in grey flitting through the beams of the Land Cruiser's headlights with dark arms, thin as wands, that stretched for the car windows. We could hear their upturned hands rattling against the bodywork as we lurched through the potholes. Only those who pressed closest seemed human and they were hardly flesh and blood, just skeletons in cloaks, the skin of their faces dragged back against the bone on a rictus of suffering and supplication. Above the noise of the engine the pleading beat like surf on the car doors.

Of all the writing in this book, that passage from Michael Buerk's *The Road Taken* is one of the finest and most terrible; and only Martha Gellhorn's account of the liberation of Buchenwald, which I have not included on the grounds that it would weigh down this work with too much horror, seems to me to match it; together with Alistair Cooke's report on Robert Kennedy's murder.

At last the three of them reached the town of Korem, where they found the scenes that would shortly electrify the entire world.

Mohamed Amin had a superb eye for a shot, and could isolate a particular figure or face with great insight and accuracy. Often it was as if he sensed what the person he had focused on would do next. His pictures were a perfect match for Buerk's ability to set precisely visualised instants against the general pattern of dreadful suffering.

His report was long, and there were relatively few basic facts which he needed to put over. That meant that the sentences could be slow and balanced and well timed, and sometimes longer than usual. In television-speak, he let the pictures breathe. When he and Mo Amin edited them, later, Michael delivered his words with clarity and insight, and a kind of angry despair, yet without an excess of emotion which might irritate the viewer. It was, I think, the best piece of television reporting in my lifetime.

Yet it was a single word in the opening two minutes of the BBC six o'clock news on 23 October 1984 which captured the horrified imagination of the millions of people watching: *biblical*. For many of us who worked in news, it was the most telling expression we could remember:

> Dawn: and as the sun breaks through the piercing chill of night on the plain outside Korem, it lights up a biblical famine. Now. In the twentieth century. This place, say workers here, is the closest thing to hell on earth. Thousands of wasted people are coming here for help, many find only death. They flood in every day from villages hundreds of miles away, dulled by hunger, driven beyond the point of desperation. Fifteen thousand children here now, suffering, confused, lost. Death is all around. A child or an adult dies every twenty minutes. Korem, an insignificant town, has become a place of grief. . . The choice of who can be helped and who can't among the newcomers is heart-breaking. There's not enough food for half these people.

He spoke of 'fifteen thousand children here now', but at that moment you see only one single child, standing alone and abandoned, with an elongated head, bald from malnutrition; you can hear him keening from fear and bewilderment as he looks round with huge unblinking eyes. Over that picture Buerk lays down the three devastating, unanswerable words 'suffering, confused, lost'. Not many people who saw that image in 1984 will have found it easy to forget in the months and years that followed. It has stayed with me ever since.

Buerk's writing is spare and simple: the longest word he uses in this passage is 'desperation'. A lesser reporter would have thrown facts and figures at the viewer; Buerk understands that nothing matters except the images, and that they simply need to be pointed up, emphasised, underlined, not overridden. Mo Amin's pictures would have been immensely strong even if some tyro had written the commentary; Michael Buerk's words made them, quite simply, overwhelming. Many journalists have tried to emulate his style and his use of words since then, but no one has succeeded. And although television is a visual medium, it was essentially Michael Buerk's writing which gave his report from Korem its gut-wrenching power.

The Playground of War

I kept a diary, which is the basis of this account – a
mixture of horror, absurdity, melodrama, human courage and betrayal. I wept when I wrote it, and there are
moments when I weep now.

Jon Swain, *The River of Time*, 1995

FOR PEOPLE OF MY generation, Vietnam was *the* story: the one
which defined what we thought about the world and ourselves.
I was certainly old enough – twenty-four in 1968 – to have gone
there to report. But it would have meant throwing up my new job
with the BBC, leaving my new wife who was pregnant with our
first child, and paying my own way to go to Saigon or Phnom Penh
as a freelance, so I didn't. I behaved responsibly, and stayed at home:
just about the last time I would ever be quite so sensible. All the
same, for months on end, I pestered my avuncular editor to send me
to Vietnam, but he clearly lacked the necessary faith in me.

It wasn't necessarily dangerous if you simply went to Saigon and
stayed there. What was life-threatening was heading out into the
countryside; and several of my colleagues made a name for themselves by doing precisely that.

One was Brian Barron, the longest-serving foreign correspondent in the BBC's history, who was first appointed to a foreign
posting in the early sixties and was never based in Britain again
throughout his career. Another was Martin Bell, one of the finest
broadcasters the BBC ever employed. And there were others, like
Michael Clayton, a tall, elegant, idiosyncratic figure who later
became editor of the magazine *Horse and Hound*, but who first won

fame in Britain by having the courage to show how scared he was during the various firefights he got himself into. At that stage viewers were still used to the clipped, impersonal style of the Second World War, and a man who insisted on thrusting himself in the way of danger while being clearly scared stiff was something altogether new and distinctly admirable. I envied them all, while remaining in the total safety of Broadcasting House.

Yet I, and large numbers of people like me, understood precisely what was going on in the Vietnam War, thanks to the reporting of one man: Nicholas Tomalin of the *Sunday Times*, which was then going through the greatest period in its long history. Tomalin wasn't a foreign correspondent in the traditional sense. He was based in London, and reported on any number of subjects, exposing a company which was selling supposedly high-quality French wines which it had fraudulently mixed with cheap plonk at a warehouse in London, and demonstrating how the 'I'm Backing Britain' campaign was unravelling. Perhaps his best-known story was the deceit and suicide of the would-be round-the-world yachtsman Donald Crowhurst, who sailed round in a circle in the Atlantic before killing himself.

But when he travelled abroad, Tomalin shifted into a different and more elevated mode of reporting. He covered the brutal regime of the Colonels in Greece, the massacres carried out by the Pakistan army against the population of what was then known as East Pakistan, and the absurd autocracy of President Marcos in the Philippines. But, most significantly of all, he covered the Vietnam War.

Tomalin was the author (in a *Sunday Times* article of 1969) of that much-quoted definition of the qualities needed for success in journalism: 'ratlike cunning, a plausible manner and a little literary ability'. He possessed all three in good measure himself, though his own literary ability was considerable; he was brilliant at capturing the genuine patterns of everyday speech in the quotes he used, while the way he structured his sentences was later thought to be worthy of an academic thesis. Tomalin read English at Trinity Hall, Cambridge, 1951–54, and was both president of the union and a highly successful editor of *Granta*, the magazine Alistair Cooke had once edited. Without realising it at first, Tomalin was part of a phenomenon which became known in America as 'The New Journalism' and was practised there by people like Tom Wolfe, Truman Capote and Norman Mailer. The *Sunday Times* opened the way to Tomalin's free-flowing style by encouraging him to break from the stodgier, more traditional type of newspaper reporting, and allowing his essays to spread over two or three thousand words. After more than a century, the *Sunday Times* was going back to the tradition of William Howard Russell. Yet there was nothing dense or compacted about Tomalin's writing. He approached his subjects as a novelist might, and his reports were always wonderfully readable.

In Saigon, searching for a different angle from the usual reportage, as a weekly journalist must, Tomalin decided to avoid the daily round of US military press briefings ('The Five O'Clock Follies') at the Rex Hotel in Saigon, which the hugely experienced Associated Press bureau chief, Richard Pyle, called 'the longest-playing tragicomedy in South-East Asia's theatre of the absurd'. The Follies promoted an entirely false picture of the war, measuring progress in terms of enemies killed: the body count. A misplaced sense of patriotism, combined with a desire to give editors back home what they demanded, encouraged most American journalists to regurgitate the version of the war which they heard at the Follies. It wasn't until the start of 1968 that Jack Lawrence of CBS, arguably the best and most perceptive of the American correspondents based in Saigon, urged the CBS anchor Walter Cronkite to come out to Vietnam and see for himself the difference between the situation on the ground and the version of it that the Five O'clock Follies presented. On returning to America in February 1968, Cronkite reported: '[I]t seems now more certain than ever that the bloody experience of Vietnam is to end in a stalemate.'

That the Americans were not winning the war, and would not, had been abundantly clear to Nick Tomalin a year and a half earlier. He managed to get himself a facility to spend the day with a colourful Texan general of the US 1st Infantry Division ('The Big Red One') as he toured a series of front-line positions in areas contested by the Viet Cong. Tomalin's hugely influential report for the *Sunday Times* appeared on 5 June 1966 under the headline:

THE GENERAL GOES ZAPPING CHARLIE CONG

At nearly 2,500 words it was considerably longer than most British newspapers would run nowadays, and it opens more like a short story than a detailed news report: 'After a light lunch last Wednesday, General James F. Hollingsworth, of Big Red One, took off in his personal helicopter and killed more Vietnamese than all the troops he commanded.'

The success of the article depends on a number of factors. The reader, perhaps like Tomalin himself, is appalled by the general's bloodthirsty attitude to the people on the ground, while sneakingly admiring his courage and being seduced by his conversation and his beautifully rendered Texas accent. In the end, like the dénouement of a piece of good fiction, we come to realise that the General has been right all along about the people he had been shooting at; and that Tomalin's own instinctively liberal notions, which are ours, have been wrong. And yet it's equally obvious why General Hollingsworth and the United States as a whole are going to be on the losing side in the war. The article is a masterpiece:

'Our mission today,' says the General, 'is to push those goddam VCs right off Routes 13 and 16. . . I guess we've been hither and thither with all our operations since, an' the ol' VC he's reckoned he could creep back. He's been puttin' out propaganda he's goin' to interdict our right of passage along those routes. So this day we aim to zapp him, and zapp him, and zapp him again till we've zapped him right back where he came from. Yes, sir. Let's go.'

The General sits at the helicopter's open door, knees apart, his shiny black toecaps jutting out into space, rolls a filtertip cigarette to-and-fro in his teeth, and thinks.

'Put me down at Battalion HQ,' he calls to the pilot.

'There's sniper fire reported on choppers in that area, General.'

'Goddam the snipers, just put me down.'

Two American F-105 jets come past and drop

> . . . a trail of silver, fish-shaped canisters. After four seconds'
> silence, light orange fire explodes in patches along an area fifty
> yards wide by three-quarters of a mile long. Napalm.
>
> 'Aaaaah,' cries the General. 'Nice. Nice. Very neat. Come in
> low, let's see who's left down there.'
>
> 'How do you know for sure the Viet Cong snipers were in that
> strip you burned?'
>
> 'We don't. The smoke position was a guess. That's why we zapp
> the whole forest.'
>
> 'But what if there was someone, a civilian, walking through there?'
>
> 'Aw come on son, you think there's folks just sniffing flowers
> in tropical vegetation like that? With a big operation on here-
> abouts? Anyone left down there, he's Charlie Cong all right.'

They spot two men running below. The General grabs his M16 and
fires a long burst at them:

> 'But General, how do you know those aren't just frightened
> peasants?'
>
> 'Running? Like that? Don't give me a pain. The clips, the clips,
> where in hell are the cartridges in this ship?'

They fire some more, then drop gas bombs: 'There's nothing alive in
there,' says the general. 'Or they'd be skedaddling. Yes there is, by golly.'

A figure in black pyjamas with no hat or shoes appears, and
after more shooting runs out: 'in each hand a red flag which he
waves desperately above his head. "Stop, stop, he's quit," shouts the
General, knocking the machine-gun so tracers erupt into the sky.'

The helicopter puts down:

> 'That's a Cong for sure,' cries the General in triumph and with
> one deft move grabs the man's short black hair and yanks him off
> his feet, inboard.
>
> The red flags I spotted from the air are his hands, bathed
> solidly in blood. Further blood is pouring from under his shirt,
> over his trousers.

He can't be more than sixteen, Tomalin thinks, and resembles a tiny, fine-boned wild animal. While one of the soldiers puts a tourniquet on him, the General pokes his carbine at the base of his shirt: "'Look at that now,' he says, turning to me. "You still thinking about innocent peasants? Look at the weaponry.'" The prisoner is wearing a webbing belt with four clips of ammunition.

When they land, they spot a bullet hole in one of the rotor blades:

> 'That's proof positive they was firin' at us all the time. An' firin' on us first, boy. So much for your fellers smellin' flowers.'
>
> The General is magnanimous in his victory over my squeamish civilian worries.
>
> 'You see son, I saw rifles on that first pair of running men. Didn't tell you that at the time. And, by the way you mustn't imagine there could have been ordinary farm folk in that house, when you're as old a veteran as I am you get to know about these things by instinct. I agree there was chickens for food with them, strung up on a pole. You didn't see anything bigger, like a pig or a cow did yuh? Well then.'

And then his final words: 'There's no better way to fight than goin' out to shoot VCs. An' there's nothing I love better than killin' Cong. No sir.'

By the beginning of the 1970s, foreign interest in Vietnam was fading. American troops were being withdrawn, and the attention of the international news media had switched elsewhere: often to Northern Ireland, which was cheaper and easier to cover. Still, during the early months of 1972 the siege of An Loc, where an American brigade was holding out against Viet Cong forces supported by North Vietnam regular units, reignited some interest. An Loc was under constant artillery fire, and the Americans were using their massive air power to disrupt the North Vietnamese build-up and to resupply the US forces on the ground. As ever when heavy artillery and air bombardment are combined, it was extremely dangerous for journalists to cover.

ITN had sent two correspondents there, the redoubtable Mike Nicholson and Richard Lindley. But Nicholson had come uncomfortably close to death when a Viet Cong rocket-propelled grenade had hit his car, passing from side to side through the boot. Although he was physically unhurt, the ITN bosses in London decided to pull him out. In his place they sent in Chris Wain, a quiet and thoughtful correspondent who was already starting to amass a good deal of experience in reporting wars and insurrections, and later moved to the BBC as defence correspondent.

Wain and his two-man camera crew drove up Highway 13 towards An Loc, until it became impossible to drive any further. They got out and walked, and sometimes they crawled on their hands and knees in order to make any progress. Yet although just being there was really dangerous, they couldn't get any decent pictures of the action all round them. 'You can't actually see much on a front line,' he said later, 'because anyone showing themselves usually attracts fire.'

Wain had taken a dislike to the way his fellow correspondents were all dressed in American jungle camouflage – he regarded it as grandstanding in order to look macho on camera – so he had chosen to wear a white shirt instead. As he wrote in a letter to me, this was an error of judgement:

> It turned out to be an excellent target-marker for the bad guys hidden in the tree-line about a kilometre away, and made me very unpopular with the South Vietnamese troops. So from then on, like virtually all the press, I wore standard US combat gear: steel-plate reinforced jungle boots to protect you from *punji* stake booby-traps; GI trousers and shirt; webbing belt for water-bottles and pouches; flak-jacket; field-dressing, morphine-shots and helmet. All of this was purchased in the Saigon flea-market apart from the morphine, which I brought out with me from the UK.

By the first week of June 1972 Chris Wain had a new camera crew from London: Alan Downes and his sound recordist Tom

Philips. All three of them had interesting backgrounds. Chris and Alan were both ex-army photographers who had served in the Royal Army Ordnance Corps; Alan had been with the army in Germany, while Chris had served with the Joint Intelligence Bureau in Cyprus during the EOKA emergency. Tom had been in the Parachute Regiment.

The eighth of June 1972 was to be one of the most important days in the coverage of the entire Vietnam War, but no one knew it that morning. The ITN team were up early because they'd heard there was fighting near the Cambodian border at a place called Trang Bang, about thirty-five miles from Saigon along Highway 1. They were the first journalists to get there, and drove into the centre of the village. There was fighting going on close by, but before they could film it a team of Vietnamese military police escorted them out. The military police left them a little way down the road, and the ITN team stopped. Chris spotted a temple on the edge of the village which was packed with frightened people who'd taken refuge there.

The team were about to start filming when they bumped into the same military police patrol. This time the Vietnamese escorted them half a mile down the road, then cut down some bamboo plants to create a makeshift barrier across the road. A Vietnamese soldier was ordered to stay there to stop them going back. By now it was getting on for ten in the morning, and they hadn't shot a foot of film. Chris knew the desk in London was expecting something from them that day, and to report back they had filmed nothing would be unacceptable.

It was raining on and off, and there was very low cloud. That meant there could be no air support for the South Vietnamese troops, and without that they were no match for their North Vietnamese opponents. Soon, though, the cloud lifted, and the ITN team went into a nearby field to get some footage of an A-37 Dragonfly dropping bombs near the ancient wall of Trang Bang. That gave them something, but after editing it would only make around fifteen seconds – just a small element in a report of say two and a half minutes. They would need a great deal more than that.

By eleven o'clock taxis were starting to arrive from Saigon, delivering various reporters, photographers and cameramen. Chris and his team no longer had the story to themselves, but at least their main opposition, the BBC, wasn't there: Mike Blakey, the BBC correspondent currently in Saigon, was off on a naval facility that day. Chris's worry was that he simply wouldn't be able to send a report to ITN that night. Nowadays he would be able to put whatever brief pictures they had shot, plus a piece to camera, into a video package with the day's material from the main news agencies – or perhaps from the television organisations ITN was affiliated with. But in the days of film, this wasn't possible: you couldn't copy other people's material, you could only use your own. You were entirely self-dependent.

The newcomers from Saigon had only been there for a few minutes when another airstrike began, this time involving two Vietnamese air force Skyraiders, dating back to the Second World War. Their tactics were unvaried. One plane would drop high explosive in order to break up bunkers and trenches, while the other, seconds later, would drop napalm to catch the survivors as they ran out into the open. There were hundreds of these airstrikes every day; they were so routine that no one bothered to film them. Chris and his colleagues watched the first plane go in at low level, and they realised immediately what none of the other journalists could know: the bombs had hit the area just behind the temple which was packed with refugees. It was a classic case of friendly fire. Alan started filming. Close by, a correspondent from a US network was watching them scornfully. His Vietnamese cameraman asked him if he wanted some shots of the attack too. The American, with whom Chris had crossed swords not long before, looked across at him.

'Hell, no,' he said in a supercilious tone, 'it's just air.'

Alan had now zoomed on the main road, which was filled with refugees frantically running towards them. The nearest of them were about 400 yards away. Over to the right, Chris could see the second Skyraider coming in low.

'Plane coming from your two o'clock,' he told Alan.

'Got it.'

Alan pulled back the zoom lever to wide-angle as the plane came swooping in, dropping four napalm cylinders straight across the road. The refugees were immediately engulfed in flame. There was the sort of heatblast you get when an oven is opened, and Chris instinctively turned away.

'Holy shit!' yelled the American correspondent. Then he shouted to his cameraman: 'Did you get that?' But the cameraman was holding his camera loosely on his left shoulder and staring down the road in disbelief. He shook his head.

Over the years in the Vietnam War there had been literally scores of these so-called 'blue-on-blue', or friendly fire, incidents, but none had ever been caught on film by a television camera. And Chris and his team had got it, close by and in full view.

The Skyraider emerged from the smoke of the napalm bombs, waggling its wings, and both planes flew off.

The ITN team rushed forward. The rain had started again, and Chris was wearing a GI poncho to protect the film-pack he was carrying. The napalm had set fire to the tarmac ahead of them, and it was still burning. Framed against the black smoke a small group of women and children came stumbling forward. They were completely silent, but when they saw the ITN crew some of the children started crying. One of them was a nine-year-old girl, entirely naked and badly burned. Her name was Phan Thi Kim Phúc. Beside them, a Vietnamese-born photographer from Associated Press, Nick Ut, was taking pictures of the group coming down the road, with Kim in the middle, her arms held out from her side, wailing (as she remembered later) 'Nóng quá, nóng quá' – 'too hot, too hot'. One of these shots won Ut fame and a Pulitzer Prize, and became one of the best known photographs in modern history.

As the little girl ran past in blind panic, Chris stopped her and gave her a drink of water, which she gulped down. She had been terribly burned. Several people emptied their water bottles over her, in the hope of giving her a little relief. The ITN team were all in shock now. And it got worse. An old woman came up, carrying the horribly burned body of an infant. It seemed to have clothing hanging down, but Chris could see it was skin.

'Alan.' Chris called out, pointing to the child.

'I can't film that,' Alan said.

'You must.'

'They won't show it. It's too awful to show.'

'We'll let London decide. You show it like it is.'

Chris knew that Alan was right, but in his outrage at what had happened he was determined that everything should be filmed. He recorded a quick piece to camera, then a commentary for the pictures. The piece to camera was too bitter and angry to be shown; ITN cut it out.

It took the editors at Associated Press some hours to decide whether to send out Nick Ut's photograph; like most agencies and media organisations, their policy was never to show full-frontal nudity. But the AP photo editor in New York, Hal Buell, argued that the news value of the picture was more important than the fact that Kim was naked, and in the end they compromised: the picture wouldn't be cropped to show her in close-up. It was sent out that evening, and appeared on the front pages of the world's newspapers the following day, Friday. It caused a sensation. So did the ITN team's filmed report. It was only ninety seconds long, but when it went out that day it had an immense impact.

On the Saturday morning Chris met Mike Blakey of the BBC. He'd been on board an American naval ship as it bombarded the North Vietnamese coast. Although the BBC had known about this facility beforehand, and had approved it, Blakey had some-how got the blame for being beaten by ITN. He was a pleasant, easy-going man, and although some television journalists would have enjoyed his humiliation and tried to reinforce it by getting another exclusive, Chris was made of kinder stuff. He agreed with Blakey that they should work in partnership – something highly unusual in British television news – in order to find out what had happened to the little girl. In the end it was Mike who discovered her. She was in the British Children's Hospital on the outskirts of Saigon.

When they got there she was lying face down on a bed with dressings on her back, arm and left hand.

Chris went out into the corridor and stopped a nurse to ask how Kim was.

'Oh, she die maybe tomorrow, maybe next day,' the nurse said off-handedly, and hurried on.

The director of the hospital told them that Kim could get more specialised treatment at another Saigon hospital, the Barsky. When they went there, the Barsky agreed to take her. But for some bureaucratic reason the people at the British Hospital had to have permission from the British embassy before she could be moved. At the embassy, the duty officer said he couldn't see why so much fuss was being made about one child. But he agreed that the switch could happen – as long as the South Vietnamese foreign ministry agreed.

Wain and Blakey headed on to the ministry. The official they saw there wasn't helpful. Moving her might show South Vietnam in a bad light, he said. And he echoed what the British diplomat had said: there were so many burned children in South Vietnam – why should this particular one get special treatment?

'I'm sorry,' he concluded, 'but I cannot agree to this.'

Chris Wain is a quiet, self-contained man, but the experiences he had gone through made him boil over. He pulled a lock knife out of his pocket and handed it to the official, hilt first.

'In that case, perhaps you'll do me a favour. Could you go round to the British Hospital and cut her throat? That will be much quicker and kinder than leaving her to die slowly in such pain.'

There was a pause.

'Since you obviously feel so strongly about this,' the official said, 'we agree to her being moved.'

As they walked triumphantly out of the foreign ministry, Mike Blakey said: 'I thought for a moment you were going to stick him.' Perhaps the Vietnamese official had thought so too.

Kim spent fourteen months in hospital and had seventeen major operations, but she recovered. After the communist takeover of South Vietnam, she became something of an anti-American propaganda icon, and went to study in Cuba, where she met and married another Vietnamese student. They planned a honeymoon in

Moscow, but when their plane stopped to refuel in Newfoundland they escaped and asked for political asylum. The Canadian authorities duly granted it. Kim and her husband settled in a suburb of Toronto and had two children. Each year, Chris Wain exchanges Christmas cards with her. So does Nick Ut.

Nick's photograph and Chris's film led directly to a UN ban on the use of napalm against civilians in 1980.

In 1975 I met another man with an international reputation obtained in Vietnam. Neil Davis, born in Tasmania, worked as a cameraman for NBC in Vietnam. At the start of the year I was covering the civil war in Angola from Kinshasa, the capital of what was then Zaire and is now the Democratic Republic of Congo. Since no BBC cameramen seemed to be available to work there with me – Kinshasa was a horribly dangerous place at that time – NBC, with whom the BBC worked in partnership, offered us Neil's services. He never minded where he worked.

Neil was a star in every way: tall, lanky, handsome, with a smile that was devastating to women. He was brave to the point of recklessness, and in each one of his work diaries – he showed me the current one in Kinshasa – he inscribed a couplet from a little-known British poet, Thomas Mordaunt, in 1763:

> One crowded hour of glorious life
>   Is worth an age without a name.

I didn't entirely agree with it then, and I don't now; but as I listened to Neil's seductive voice (he exerted his charm on men as well as women, just as Byron did) and listened to his stories of being shot and blown up in Vietnam, and saw some of his scars, I could see the attraction.

We had an extraordinary couple of weeks together, during which we ran considerable risks and became very close. We uncovered a story which involved a British mercenary calling himself 'Colonel Callan', who had murdered a number of his own men in cold blood for refusing to obey orders. Colonel Callan was working for a rebel group, the FNLA, which was holding my passport. (When I arrived in Kinshasa I was only allowed in because I had pretended to be an FNLA mercenary, and they had taken my passport away.) By this stage the FNLA knew that Neil and I had information about Callan which would destroy it as a movement – and the only way I could leave the country was to get my passport back from the FNLA compound. It was a frightening place, where executions were carried out almost every day. And yet Neil volunteered out of sheer affection and generosity of spirit to go with me and help me in the search for my passport.

We both thought we would be caught and executed, but in the absurd, bathetic way of real life we arrived there at lunchtime and the desk was unmanned except for a young kid who knew nothing about us or Colonel Callan. He handed over my passport without a word.

'I can't believe you took the risk of coming with me,' I said to Neil as we drove away.

'Couldn't let you do something like that on your own without your Uncle Neil,' he said, turning his head to me and smiling that brilliant smile of his.

We agreed that I would fly out to Europe while he stayed on in Kinshasa. When I got there I would contact him and we would simultaneously break the remarkable story we had stumbled on. It was Neil who suggested the plan, and I trusted him. It didn't work out like that, though. The moment my plane took off, Neil got onto NBC in New York and gave them the full details. It took my plane twelve hours to reach Brussels, so I was badly beaten on my own story.

A few weeks later, knowing how angry I was, he wrote me a letter. It was soothing and, like him, faintly seductive, and it ended with a key piece of advice: never leave a good story before it's over.

By chance, three years later, we found ourselves on the same plane from Johannesburg to what was then Lourenço Marques in Mozambique. Neil spotted me, walked down the aisle, and put his hand on my shoulder.

'Don't tell me you're still angry with me,' said the familiar voice, and of course I couldn't.

We had a superb meal of Lourenço Marques prawns that night, sitting at a pavement table outside the best restaurant in town; and for a few hours we were back as we had been, making the same jokes and laughing enough to make the other diners look round and stare. At the end we shook hands and went to our respective hotels. I didn't see him again: a few years later he was shot dead while covering a small-time coup attempt in Thailand.

I never forgot his advice: don't leave a story till it's over. I remembered it when the BBC ordered me not to fly on Ayatollah Khomeini's plane from his exile in Paris to his triumphant reception in Iran. I remembered it when I was instructed to leave Baghdad on the night before the first Gulf War began, and everyone assumed we would be bombed into oblivion. And I remembered it in Belgrade in 1999, when the nastiest of the Serbian extremist groups threatened to come to our hotel and cut our throats, and there was a mass exodus of Western journalists. The advice proved right on each occasion, and it had a far greater effect on my career than his brief betrayal did.

According to the foreign correspondent Jon Swain, Neil Davis hung a plaque in his Saigon apartment which read: 'When you walk with me, do not walk behind me for I may not always lead. Do not walk in front of me because I may not always follow. Walk beside me and be my friend.'

I still feel proud to have walked beside him, even briefly.

Jon Swain, Neil Davis's friend, is a quiet, thoughtful man who was the *Sunday Times* correspondent in Southeast Asia during the Vietnam War, and has remained a brave and effective reporter ever since. The book he wrote in 1995 about the war in Cambodia, *The River of Time*, became a classic: haunting and deeply sad. A character based on him appears in the film *The Killing Fields*, which charts the terrible ordeal of Dith Pran, the translator and fixer who worked for Sydney Schanberg of the *New York Times*. Dith Pran saved the lives of Schanberg and Swain, and very nearly lost his own in doing so.

In *The River of Time*, Swain says it wasn't simply journalistic ambition which decided him to fly back into Phnom Penh in the last moments before its fall, nor a zest for adventure:

> An irresistible impulse propelled me out of the security of my hotel room [in Saigon] that Sunday morning, into a taxi and to the airport, just in case the plane – any plane – was going to Phnom Penh...
>
> Cambodia had given me so much. In Phnom Penh, I had lived through intensity and exaltation I had never before known. Now that the dream was ending, I had no moral choice but to share its fate.

It took a great deal of effort to persuade the authorities to allow him on board an elderly DC-7 which was waiting to leave for Phnom Penh. There were just a few passengers, including Jean-Jacques Cazaux of Agence France-Presse, and an 'odiously smug' East German diplomat who was to find out the hard way that the Khmer Rouge had no affection whatever for Soviet bloc officials. The journey took an hour. Then Swain and the others stood on the tarmac at Pochentong airport and watched the DC-7 take off again, their last link with the outside world.

Swain's next hours and days were passed in a welter of dreadfulness, which he has never been able to forget. 'I was,' Swain says, 'overdosing on horror.' He insisted on going back to an asylum for the mentally ill in Tak Mhau: 'one of the most heart-wrenching places I had seen'.

> With the buildings trembling from the shock of rockets and shells, one had to ask who was more insane – these pitiful human creatures, one of whom clasped a simply carved wooden figure of a bird in his hand (I like to think it was a dove of peace) – or the soldiers killing each other outside?

Swain, together with Sydney Schanberg and the intensely loyal Dith Pran, stayed at the post office all night long, filing their reports until dawn. In the end, shouting against the din of gun and rocket fire, Swain realised his line to London had been cut:

> An hour later, the city fell. The chief telex operator, who had worked through the night to send out last despatches to the world, learned that his little girl had been killed by artillery fire near Chamcar Mon Palace and his wife had been fatally injured. Dressing hurriedly, uttering not a word, he went out. As he passed us, a limp figure in the sunlight, we averted our eyes.

Swain, Schanberg and Dith Pran went to the Preah Ket Mealea Hospital, where 2,000 people were lying injured. The doctors hadn't turned up and the plasma bottles and saline drips were emptying fast.

> People were bleeding to death in the corridors. The floors of the wards were caked with blood. The hot, foetid air was thick with flies – the sight of these swarming over the living and the dead, over the anguished faces of those who knew they were doomed to die, churned my stomach and made my mind reel.

> Outside, in the hospital grounds, half a dozen Khmer Rouge soldiers stopped their car and forced them out, waving their guns at them. Some of them were as young as twelve, hardly bigger than their AK-47s. They were, Swain says, 'super-deadly':

> Their leader's eyes were coals of hate. He was screaming and ranting, foaming at the mouth. He held his pistol against my head, finger firm on the trigger. My hands were high in the air and I was paralysed with fear. My camera, notebooks and other belongings littered the ground where the Khmer Rouge had thrown them. The seconds ticked by.

Dith Pran kept up a soothing flow of words in Khmer. Swain, Schanberg and an American photographer called Al were forced into the back of an armoured personnel carrier. Pran was told to go, but he and their driver, Sarun, both insisted on staying. Just before the hatch and door were bolted, Pran managed to get in as well. The assumption was that the Khmer Rouge soldiers would throw in a hand-grenade and finish them all off. They were driven around the streets for nearly half an hour. Then the vehicle stopped and they were told to get out. This is it, they thought: they were going to be executed.

But Dith Pran talked and talked to the soldiers, softly and firmly. These were neutral observers, he said, journalists who were here to witness the historic liberation of Phnom Penh. Slowly, his insistent arguments had their effect. The tension relaxed.

There were plenty of horrors still to come. Jon Swain says he is still haunted by the memory of the staff at their hotel, clutching imploringly at their arms and saying: 'Don't abandon us.' There was nothing that could be done to save them. Most of them were murdered in the savage way of the Khmer Rouge.

In the end they had to say goodbye to Pran. Sydney Schanberg loaded him with several thousand dollars and Swain gave him the rest of their food. He was taken away, while Schanberg and Swain were allowed to leave: 'We had been unable to save those who had saved us. We were protected simply because our skins were white. I felt ashamed.'

Extraordinarily, Dith Pran survived the Khmer Rouge killing fields – a phrase he himself coined. He managed to conceal the fact that he was a middle-class intellectual, and pretended he had been a taxi driver. After four years of starvation and torture, Pran was saved by the Vietnamese invasion of Cambodia and the collapse of the Khmer Rouge government. Altogether more than fifty members of his family had died.

Pran escaped to the United States. He was reunited with Sydney Schanberg, and the *New York Times* hired him as a photo-journalist. He died in 2008 of pancreatic cancer at the age of sixty-five.

The Cambodian actor, Haing Somnang Ngor, who played him in the film *The Killing Fields*, was murdered in 1996 by armed robbers in Los Angeles when he refused to hand over a locket containing a picture of his wife. She had died when they were prisoners together in a Khmer Rouge concentration camp.

A couple of months after our time together in Kinshasa in 1975, Neil Davis also found himself in Phnom Penh, days before it fell. He and an NBC correspondent, Jim Laurie, decided to get out, leaving behind them many people they had come to know and love. Laurie went back to America, but after a week he flew back to Saigon just as the regime there was starting to collapse:

> I decided, come what may, I would not again be 'evacuated'. I would witness in whatever way I could the last days of the Vietnam we knew and the first days of whatever kind of nation the Vietnamese would build for themselves.
>
> My decision was largely emotional. I was influenced by the pain of Cambodia. I was also hugely curious about what lay ahead.

Neil Davis had already decided that he wasn't going to leave Saigon, and he was a big support for Jim Laurie, who was fourteen years his junior. Neil joked that they were progressive journalists – no Vietnamese communists would harm them.

'If you get into trouble, Jim, just tell the *bộ đội giai phong* [liberation soldiers], that you are *Úc dai loi* [Australian] and wish them G'day!'

The big media organisations behaved as they often do on such occasions: they ordered the members of their staff to leave Saigon, and left their bureaus in the charge of freelances for whom they would have no great responsibility, financial or legal. CBS put its office into the hands of a British teacher and writer, Eric Cavaliero. The *Washington Post* asked a young freelance called James Fenton to look after their interests. He later became one of Britain's leading poets, and professor of poetry at

Oxford; it was he who wrote the poem from which the title of this book is taken.

The great majority of foreign journalists left. Many were involved in the panicky, ill-organised evacuation from the roof of the US embassy. Among them was a television producer, Robert Wiener, whom I came to know in Baghdad in 1990 and 1991, and whose excellent memoir of that period was turned into the feature film, *Live from Baghdad*. I once asked him why he was staying on in Baghdad. 'Because I left Saigon,' he replied crisply, 'and I've spent the whole time since trying to make up for it.'

Around seventy journalists remained. Some didn't intend to, including thirty-seven Japanese who failed to make it to the helicopter pick-up points. Others were absolutely clear in their minds that staying was the right thing to do: Peter Arnett, for example, who became known around the world for his reporting with CNN and for his later decision to remain in Baghdad in 1991 during the first Gulf War. He, George Esper and Matt Franjola refused to leave the Associated Press bureau in Saigon. Their competitors at United Press International, Alan Dawson (a Canadian), Paul Vogle (American) and a photojournalist, Hubert van Es (Dutch) also stayed. Van Es was to take the best-known photographs of Saigon's fall.

The French and British, in particular, were well represented in the group of stayers: the magnificent Sandy Gall of ITN, whose work later on in Afghanistan and on behalf of the Bushmen of the Kalahari made him one of the great modern foreign correspondents; Stewart Dalby of the *Financial Times*, who could easily have pleaded that this was scarcely an economic story; and Julian Manyon, a free-lance at the time who later became a famously assertive reporter for ITN. Others who remained included Nayan Chanda of the *Far East Economic Review*, and Tiziano Terzani of *Der Spiegel*. For the BBC, Derek Wilson, the Corporation's Southeast Asia correspondent, together with Brian Barron and Brian's redoubtable, elegant and charming cameraman Eric Thirer, were all determined to stay.

Altogether, it was an impressive group. Not one of them stayed in Saigon for their health or their personal profit. It was a deep sense of duty that kept them there.

The Viet Cong and the North Vietnamese soldiers were more civilised than the Khmer Rouge, but there was always the danger that they might decide that the journalists were American spies, and shoot them out of hand. The real enemy was panic. It's hard to stand out against the feeling of mass fear, and decide to go your own way. Those who want to go often use all types of moral persuasion to get the others to come with them.

Later, Jim Laurie wrote on his website:

> We watched the last American helicopter lift off from the roof of the American Embassy just before eight in the morning on April 30th. I interviewed distressed Vietnamese in the street below displaying US identification cards pleading with us for help in escaping; help I could not give.
>
> Other Vietnamese staggered to the embassy roof to wait for helicopters that never came. Frustrated and angry Vietnamese clearly showing emotions of betrayal began looting the US Embassy floor by floor, taking away everything they could.
>
> I raced to the NBC bureau to report at 9:45 am in Saigon the 'unconditional surrender' of Saigon by General Duong Van Minh who had been President of 'the Republic of Vietnam' for only two days.
>
> The scratchy live broadcast lasted until a little after ten Saigon time, when all communications with Vietnam were severed.

Brian Barron and Eric Thirer had also been airlifted out of Phnom Penh just before it fell, like Jim Laurie and Neil Davis. They had made their way to Manila, to catch what proved to be the last international flight into Saigon. They were almost alone on the Pan Am plane. Barron and Thirer sat grandly up in first class; something the BBC usually forbade outright. But since they thought there was a very good chance they'd be killed, the prospect of being ticked off for wasting licence fee-payers' money didn't

Neil Davis, NBC's star cameraman in Vietnam: charming, deeply competitive and extraordinarily brave. His trusty CP-16 camera rests between his feet on this military helicopter and his emergency medical pack is ready to hand.

Foreign journalists hurrying to leave Saigon as it fell on 29 April 1975: one of the century's greatest events. It's hard to blame them, but as Neil Davis always said, 'Never go till the story's over.'

Dith Pran in later years. His courage in staying with Sydney Schanberg and Jon Swain when the Khmer Rouge captured Phnom Penh saved their lives at the risk of his own.

Corbis Historical / Getty Images

The redoubtable Don McCullin, photographed in a quiet moment during the battle for Hue in South Vietnam in 1968, one of the most dangerous episodes of the entire Vietnam War. Four decades later, in his eighties, he is still covering wars.

The greatest scoop of the twenty-first century so far. Jürgen Todenhöfer, the 74-year-old German journalist and former politician, interviews the German-born Islamic State volunteer Abu Qatadah in the IS capital, Mosul, while heavily armed IS guards look on.

Anthony Loyd of *The Times* after being beaten up and shot by a Syrian rebel commander, Hakim Anza, in 2014: a self-portrait taken from his hospital bed on a mobile phone. The incident didn't stop him working as a war correspondent.

The doyenne of the profession. Marie Colvin died in February 2012 when the Syrian army pinpointed the building in Homs from which she was reporting by satellite phone, and shelled it. She is pictured here with the photographer Paul Conroy, who was with her when she was killed.

The author with producer Peter Leng and camerman Duncan Stone introducing the BBC programme *The Editors* from a forbidden setting overlooking the river Tigris in Baghdad: not an altogether sensible place from which to film.

loom particularly large in comparison. They had scarcely troubled at any point to discuss the pros and cons of going back to Saigon; for them there were no cons.

'We were young,' Thirer says now, 'why would we want to stay away? I don't think we ever bothered to talk about it.'

Halfway through the flight the captain came out and explained that the plane had just been requisitioned by the US government, so the basis of their insurance as passengers had changed. They didn't really care. When they landed in Saigon they went straight to the Caravelle Hotel, as they always did. The windows of their rooms vibrated to the heavy thump of shells falling on Tan Son Nhat airport, five miles away.

Barron and Thirer carried on working, though by now it was impossible to send their material out of the country and on to London. The best place to film the fighting from was a place nicknamed Newport Bridge, so they got a driver in an ancient Buick to take them there. They fixed a Union Jack to the radio aerial in the hope it might give them some protection. It didn't. A South Vietnamese officer, 'freaked to the point of madness' as Barron later put it, threatened to shoot them if they didn't hand over the car. They managed to get all their gear out of it, and kept on walking in order to get away from him. The next day they went back to Newport Bridge and found that the Buick had been used to block the road. It had been squashed as flat as a soft-drinks can by a passing tank.

On the morning of the day the city fell, the phone system finally collapsed. Barron and Thirer raced to the main post office, where an amazing woman called Madame Lin single-handedly worked the elaborate system for calling up a radio 'circuit'. Barron could speak to the BBC traffic desk in London, and record a despatch. He could also speak to the foreign editor, John Huston, a gentle, erudite Irishman who, with the full authority of the BBC management, had ordered him and Thirer to leave some days before: to absolutely no effect, of course. Now, down the line to Saigon, Huston was able to hear everything that was happening.

The lights were cut, and Thirer, standing near the window, was the first to see men wearing North Vietnamese uniforms swarming around by the entrance to their building. Barron was giving a live commentary to London. He wrote later: 'There was a thunderous knocking at the door. Two polite but unsmiling North Vietnamese officers stood there. "Gentlemen, this radio station is now closed. We have taken control," one of them said. That was the last broadcast anyone did from Saigon. The war was over.'

Suddenly the building started to shake, and the microphone suspended from the ceiling began to swing from side to side. A squadron of fighter-bombers which had defected to the rebels' side was dropping bombs on the presidential palace, not far away. Thirer snatched up his faithful CP-16, one of the most reliable cameras ever used for television, and they ran down the stairs into the street. Neil Davis and Jim Laurie of NBC had arrived at the palace a minute or two earlier, and Neil got the key shot of a North Vietnamese tank bursting its way through the ornamental gates. Thirer's pictures were magnificent, and later won all sorts of awards. The North Vietnamese soldiers let off round after round of cele-bratory gunfire into the air, and the Viet Cong flag was soon flying over the palace.

In the afternoon, Davis and Laurie went out to film North Vietnamese troops carrying out a mopping-up operation near the American embassy. For Laurie, the sudden switch in circumstances was weird:

> Having covered the war on the American side, it seemed surreal to be creeping forward into a small park, routing out a pocket of resistance from a few soldiers of what our new companions called 'American puppet troops'.
>
> We filmed the body of a South Vietnamese officer lying next to his army jeep. Most 'Saigon troops' had shed their uniforms and retreated into civilian life. Scattered uniforms lay strewn along the street.

There were no communications of any kind now. Soon, Laurie heard the newsreader on the BBC World Service say: 'Four days after the fall of Saigon, there is no word on the fate of more than 70 foreign journalists trapped in the former South Vietnamese capital.'

The NBC, BBC and ITN teams were going out all day long, filming whatever they could in order to have the material for a Saigon diary, when it could finally be shown. Sandy Gall had obtained some particularly good footage. He and Brian Barron greeted each other in friendly fashion whenever they bumped into each other, either at the Caravelle Hotel or out in the street, but they didn't socialise. They were both too competitive for that.

Conditions were relatively good in the hotel: there was still coffee, croissants and papaya every morning, and *oeufs sur le plat* for the Anglo-Saxons. Eric Thirer, however, was getting more and more sick, and neither he nor Barron could work out what was wrong with him. Barron went out to a pharmacy and described the symptoms. He brought back a packet of pills inscribed in Vietnamese writing which neither of them could understand. Thirer took the pills but, far from helping, they seemed to make him feel lower and more debilitated than ever.

In the end, one of the Western journalists managed to make contact with a North Vietnamese charter company, and an elderly Russian-built Ilyushin landed at the damaged airport in Saigon to take everyone out. Tickets cost $120. Scarcely any of the journalists wanted to stay now; all their concentration was on bringing their material out to the world. The plane flew them to Vientiane, but they needed to get to Thailand, and the border was closed. Eventually money changed hands, and a Thai official escorted them across. They could then fly wherever they wanted.

Brian Barron went directly to London, and his material was turned round quickly and put out as a documentary. Sandy Gall also headed for London, but had a nasty shock when he arrived. There was a strike at Independent Television, and his material couldn't be transmitted until well after Brian's. After all Sandy's courage and immense hard work, his efforts were thwarted by someone else's dispute about pay and conditions.

Eric Thirer went back to his base in Hong Kong, but his condition seemed to be worsening. Barron insisted he should come to London and be checked out by the Hospital for Tropical Diseases. They found that he had hookworm, an unpleasant and debilitating infection which can lead to severe anaemia. He'd probably picked it up in Cambodia. After treatment, he recovered completely.

The mysterious medicine which Brian Barron had obtained for him in Saigon turned out to be Valium.

ELEVEN

Civilian Targets

In the midst of despair, such generosity and spirit, from
the people who cared for their elderly neighbours, even
if they were from the 'wrong' ethnic group. Who insisted
on coffee for their visitors, when it probably cost more
than gold, or who stood in line for water at dawn and
carried it up who knows how many flights of stairs to
ensure everyone appeared with clean hair and clothes.

Emma Daly, *Independent*, 1995

FOR SOME REASON, IT has always been rare to find foreign correspondents who have the two chief qualities of their trade in
precisely equal measure: the dogged adventurousness to find out
remarkable and extraordinary things, and the writing ability to
make them come alive to their readers or viewers. Most of us have
usually been better at one or other of these. One foreign correspondent who has always been able to balance the two is Anthony Loyd
of *The Times*.

Loyd started out as a soldier, serving five years in the Royal Green
Jackets in Northern Ireland and the first Gulf War. For nearly a
quarter of a century since then he has reported on up to twenty
wars; the precise number depends how you differentiate between
different phases of conflicts like, say, the one in Syria. He wrote a
bestselling book called *My War Gone By, I Miss It So*, whose title
irritated me until I realised it was a deeply sensitive account of what
it is like to experience combat and fear, combined with his struggles
with various types of addiction. It wasn't until 2001 that I met him.
He and a photographer, Seamus Murphy, turned up at a building

my team and I had requisitioned close to the front line north of Kabul, in the weeks before the fall of the Taliban. (Murphy took the photograph of me on the cover of this book.) Like old soldiers, we had made ourselves relatively comfortable in our building, and there was resistance among some of my colleagues to allowing a couple of outsiders to stay with us. In the end everyone agreed, and Loyd and Murphy settled in. Each day they went out, searching for stories and finding them; and each evening I listened to the tales of what they'd done.

That was when I started to appreciate Loyd's deep sensitivity to the subjects he covered: far deeper than most journalists would care to go. As he approaches fifty, he has made the war in Syria and Iraq his own. There has been plenty of first-class coverage from Syria, including by my own colleagues, people such as Ian Pannell and Paul Wood, but the quality of Loyd's writing has an almost hypnotic feel to it which goes way beyond normal reporting, a sophistication which most journalists would feel inhibited from displaying.

Here, for instance, are extracts from a despatch which he sent to *The Times* from Amiriyat, outside the town of Fallujah, not far from Baghdad. It appeared on 12 March 2016 under the plonking head-line 'Panic and brutality in fight for Fallujah':

> A severed head lay at my feet. It belonged to a teenage storm trooper, part of Islamic State's elite forces, no more than seventeen years old. The skin on his face was quite unblemished, and soft with youth, though his long black hair was matted and tangled. The features were Asian, suggesting those of steppes far from Iraq. Despite the abhorrence of it all, I could see that, in life, he would have been handsome.
>
> When I saw first saw that head lying in the dust, beside the corpses of two Isis fighters near the gates of a Shia militia base east of Amiriyat Fallujah, it was on its side. Later, after a group of grinning militiamen had stopped to take photos of themselves with the head and the bodies, putting their feet on the flesh, raising their guns like big-game hunters in Hell, someone placed it upright.

Such are the fruits of victory on the ground in Iraq today, though you will likely not find such details in the glib, anaesthetised coalition reports detailing air sorties flown, bombs dropped, targets destroyed; a ruined town liberated by Iraqi government forces here, or lost to Isis there.

As we stood in the afternoon heat beside the head, it seemed we existed in parallel realities, those militiamen and I. They took photos and smiled and jeered. Among themselves, they exalted in the trophy. But they forbade me from photographing that dark tableau, in case it be judged from outside.

'No photos of the head,' they warned, even as they laughed.

The contradiction was almost as grotesque as the mutilation: they took joy from a wrong within that they also knew was unacceptable to the world without; a world that included coalition fighter jets that had bombed Islamic State in the very same battle that the beheaded youth had died. . .

Nevertheless, as so close a witness to this small atrocity, I could understand, looking from head to torso, why beheading has become such a popular practice on the rage-filled battlefields across Iraq and Syria. The action uniquely disintegrates a man's physical value, destroying him more completely than any blast or shell can somehow do; conjoining annihilation and desecration with the triumph of hate.

Some news organisations are mildly nervous about scoops; especially those which have a high reputation for accuracy and are unwilling to put that in jeopardy. In 2010 – it was only a minor story, but one in which I take a certain amount of pride – my producer, Oggy Boytchev, plus a cameraman, a translator and a security man, drove westwards out of Baghdad to go to one of the most dangerous places in Iraq: Fallujah, close to where Anthony Loyd was reporting.

We had heard that the hospital there had been reporting a disturbingly high level of birth defects as an apparent result of some armaments used by the Americans in the two big battles for Fallujah a few years earlier. The allegation was that the Americans had fired shells with depleted uranium warheads. No Western journalist had gone to cover the birth defects story, because the town was in the hands of Islamic extremists and it was regarded as too risky. But sitting in the BBC's Baghdad bureau day after day, only an hour's drive from Fallujah, and finding my eyes resting constantly on the map on the office wall, made me more and more determined to go there; and when we heard that a medical report was about to come out in London, suggesting that the number of birth defects was higher than ever, I decided I couldn't live with my conscience if we didn't head out there.

The journey was pretty hair-raising, but we started to get what we needed within minutes of reaching the hospital. A doctor whom I stopped at the entrance to the paediatric ward was clearly very nervous. The staff were scared of upsetting the Iraqi government and the Americans, as well as the Islamic extremists who were now running Fallujah. Nevertheless she answered my questions when I put them to her on camera:

'How many cases of birth defects do you see on the ward?'

[No answer.]

'One or two a week?'

'No, no, no, two or three cases a day.'

'What is it that happened in Fallujah that means that these defects exist in such numbers?'

'I am a doctor. I have to be scientific in my talk. I have no proof and nothing documented, but I can tell you that, year by year, the number is increasing.'

After that we went off to film in the wards, and in various houses around the town. Again and again we found babies with serious genetic malformations, children with too many toes and fingers whose heads lolled and whose eyes were unfocused and dull. We were shown dozens of photographs of dead children whose condition meant they couldn't possibly have survived: one of the babies had three heads. It was impossible, given the security problems, to carry out any proper widespread investigation, but it seemed pretty conclusive that the worst defects happened to families who lived near the river and got their drinking water from there. The Americans had bulldozed the rubble from the buildings destroyed in the fighting into the river at that point.

If you go to any hospital, even in Western Europe or the US, you will find genetic disorders that lead to deformity or death: but not, I knew, on this disturbing scale. We couldn't state as fact that the fierce spike in birth defects was caused by the American attacks on Fallujah; but we could report the position as we found it, and we used the doctor's words to show the scale of the problem. And we could report that other people had blamed the phenomenon on the American weaponry, without making any judgement about whether this was true or not.

That night we sent our report to London, but I could see that the people there were nervous about it.

'If this is true,' one editor said – never a good opening line in a conversation – 'why haven't the *Guardian* or the *Independent* done something about it? They're usually very strong on this kind of story.'

The explanation was that it was really dangerous to get to Fallujah, of course, and that only the BBC had the security resources to make the journey. Since we had strong research back-up from doctors and academics in Britain and Iraq, I had no anxieties about it.

That night the story was the lead on the various news bulletins right across the BBC's range of outputs. I was grateful to the various editors who decided to give it that degree of prominence, given the uncertainties which they may have felt. With hindsight, it's clear that the story was correct and it was absolutely right that the BBC should have put its entire weight behind it. Still, there were shoals of complaints, both from British people and from Americans. Maybe this was because the victims were children. People who might not have objected so much to a story about physical damage to adults were incensed to be told that the actions of the American military could possibly have damaged children in this disturbing way. A senior figure at the US embassy wrote to complain: '[T]he story was thinly sourced and seemed to be driven more by images than facts or research. My office facilitates hundreds of interviews, embeds, visas and meetings for BBC journalists every year, because you are a quality operation. This story, however, was nowhere near BBC standards.'

The *Independent*'s correspondent Patrick Cockburn picked up the story the next day. If some others had done so, the BBC's collective mind might have been made easier. What really seems to have caused the worry was the feeling of being out in the open with no back-up.

As scoops go, however, that was a pretty moderate affair; even I have had better. The rest of this chapter is dedicated to scoops in the traditional sense: journalistic achievements which have attracted attention right around the world.

In July 1992, when the war in Bosnia was reaching its height, Penny Marshall, Ian Williams and Ed Vulliamy from ITN, *Channel 4 News* and the *Guardian* respectively managed something no other journalists at the time had done: they reached the concentration camps which the Bosnian Serbs had set up to hold Bosnian Muslim and Croatian prisoners at Omarska and Trnopolje. Getting there was an enviable achievement. The Bosnian Serb President, Radovan Karadžić, gave them one of his loose and usually meaningless promises: they could visit the camps and see everything they wanted. They knew how little the promise signified, but they went there anyway and tried to persuade the camp guards to let them in.

All that happened at first was that they were allowed to see the canteen and a few prisoners being forced to run around. But they kept on demanding that the guards should honour Karadžić's promise to them, and eventually they were driven to Trnopolje. There a large group of prisoners had gathered behind a straggling wire fence, and the cameraman was able to film them without too much restriction. Several of the prisoners were strikingly emaciated, especially Fikrit Alić, whose half-naked body was almost skeletal;

he looked like a prisoner from Bergen-Belsen. The Bosnian Serb guards failed to stop Ian Williams talking through the wire to the prisoners, and although they were nervous about speaking out, it was clear that there was a good deal of ill-treatment here.

In the ITN pictures Trnopolje looked like a death camp, and men like Fikrit Alić seemed to be in the last stages of malnutrition. In fact it was a holding camp where the prisoners were often beaten and badly treated, but it wasn't a place of extermination. The Bosnian Serbs were perfectly capable of murdering large numbers of people because of their race, as they showed later at Srebrenica, and perhaps Trnopolje was a foretaste of that. World opinion certainly thought so. What had previously looked like a small and nasty three-way war, marked by ethnic cleansing and cruelty, now appeared in a different light; the Serbs were seen by many people as the equivalent of Nazis. After the reporting of Penny Marshall, Ian Williams and Ed Vulliamy, the reality of the war seemed clear.

Later a small, intelligent, highly readable magazine in London, *Living Marxism*, printed an article by a German journalist which threw doubt on the pictures. ITN, feeling it had to defend its journalists, sued. *Living Marxism* lost the case, and had to pay damages which were great enough to drive it out of business. I knew and liked the magazine and its editor, and felt that a big, well-funded organisation like ITN shouldn't destroy a worthwhile magazine, whatever the reason; so I sided publicly with *LM*. It was a mistake on my part, of course, because it seemed to put me on the side of those who thought there was something wrong with the pictures from Trnopolje.

There was clearly nothing whatever wrong with them. If I had been with a team which obtained them I would have felt justifiably proud, and Penny Marshall and Ian Williams used the story in a restrained and thoughtful way. The outside world might have thought Trnopolje looked like a Nazi death camp, but neither ITN nor *Channel 4 News* used the kind of emotive language which might have encouraged that association. It was a remarkable scoop, from which the Bosnian Serbs never recovered, and Penny, in particular, won the television industry's plaudits for what she had done.

———

Reporting from Iraq during and after the invasion of 2003 was, I suppose, a later generation's equivalent of reporting from Vietnam. Sixty-three journalists died in Vietnam; 173 died in Iraq. By comparison, during the siege of Sarajevo, 1992–95, nineteen were killed. Yet the peculiarly difficult circumstances of the siege, with its ever-present danger and the cruel suffering of the inhabitants of the city, makes it stand out in the minds of many of us in a way that Iraq, with all its horrors, never quite did. Life in the Holiday Inn, the ugly yellow block jammed in among Sarajevo's otherwise attractive buildings, was full of privations, which many of us endured for long weeks at a time. Yet because it was the one main centre for the correspondents covering the siege, it was also a place of great comradeship. It was there that I first met Christiane Amanpour, whose career took off spectacularly when she corrected and challenged President Bill Clinton live by satellite, demanding to know what he was going to do about the obscenity of the siege. I've liked and admired her ever since: her sense of rectitude and her love of her father's native country, Iran, have been two strong reasons for this, but she is also great fun.

John Burns, the *New York Times* correspondent there, became a lifelong friend of mine. British-born, tall, with a mane of bushy hair which I've watched change over the years from dark to grey-white, he was probably the most intellectually gifted reporter there. He insisted on staying in Sarajevo for long and physically exhausting stretches of time, just as later he insisted on living in Baghdad during the worst years, rather than merely visiting as so many of us did. His delightful wife Jane, also British, was *The Times*'s bureau manager, and she turned a large Baghdad villa into an English country house at the paper's expense, on the grounds that the people who had to work in so difficult a place deserved decent living conditions. The

BBC lived close by, but our villa was rough, cheaply furnished, and deeply uncomfortable by comparison.

I'd known and liked John in the past, but when I first arrived in Sarajevo and settled at the Holiday Inn it irritated me to see, in a place where there was so little food and everyone went hungry, that the waiters served him with two eggs every morning at breakfast. I assumed this was the result of some sort of graft. It was only later that I discovered he was recovering from treatment for cancer, and that his doctor had told him to eat protein regularly if he insisted on going to a warzone during his convalescence.

All of us, John included, had to exist on one proper meal a day. Dinner at the Holiday Inn was, in spite of the surrounding circumstances of the war, an immensely sociable affair. Noise and a fierce cloud of cigarette smoke hit you in the face as you pushed open the doors, but the pickings were slim: a bowl of thin, watery soup with a piece of blackish bread, a small chunk of some nameless meat with a single scoop of rice, and a weird pudding: a square of coconut cake topped with bitter chocolate, two inches by one and a half, which never changed throughout the siege and always seemed to stay the same size.

I usually sat with my own team, but sometimes I would excuse myself and go and sit with John Burns or Christiane or Janine di Giovanni. Janine wrote about it all afterwards in her book *Madness Visible* with considerable nostalgia:

> The food was disgusting and I didn't bathe for weeks, but the comradeship of the journalists reporting the war was fierce. I met some of my closest friends there, as well as my future husband. We were bonded together forever because of the siege and the sorrow of watching this beautiful and brave city get pummelled.

> I go back often to Sarajevo now, but I have only stayed in the Holiday Inn one time since the war ended. I was too tormented by ghosts – and it was strange to turn on a switch and have electricity, strange not to see half the hotel open to the air because it had been blown apart by a bomb.

However, I did search for all the waiters that I had known during the war – the ones who used to play soccer at night in the cavernous dining room because the shelling and sniping made it too dangerous to go outside. How I loved their courage, their dignity, and the fact that they wore freshly cleaned white shirts and bow ties while they served us rice and rock-hard bread for dinner.

There was no enjoyment in reporting from Sarajevo – it made you too angry for that, and life was too cheap – but there was a fierce satisfaction about going there. And you formed intense friendships which became permanent.

For me, one such friendship was with Kurt Schork, the Reuters correspondent in Sarajevo. Studious, bespectacled, he looked more like a professor of law at an American university than a journalist; but he was quite extraordinarily brave, and was swept on by a fierce moral sense that the siege was intrinsically wrong, and that it was the duty of the world's supposedly civilised nations to bring it to an end as soon as possible. He and I had long discussions about it – he was too pleasant to call them arguments – and although we didn't necessarily agree about how to bring the siege to an end we remained good friends. Kurt wanted immediate armed intervention; I believed in a combination of military and diplomatic pressure. Sometimes John Burns, whose opinions lay somewhere in the middle, would join in. Outside, from time to time, the shells would fall, and once Kurt and I had to rush out and report on the fatalities from a nearby explosion; but the quality of our discussions was always high, and I came to enjoy them hugely.

Kurt had an interesting background for a journalist. He was born in Washington, DC, in 1947, and went to Oxford as a Rhodes Scholar in 1969, the same year as the future President Bill Clinton. He became a property developer after returning to the US, then gravitated to politics as an adviser. After that he went to the New York City Transit Authority where he became chief of staff. But none of these things seemed to satisfy him, and eventually he switched to journalism. Reuters hired him, and he found himself in

Sarajevo, where he quickly became one of the dominant figures in the foreign press corps.

In May 1993, Kurt stumbled on a story which he made his own. For him it summed up the tragedy and waste of the siege. Just about every newspaper around the world which took the Reuters service printed it, many in full. It was one of the most successful despatches in the agency's history. Everyone knew it as the 'Romeo and Juliet story':

SARAJEVO, May 23, 1993
By Kurt Schork
Reuters

Two lovers lie dead on the banks of Sarajevo's Miljacka river, locked in a final embrace.

For four days they have sprawled near Vrbana bridge in a wasteland of shell-blasted rubble, downed tree branches and dangling power lines.

So dangerous is the area no one has dared recover their bodies.

Boško Brckić and Admira Ismić, both 25, were shot dead on Wednesday trying to escape the besieged Bosnian capital for Serbia.

Sweethearts since high school, he was a Serb and she was a Moslem.

'They were shot at the same time, but he fell instantly and she was still alive,' recounts Dino, a soldier who saw the couple trying to cross from government territory to rebel Serb positions.

'She crawled over and hugged him and they died like that, in each other's arms.'

Squinting through a hole in the sandbagged wall of a bombed-out building, Dino points to where the couple lie mouldering amid the debris of Bosnia's 14-month civil war.

Boško is face-down on the pavement, right arm bent awkwardly behind him. Admira lies next to her lover, left arm across his back.

The government side says Serb soldiers shot the couple, but Serb forces insist Bosnian Moslem-led government troops were responsible.

'I don't care who killed them, I just want their bodies so I can bury them,' says Zijah Ismic, the dead girl's father. 'I don't want them to rot in no-man's land.'

. . .

The university chemistry students dated for seven years before moving in to live together nine months ago.

With his father dead, no one would have blamed Boško had he left Sarajevo when his mother and brother fled before war broke out last year.

Instead, he stayed in the city.

'He had no one here, just Admira,' explains the dead girl's mother.

'Boško stayed in Sarajevo because of her. Admira wanted to repay him by travelling with him to Serbia.'

. . .

'Love took them to their deaths,' Ismic says of Boško and Admira.

'That's proof this is not a war between Serbs and Moslems. It's a war between crazy people, between monsters. That's why their bodies are still out there.'

On 24 May 2000, seven years and a day after Kurt had sent that despatch, he was driving down a road through the Sierra Leone bush in a car which also contained a Spanish cameraman who worked for APTN, Miguel Moreno de Mora, and two other Reuters journalists, Mark Chisholm, a South African cameraman, and Yannis Behrakis, a Greek photographer. Their car ran into an ambush, and Schork and de Mora were killed; the other two were injured.

Schork had left a will which stipulated that after his body had been cremated, his ashes should be divided into two parts and placed in two wooden boxes. One box was buried beside his mother in Washington, DC. The other was taken to the Lion

Cemetery in Sarajevo, and placed in a grave beside that of Boško and Admira.

———

Lyse Doucet seems to me to be the ultimate freelance within the regimented vastness of BBC News. She fits in, but no one has managed to make her a natural company person. She hunts down her own stories, rings her contacts constantly, pushes for information, for access, for interviews. People smile when they hear her exotic accent on the other end of the line, because she is warm and jolly and has an amazingly capacious memory for their personal details.

Her name and background are exotic too: she was born in the Canadian province of New Brunswick, of ancestry which included Mi'kmaq, a First Nations grouping, and Acadian, the descendants of French settlers along the North American coast who were forced out by the British between 1755 and 1764 in what became known as the Great Expulsion. Some emigrated to the territory of Louisiana, where they were called Cajuns. Lyse was brought up speaking English, but she is a fierce defender of the peoples she sprang from. Once, when she was introduced to Prince Charles, she immediately raised with him the case of the Acadians, and demanded that Britain should give them redress. It didn't stop the establishment from awarding her an OBE.

Lyse began her career as a foreign correspondent in West Africa in 1983, reporting for the Canadian media and then for the BBC. In 1988 she went to work in Pakistan, but the BBC correspondent there said he didn't want her intruding on his patch and she was forced out; Lyse's remarkable work rate and her ability to excavate stories can be a serious challenge to anyone more conventional. Leaving Islamabad was the best thing that could have happened to her, because she managed to get a rare visa to Kabul. She arrived there on Christmas Eve, 1988, to start reporting.

Afghanistan was just about to go through one of its greatest upheavals. In February 1989 the Soviet troops who had invaded nearly ten years earlier were withdrawn, and the pro-communist government of President Najibullah was left alone to fight the mujaheddin, who had won their long fight against the Russians. It was a chaotic and exciting time, and Lyse Doucet's voice with its strange, charming vowels was heard every day on the radio.

In June 1989 I was in Kabul with the renowned combat cameraman Peter Jouvenal. We had been secretly infiltrated into the city by one particular mujaheddin group, Harakat-e-Islami. After an extraordinary few days of driving round the city undercover and interviewing dissidents within the governmental structure, the secret police discovered where we were and staged a raid on our safe house. There was a shoot-out, and we were spirited away in a taxi driven by a Harakat supporter.

On our way to the outskirts of Kabul, where we would be able to make our escape into the mountains on foot, we passed the turning to the InterContinental, the only modern hotel in Kabul at that point. Jouvenal muttered to me that Lyse Doucet was based there.

'We ought to go and have tea with her,' he said jokingly.

As I watched the box-like bulk of the InterCon jutting out over the hillside, I was filled with a sense of longing for the sheer normality of sitting in the hotel lounge and drinking a civilised cup of tea with a colleague, after all the rough living and risk we had endured for the past few weeks. I was desperate to tell the driver to turn off, so that we could go and ask for Lyse's help. She would of course have given it – I know that now – but all three of us would have been arrested within minutes. So I turned my face towards the mountains and we drove on; to safety, as it turned out. Still, Lyse (whom I hadn't actually met at that stage) and the tea of course, were a tremendous draw to an anxious fugitive.

The events of 1989 gave Lyse a major story, and she showed she could cope with it with grace and skill. So when the Islamabad job didn't work out for the correspondent who had objected to her presence, it was offered to her. She accepted, but cannily insisted that she should also cover Afghanistan and, later, Iran. Lyse was to stay in the region for five years.

She first met Hamid Karzai, who later became Afghanistan's president, in 1988 when he was in exile in the city of Quetta. At that stage she was freelancing successfully for the BBC from the city, although the BBC had been certain there would be no stories there; predictably, Lyse's industry and sheer instinct proved them wrong. Karzai became a personal friend. Before the al-Qaeda attacks on New York and Washington in September 2001, he was a deeply worried man; Pakistan was unhealthily friendly with the Taliban government in Kabul, which was demanding Karzai's extradition, and he was afraid the Pakistani government might agree.

The 9/11 attacks changed all that. The Americans and British were casting round for a new Afghan leader who would set up a post-Taliban government. Their previous nominee, Abdul Haq, had been murdered by the Taliban after being captured in the mountains outside Kabul. Among Lyse's many scoops at that time was the first reaction from Karzai to the news that an international conference in Bonn had proposed him as Afghanistan's interim leader. In a letter to me, she wrote:

> I immediately called Karzai on his satellite phone for his reaction. He replied, 'Am I the new leader?'
>
> 'Haven't they told you?' I asked.
>
> 'I've been fighting,' he said. He asked if I was sure it was true, which made me a bit nervous. But I said I'd heard it on the BBC. So I asked for his reaction, in case it *was* true. And in true Karzai form he simply said 'That's nice.' When I reported it I was tempted to say 'very nice', but that wasn't what he said, so I reported his reaction faithfully. A short time after, news emerged he had been injured by an errant US air strike that morning. But he didn't mention it during our call.

A year later, the BBC asked Lyse to make a report to mark the anniversary of 9/11. She came up with the idea of taking a close look at Hamid Karzai, who was still the darling of the West. Karzai, who always enjoyed media attention, agreed to do it. The cameraman was to be Phil Goodwin, a big, highly intelligent man, Cambridge-educated, who had opted for camera work after some years as a producer and as a BBC correspondent. It was an unusual move, but Goodwin was always his own man. His ability to shoot beautiful pictures was undoubted, and he had a courage and a determination which made him hugely valuable on a shoot. He had his own views, and was never shy about making them known.

Lyse describes what followed:

> We hung around the lovely Palace, day in day out, filming all the turbaned tribal delegations arriving en masse from the provinces, the launch of a new currency, the visits of ambassadors and spy chiefs. Then one day Karzai said he was going to Kandahar for the wedding of his half-brother, Ahmed Wali. No media were allowed, but we were told we could come along.

At this stage, although the security position was hugely unsettled in Afghanistan, Karzai's close protection team was still being trained, and his American bodyguards were constantly begging Washington for armoured vehicles to travel round in. Karzai made things even harder for them by wading into the crowds to shake hands and standing up in open-topped vehicles.

He and his entourage, which included Lyse and Phil Goodwin, had just finished inspecting the mansion in Kandahar where Mullah Omar, the head of the Taliban, had lived. The convoy was pulling out, with Lyse in a car near the front. Phil filmed Karzai's vehicle as it drove out of the compound.

> Karzai had been leaving in his SUV, which was a few vehicles behind us. A young man leaned forward in the crowds to greet him. The young boy's dream had been to work for the President. The President leaned out the window toward him.
>
> At that moment another young boy, whose mission was to kill Karzai, moved in and opened fire. Phil just kept filming even as the shots rang out. When he was shouted at to take cover, he went just inside an open building on the other side of the convoy and calmly and bravely kept filming.

Incidents like this are usually impossible to film properly; just think of the patchy, deeply unsatisfactory coverage of John

F. Kennedy's or Anwar Sadat's assassination. Because no one is expecting it, it takes a relatively long time for the person working the camera to realise what's happening, and the chances are very strong that it won't be switched on or focused at the key moment. Assassination attempts are usually marked by pictures of the aftermath – the camera moving round all over the place, the chaos as people shout and push and panic.

Phil Goodwin's coverage was entirely different. Now, as you watch it, you almost have the feeling that it's part of a feature film. Steady and clear, it captured every part of the action with a remarkable calmness: no excitement, no shaking, no crash zooms. Phil's camera was running before the shooting took place, and he carried on filming until the entire incident was over. Later, a number of security agencies used his pictures on their training courses, to demonstrate how not to protect a president.

The whole group was rushed to the main US base outside Kandahar, where American Rangers surrounded them. For her report, Lyse needed to get Karzai's reaction to the murder attempt, so with the camera running she and Phil went into the room where he was sitting. Lyse, who is instinctively warm and caring, warned Phil that she wouldn't be able to speak to Karzai as though this were just another incident; she would have to greet him as a friend. But he filmed it carefully, so that the more personal part of the interview could be cut out.

How was he, Lyse asked Karzai?

"'I'm fine," he replied. I then said something to the effect that "someone just tried to kill you". "Really?" he replied; more classic Karzai. We wondered later if he was still in shock.'

Calls soon started flooding in to Lyse from all round the world. The BBC, not realising that she was with Karzai, rang to tell her there were reports in Kabul that there'd been an attempt on his life; did she know anything about this?

She and Goodwin flew back to Kabul during the night, then edited and sent their report very early in the morning. Karzai asked to see the raw footage, and spotted that it hadn't been an American bodyguard who'd saved his life (though an Afghan-American close protection man sitting in the car behind Karzai had fired out through the window); it was the Afghan boy who loved Karzai and had shaken his hand. When the shots rang out he'd jumped on the assassin and lost his own life in saving Karzai's. This was important to the new government, of course: the leader's life had been saved by an Afghan, not by an American.

The report which Lyse Doucet and Phil Goodwin compiled was one of the best pieces of action filming ever seen; and what was remarkable about it was the way in which both of them kept their heads all the way through and stayed utterly calm. Before the BBC team left Kandahar for Kabul, Lyse turned to Karzai's half-brother, Ahmed Wali, and said: 'What a day this was!'

'Of course it was a big day,' he answered; 'it was my wedding.' Following Afghan tradition, his bride hadn't even been there. Celebrations in the old style like this are all-male affairs.

The BBC high-risk team rang Lyse later and asked if she had been wearing body armour during the attack.

'No,' she said. 'We were at a wedding.'

I can hear the studio in London through my earpiece. 'Alex, we can see you, coming to you in ten seconds. . . nine, eight, seven, six, five. . . And now we can cross live to Tripoli, where our correspondent is with the rebel convoy heading into the town, Alex. . .'

We'd done it. I start babbling about the scene, telling him these people are welcoming the Opposition fighters, there is no resistance, and the gunfire they can hear is celebratory gunfire – men firing their weapons into the air but not at each other, not at anyone intentionally. There are bullets flying everywhere, though, and showering the back of the pick-up. It's dangerous in its own right. Several land on Jim's arms as he is trying to hold the camera steady. He holds fast and they singe his skin. Afterwards he's left with a lot of red weals on his forearm. I feel one land next to me and stupidly I pick it up and drop it instantly – it's burning hot.

As quoted in Alex Crawford's *Colonel Gaddafi's Hat*, it was one of the biggest scoops of recent times: the fall of Colonel Gaddafi's capital, Tripoli, to the rebel forces. There were plenty of foreign correspondents in the city already, but they were penned in at the five-star Rixos Hotel, where the government had kept them virtual prisoners. Only one correspondent entered Tripoli with the rebels and ended up in the central square: Alex Crawford, together with her team from Sky News.

Compared with the stock characters of foreign news reporting, Alex seemed an unlikely figure: aged forty-eight at the time, with four young children. She had been a foreign correspondent for only six years when Tripoli fell, and during those six years she had been the Royal Television Society's journalist of the year no fewer than three times. Driving into Tripoli would give her a fourth award.

People who are interested in working in front of the camera for television news tend to think that being a presenter is the thing to aim for. In fact, presenting is a difficult job without all that many rewards. 'Nothing more than reading autocue,' people often say, yet it's much more than that. The art is to read autocue while seeming to be making it up as you go along; plus showing that you have a personality. When things go wrong and the ratings fall, you are more likely to get the sack than anyone else. Worse, your daily existence is tiring and stressful without being particularly enjoyable; and the greatest satisfaction is to get through an entire programme without any glitches.

Alex Crawford understood right from the start that for her the best job in television news was to be a foreign correspondent. She was turned down no fewer than four times for the job, but never gave up trying. When someone asked her, on one of the many television and radio interviews she did after Tripoli, how she'd managed to succeed, her answer was a straightforward one: 'Never take no for an answer.'

Her background was complex and interesting. Her father was British, her mother Chinese. She was born in Nigeria, lived as a child in Zambia, was educated for a time in Rhodesia – now Zimbabwe – where the children learned 'terrorist drill' as well as fire drill. She did some training on the *Rand Daily Mail* in Johannesburg, an excellent, liberal newspaper which was eventually forced out of business by the National Party in white South Africa. Moving to Britain, she worked on the *Wokingham Times*, a small local paper which nevertheless produced a remarkable number of top journalists. She went to BBC Radio Nottingham, then reached the BBC newsroom in London, but as a sub-editor. The work, she said later, was deadly dull.

The BBC didn't seem likely to make her a foreign correspondent, so she left a good job there and went to a less secure one at TV-am, which was plagued with strikes, and had no real money and a short future. From there, in 1989, she went to Sky News when it launched. Those were exciting days, when a buccaneering team of Australians showed the more staid Brits how to run a twenty-four-hour show. There was a lot of energy, and, compared with BBC and ITN, the staff were young, vibrant and rebellious. For ten years Alex took time off to have her children, but she came back each time, still wanting to be a foreign correspondent and, more especially, to get back to Africa. And in the end, after a great deal more refusal to take no for an answer, it worked.

Some top correspondents are fired by a desire to beat the opposition. Television news is one of the most competitive occupations on earth, and winning is, if not everything, then certainly highly important. Alex Crawford seems not to be made that way. Her concern is to be there, to get the story; the rest doesn't matter so much.

In Libya, getting into Tripoli as she did wasn't simply a slice of good luck, though luck always seems to enter these things somewhere. For Alex, it was the result of hard work and careful marshalling of her contacts in the opposition. The rebels who took her to Tripoli knew her, because she had spent time with them and got their message out to the world. As a result, they all respected her.

Now she had driven into the city with them and was broadcasting live via a gadget called a BGAN, which stands for Broadband Global Area Network and utilises the Inmarsat satellite system. It is the size of a laptop, and in 2011 was by far the best equipment available. The problem was keeping it powered up, since live broadcasting drained the battery very fast. Alex's producer had the answer: a gadget which plugged the BGAN into the cigarette lighter of their vehicle. It worked perfectly:

> I'm trying to reassure the viewers, who I know in the past have been horrified at the sound of gunfire behind me and do worry about my crew and our safety. I am also bearing in mind that my boss, John Ryley – who is Sky's Head of News – is monitoring these pictures as they are coming in and he will want to know that everything is under control and I am not jeopardising any of my team's safety. He wants to count us all back.
>
> 'I am wearing this flak jacket and helmet not because I am afraid or fear for our safety,' I say on air, 'but because there are so many bullets flying around due to the celebratory gunfire.'
>
> The pictures and audio we are sending from the back of the pick-up go through a 'gallery' in London which acts as mission control. The gallery is full of the essential behind-the-scenes staff who actually make sure our reports and broadcasts get on air. 'We're staying with you, Crawfie,' says the producer in London, Adam Jay. 'The pictures are great.' That's all I needed to hear.

The other big television news organisations all carried out postmortems in the days that followed, trying to work out how they had been beaten by Alex Crawford and her small team. The BBC had a much larger group of people, but they were imprisoned, almost literally, in the Rixos. Sky is a small, highly efficient organisation whose watchword is flexibility. Its audience is tiny, but it makes up for that by attracting attention. Above all, it isn't burdened with the need to produce a programme of record. The BBC, by contrast, has a huge audience worldwide, which it has built up because it has a large staff of highly qualified correspondents everywhere, and it carries the weight of responsibility heavily. It is the difference between a motorcycle courier and a bus. Often, those of us on the bus would love to hop off and weave our way on a motorbike through the traffic; but in the end we stay on because of the service we provide. There's no doubt which is more fun, though.

Once, long ago, working for BBC television news was much like working for Sky is today. You made your own decisions, you took your chances, and because you felt (as Alex Crawford and her colleagues from Sky feel now) that your efforts, and your efforts alone, would decide whether your organisation succeeded or not, you made yourself the master of the story, finding your contacts and working on them until the story reached fruition. Now, in big organisations, the decisions are increasingly made in London, and the correspondents on the spot are told what to do. Their sense of personal responsibility is vitiated. The real enjoyment of being a television foreign correspondent belongs to the free agents: people like Alex Crawford.

The camera has been set up on the top of a building, looking down along the length of one of the main streets in Mosul, the third biggest city in Iraq, which was captured from the Iraqi army by a small force of Islamic State fighters in the summer of 2014. It is now the capital of the caliphate which Islamic State has set up across Syria and Iraq. The camera is facing west, and the sun is setting in the centre of the picture: this is not a good position from which to film an interview. In front of the camera stands an over-weight young man with a scrubby, gingerish beard, glasses, and a Bedouin scarf tied round his head. A leather holster hangs under his left arm, with a handgun in it. The other man, his interviewer, is elderly. He too wears glasses and a Bedouin scarf. By coming here, he has achieved something no other Western journalist has managed: he has found his way into the heart of Islamic State and will return to tell the world about it. It is one of the great scoops of the new century.

Jürgen Todenhöfer, at seventy-four, has been a German judge, and a member of the European Parliament. His career has been a distinguished one; and now he has turned journalist and taken the extraordinary risk of coming to the most dangerous place on earth for Westerners. On top of this, he has raised the stakes by bringing his son with him to carry out the filming and do the rest of the technical work. Despite the scarf round his head, Jürgen Todenhöfer is not disguised in any way. Everyone knows exactly who he is, and why he is here. He has put his life, and the life of his son, into the hands of Islamic State – the organisation whose members have sawn off the heads of their prisoners on camera, lingering greedily over the spurting blood, and burned a Jordanian pilot alive in a cage. These are people whose trademark is cruelty and blood lust.

Behind the speakers, three armed men are standing with their backs to the setting sun. They are wearing black clothes and black balaclavas which hide everything but their eyes. They look very much like the men who beheaded the Western journalists and the aid workers.

The man whom Todenhöfer is about to interview is also German. He had a conventional Protestant upbringing, but converted to Islam in his late teens and managed to get to Syria to join Islamic State. Although he looks flabby and out of condition, he seems to have been a brave fighter, and was one of the small Islamic State force which captured Mosul from 30,000 soldiers of the Iraqi national army in June 2014. His Islamic name is Abu Qatadah. Behind him the gunmen look around listlessly; they can't speak German, the language in which the interview is conducted, so they quickly become bored. In the background, cars drive up and down the main street of Mosul. It could be anywhere in the Middle East, except that it's a city in the hands of the most extreme organisation on earth.

The interview is a long one, and lasts through sunset and well beyond. It doesn't reveal any new facts, and the German convert who is speaking doesn't do much beyond repeating the standard, threat-laden discourse of Islamic State; but what is remarkable is the way in which, despite this menacing atmosphere, Jürgen Todenhöfer puts the questions that demand to be put. The temptation, when you are surrounded by deeply hostile people, is to moderate your questions; it is something everyone in this position needs to fight against. You have to remember that you will be watched by people sitting in the total safety of their own homes far away, who will be scandalised if you don't put the questions toughly. Todenhöfer doesn't seem to feel the pressure. The shot is framed to show him standing face to face with Abu Qatadah, and you can see that, from time to time, Todenhöfer looks quite irritable at the kind of answers he is getting. His questions aren't aggressive, but they are strong and insistent: he doesn't let Abu Qatadah get away with anything. Altogether, it is probably the most enlightening exchange which any Western journalist has had with Islamic State. This is a shortened version of the interview accessible on YouTube:

TODENHÖFER: What will IS do once it has conquered large parts of Syria and Iraq? Will it keep going?

ABU QATADAH: The main goal of IS is to establish the Sharia of God (may He be glorified and exalted), in both Iraq or Syria. We have now witnessed various extensions of IS power in Libya, Sinai, Egypt, Yemen and also to the Arabian peninsula, to so-called Saudi Arabia. We don't have frontiers, we only have front lines. That means the expansion will not stop.

TODENHÖFER: So that means you also want to conquer Europe one day?

ABU QATADAH: No, no, we *will* one day conquer Europe. We don't just want to, we're going to. And we are sure about that. [Laughs.]

TODENHÖFER: What is the role of the different religions within the IS [Islamic State]? What rights do Christians and Jews have?

ABU QATADAH: In the IS Jews & Christians and some scholars say even the fire worshippers have the possibility to pay the Jizyah, a per capita protection tax. If they pay that, they are protected from us and of course they are protected in their religion. Everything that is part of their religion can be practised. If they don't pay the Jizyah they will all be killed.

TODENHÖFER: Killed?

ABU QATADAH: Yes, or expelled...

TODENHÖFER: Will you kill all Muslims in Europe who don't adopt your religious beliefs?

ABU QATADAH: He who doesn't adopt our religious beliefs, who doesn't adopt Islam, if he persists on his wrong path, then there is no other option but the sword.

TODENHÖFER: These statements you are making are very hard.

ABU QATADAH: These are not just statements that I make, this is the verdict of Islam. The verdict for apostasy. Every apostate will be killed.

TODENHÖFER: You, the IS, have beheaded people in dramatic ways, and you have filmed it. You have introduced slavery. You have enslaved Yazidis. Do you consider the beheading of people and slavery a progress for humankind?

ABU QATADAH: That's a part of our religion, to teach the infidel the fear which they should have towards us. And we will continue to behead people. No matter whether they are Shi'a, Christian, Jews or anything else. We will continue to practise this. And the people should think about it.

TODENHÖFER: Do you consider slavery progress?

ABU QATADAH: Definitely. Progress, help, and so on. Slavery always existed. It existed under Christians and Jews.

TODENHÖFER: You used to be a German Protestant and you became a Muslim. And now you are in Mosul, which you helped to conquer. Will you go back to Germany some day?

ABU QATADAH: We will definitely go back, and we won't be joking. We'll bring our weapons and our fighters with us, and we'll kill anyone who doesn't accept Islam or else pay the protective tax.

The essence of Jürgen Todenhöfer's exclusive lay, not in the details of his interview with Abu Qatadah – such things can be gleaned from any of the half-baked websites which support Islamic

State – but in the fact that he was able to get to Mosul, spend ten days there, and leave in safety. An unknown number of other journalists have travelled to the territory occupied by IS, but have either been held prisoner or been murdered in particularly grue-some ways.

Todenhöfer's method of going about it – his M.O. – was to write to the eighty or so German jihadis he could find on Facebook to ask if he could interview them about their reasons for leaving Germany. Fifteen replied, and one of them said he could put Todenhöfer in touch with the IS 'media department'. Over a period of seven months in 2014, Todenhöfer had a total of more than twenty hours of discussions with this man over the internet, discussing questions of ideology, war, and the beheading on camera of the American journalist James Foley. And of course they talked about Todenhöfer's safety if he went to meet IS; he stressed that he would only go if he had realistic guarantees.

Finally he was given an undertaking from the office of the caliph-ate, the top governing body of IS, that he would be allowed to come and go. Todenhöfer had no idea whether this was genuine or not; it could, he said later, have been fake. But after his long discussions with the IS intermediary he decided he could trust their assurances. 'I didn't see any reason why they would spend so many months in discussion with me just to get me and then to cut off my head. That was not logical to me.'

It was an act of faith on Todenhöfer's part, that sudden mental lurch that journalists who find themselves in this sort of posi-tion sometimes experience. Others – Daniel Pearl, for instance, the American correspondent who was brutally murdered by al-Qaeda in Karachi – had the same feeling, that he could trust his interlocutors. In the end, reason and common sense take a back seat, and other, less reliable and less quantifiable faculties take over. But it was an enormous gamble; nowadays, no big news organisation I know in any Western country would allow one of its employees to do this. Todenhöfer's great advantage was that he didn't have a boss to convince; and perhaps (I write this at the age of seventy-one) a seventy-four-year-old journalist feels that he has less to lose than a younger one. But it was an act of great courage:

> They knew that I had made very negative comments on them before. They knew I had met [President] Assad [of Syria]. I told them clearly that 'I am not on your side', and they said, 'Yes, that is not our problem, we don't care about your opinion, we want you to tell what you have seen here, not the opinion that you had beforehand.'

The whole experience was dangerous and unpleasant. Sometimes – on their last day, for instance – Todenhöfer and his son, the photographer/cameraman, had no food or water at all. In Mosul, as they were driving through the town, an American drone identified someone they were with, and a bomb followed very soon afterwards. When they got back to Raqqa after spending some time in Mosul, they were delayed by three days. That saved their lives: two days before they arrived a Syrian bomb destroyed their apartment.

Ultimately, the reason why Todenhöfer went through this extraordinary experience was not to make money, nor to capture the world's attention for himself. It was for an ideal. At the end of the interview which he and his son filmed with Abu Qatadah on the rooftop in Mosul (extremely risky, one would have thought, with the drones buzzing round overhead), Todenhöfer put a written statement in German and English on the screen. It showed not only how much conscientious thought he had put into the entire project, but also his reasons for risking his life in this way:

> I have long thought about whether I should post this interview with Abu Qatadah, the German jihadist. But you can only defeat your opponents if you know them. For me, what Abu Qatadah represents has nothing to do with the compassionate Islam, represented by 99.9 per cent of our fellow citizens. It is with these moderate Muslims that we should ally ourselves to end the ideological kidnapping of their great religion by extremists.

Islam is a religion of justice and mercy; it has nothing to do with terrorism.

For me, as a lifelong foreign correspondent, these words and the courage with which Jürgen Todenhöfer went to the most dangerous place on earth, and managed to return, make him one of the best and bravest of all the people I have described in this book. The rest of us can only stand back and admire what he did.

TWELVE

Back-Up

> The correspondent is just the one the viewer sees. People
> forget the other ones, who put the correspondent there
> and make sure he does what he's supposed to do, when
> he's supposed to do it. But they're there, all right.
>
> Brian Barron, in conversation with the author, 1977

IT'S RARE FOR THE foreign correspondent to work entirely alone.
He or she usually depends on the help of a local fixer, a translator, a driver, or in some cases even a bodyguard. Newspaper or radio
correspondents, being solitary, often join forces with their competitors and share the services of fixers or drivers; it's both cheaper and
safer. Television correspondents, by contrast, work independently.
They usually have their own small team – a cameraman or -woman
and perhaps a producer – as well as local helpers. Each member
of the group will have a different perspective on the work they do.
Being part of a small team tends to act as a real strength for a correspondent. Reporting can be a fairly lonely business, with constant
decisions which often need to be made on the basis of inadequate
information and a lot of guesswork.

When I was working in Africa as a foreign correspondent for
radio – one of the lonelier professions – I came across a correspond-
ent-and-producer team that gave me grounds for a good deal of
envy. Richard Lindley and Robin Denselow worked for the BBC
current affairs programme *Panorama*, and tended to specialise in
reporting on Africa. They were a formidable pair: Lindley, the correspondent, Cambridge-educated, tall, well dressed in neatly pressed
khaki, impossibly handsome; Denselow, in those days the producer

(he later became a correspondent in his own right), educated at New College, Oxford, and with a wide range of outside interests, which included reviewing rock concerts for the *Guardian*. I was impressed by each of them individually, and even more so by the way they worked together. What must it be like, I wondered, to have someone to debate everything with, to plan your strategies with, to prove that two heads were indeed better than one, to enjoy that degree of companionship and trust?

I met them in the Angolan capital, Luanda, where they were reporting on the civil war between the MPLA, the FNLA and UNITA. In the fading heat of the evening we sat in a bar nursing our drinks and talking about the situation. I was only a little younger than they were, but my status as a radio correspondent put me several notches below them, as representatives of the grandest current affairs programme in British television. It was then that they told me of their experiences a year or so earlier, when they were caught without the necessary accreditation.

They were locked up in a highly unpleasant gaol close to the airport, where prisoners were routinely beaten up or executed. The section where they were held contained two hundred or more prisoners, and there was only one filthy latrine for them all. Lindley and Denselow, as the only white men there, were ordered to clean it out. It was the most disgusting job either of them had ever been forced to do, but they decided to make the best they possibly could of it. Laughing and joking, they marched down to the latrine with their mops at the slope and set about cleaning it up, singing American spirituals at the tops of their voices as they scraped away the accumulated filth of years. Their energy and enthusiasm earned them the praise and applause of the entire prison; and when they were released soon afterwards they were given a joyful send-off.

This story stayed with me long afterwards, as an example of what teamwork could achieve. I had often asked my bosses for a full-time producer, but was always told it was impossible. It wasn't until the 1990s that a namesake, Paul Simpson, was given the job of travelling with me to work on our reports. Soon afterwards my new wife, Dee, was made the producer of a programme we had devised together, known immodestly as *Simpson's World*; she was paid peanuts for her work, but the programme covered the cost of her air travel, and since she shared my room and ate with us, her living costs were quietly buried in the general production budget. So we were happy.

The result was that three people called Simpson would fetch up at each new hotel. Paul and Dee were more or less the same age; I was a couple of decades older. As they always do, the staff at the reception desk would make up their minds about us as we stood there: I was Paul's father, they assumed, and he and Dee were a couple. It was always a pleasure to watch their faces as Dee and I went to one room, and Paul to another. The programme continued for ten years even when Dee suffered a series of miscarriages. When, finally, she became pregnant again, I insisted that she should stay at home and nurse the pregnancy through to term, even if it meant there would be no more *Simpson's World*s. By the time our little son Rafe was old enough for her to start travelling again, there had been a change of management at the BBC and the programme was discontinued.

For five years after that, Oggy Boytchev worked as my producer. During an undercover trip to Zimbabwe, where the BBC was banned, one of my favourite cameramen, Nigel Bateson, explained to the manager of a hotel where we were staying undercover that I was Nigel's eccentric English uncle, and Oggy, born in Bulgaria and given political asylum in Britain in the 1980s, was my Bulgarian butler. At the end of the five years he took a generous BBC redundancy package, and was obliged to leave me in Tripoli during Colonel Gaddafi's losing battle against his enemies in 2011.

At that stage the BBC's foreign editor, Jon Williams, decided to team me up with a producer who had been working for television news for more than twenty years, but whom I had scarcely met during that time. Peter Leng, a former exhibitioner at St John's College, Cambridge, was twenty years younger than I. That apart, our backgrounds weren't altogether dissimilar: we had both started out as middle-class south Londoners with a love of travel. Peter's abiding interest had been India, and he had studied Indian history at Cambridge. Like me, he had three children, though mine came from two marriages and his from only one. His youngest son was called Ralph; my son was called Rafe. Peter was quiet and thoughtful, but steely; I was much more flashy. As a result, perhaps, our partnership worked rather well. There were never any fireworks between us and like a married couple we soon started to anticipate each other's ideas and intentions. We first met when I invited him, rather primly, to tea at Fortnum & Mason's; it was just about the last predictable thing we were to do.

Over the years that followed, Peter and I have done some remarkable travelling, from Iraq, Afghanistan and Libya to Russia, China and Nigeria. Together, we devised the first news programme on BBC domestic television for thirty years. It was called *The Editors*, and drew on the formidable talents of some of the BBC's best journalists. Although it was buried late at night, around 11.30, it was good enough to persuade nearly a million people to stay up and watch it. Half of them actually turned their television sets on for it, and it often got double the audience of the *Newsnight* programme which went out immediately before it.

It didn't last, even though it cost remarkably little and was probably the least expensive news and current affairs programme on British television. We insisted that everyone who made a film for *The Editors* had to address a particular question, and answer it clearly and well – not merely give it the 'on-the-one-hand-and-on-the-other' treatment. The most controversial question of the programme's year-long run was one that Peter and I set ourselves to answer: did white people have a future in South Africa? Merely posing it gave rise to howls of rage on all sides there; the ruling ANC was infuriated by it. So were many white South Africans, whether liberals or old-style conservatives, because it undermined their confidence in the future. Only a few thoughtful people, black and white, gave our film their support; yet it proved remarkably prescient.

Over the next few years, demonstrators on university campuses and city centres started demanding the dismantling of statues to former heroes of the Afrikaner and British-descended communities. 'You are not African,' a well-known black commentator wrote to a white one in an open letter in the *City Press* newspaper. Some tried to stop the teaching of Afrikaans, which had formerly been the language of apartheid but was now attempting a comeback as one of South Africa's official languages. In response to all this, white racism showed its face on a number of South African campuses. The economic position of white people in South Africa was declining as the rand fell, and the exodus to Britain, Australia, Canada and the US increased. Three years on, many more people in South Africa would probably think it was a reasonable, if still unsettling, question to ask; and asking unsettling questions is surely one of the more important aims of journalism. Unless, of course, you want to be the stooge of a particular party or government.

Since the reporting of news is often a collegial business, it would be good at this point to hear the stories of some of those who work alongside the foreign correspondent: producers, translators, cameramen, photographers.

THE PRODUCER'S STORY

It was Boxing Day 2004, and in sweltering Singapore, the man who later became my producer, Peter Leng, was out with his family ice-skating. A single beep from Peter's mobile phone put an end to that. The BBC correspondent in Bangkok was messaging: 'Four tourists dead in Phuket from tidal wave.'

At first, information was slow and it was hard to be certain how serious things were. The correspondent, Kylie Morris, was despatched to Phuket with her producer, Annie Phrommayon, to find out. As the hours passed, it became more and more clear that this was a disaster on a huge scale. That evening Peter, together with the BBC's Asia correspondent, Andrew Harding, and a cameraman, Jone Chang, from a well-known Singaporean journalistic dynasty, gathered at the airport to fly to Phuket to join Kylie and Annie.

In my experience, you go through a variety of emotions at a time like this. Abandoning the family tugs at the heartstrings, and you sometimes feel distinctly nervous at the prospect of whatever you're heading into; but meeting your colleagues and settling in to the atmosphere of jokiness and friendship quickly sets up its own atmosphere around you. They become like a kind of alternative family, people you like and trust and share a variety of experiences with. By the time you're sitting on the plane, the transition is complete. Home is shut off for a fortnight or so; a new reality has taken over.

It's very much harder for those whom you have left behind. The person you live with stands waving on the doorstep and watching as the taxi carrying you and your suitcase drives off down the street. Then he or she turns back into a home which, after all the bustle and panic of hasty packing, has suddenly become silent and empty. They, not you, have to make the adjustments. My ten-year-old son's teacher once told me: 'I always know when you're away reporting somewhere. Rafe looks out of the window more, and he's quieter than usual.' Being a foreign correspondent is a deeply selfish occupation. You make all the moves and have all the experiences, while the people at home pay the real price.

Phuket proved to be merely the first and easiest step for the team. What had started as a report on a small-scale, mostly European tragedy quickly widened. Reports from Aceh province, far away in northern Indonesia, started trickling in. An unthinkable catastrophe had plainly occurred: thousands dead, entire communities wiped out. Phuket was no longer the place to be: Aceh now seemed like the centre of the story. Rachel Harvey, the BBC's correspondent in Jakarta, together with her producer, Becky Lipscombe, went straight to Aceh, accompanied by a Singapore-based cameraman, Joe Phua. Joe, another scion of the great camera clan there, is a close personal friend of mine. In 2001, when the BBC went into Kabul as the Taliban fell, Joe hobbled along with us. He had broken a metatarsal in his foot a few days before, but, dosed up with heavy-duty painkillers, he refused to stay behind and got some of the best pictures of that day.

Thanks in part to the quick thinking of another friend of mine, then the BBC's foreign editor, Malcolm Downing, Rachel's team got to Aceh well before any other international journalists, and started sending back reports on the disaster which had followed the tsunami. What had happened in other countries, Thailand, Sri Lanka and India, was terrible enough; the BBC was now revealing to the world that what had happened in Aceh was cataclysmic.

For Peter and his team, a complicated series of manoeuvres now followed. The highly successful BBC cameraman, Darren Conway, invariably known from his initials as DC, joined Andrew Harding and they went straight off to Banda Aceh. Peter had to go back to Singapore to pick up supplies. A story as big as this, far from any main population centre and with disease and starvation as its accompaniment, would require enough food and bottled water to last for at least a week before new supplies could be brought in. Each member of the team brought a sleeping bag and a personal medical kit, but knowing the dangers of disease Peter bought a big batch of Dettol hand cleanser, plus basic medicines. He also gathered together quantities of tinned chicken soup, plus as much in the way of fresh fruit and vegetables as he could pack and take on a plane. The excess baggage costs were huge.

There were other problems. A separatist struggle had been going on in Aceh for many years, and the whole area was out of bounds to foreign journalists. Andrew and DC reached Medan, the only international airport on the island of Sumatra, but were barred from going any further. After a while, though, some skilful diplomacy got them in, and Peter soon managed to get the blue military cards that were required for the BBC people who followed. Soon, the BBC had set up a beachhead in Banda Aceh and was broadcasting live. It was a triumph of planning and hard work.

The entire coastal area of Aceh had been entirely devastated. Not a single building seemed to be untouched, so finding somewhere for the team to live and work was an immense problem. Everywhere they looked, the mud-covered ground was littered with the belongings of people who had died or fled. Peter found himself examining the pitiful photo albums which were all that remained of entire lives and families, or looking at the toys which had been swept up by the flood and left lying in the mud. The whole coast was deserted: no police, no soldiers, no relief workers, and few surviving inhabitants.

The team took over what was left of a house on the edge of the area the tsunami had destroyed. The survivors were packing up their belongings and leaving, so Peter rented three more houses nearby and hired local people to clean out the mud and debris from them. There were jobs for other local people too; he hired four cars and drivers, and motorbike riders to pick up equipment and video cassettes. He even found a cleaner to look after the BBC houses.

The business of transmitting reports back to London presented some difficult technical problems. There was a local telecoms building with a large satellite dish which had survived, though there was thick mud everywhere. Joe Phua managed to get the station up and working, and the team was on air quickly. Broadcasting live soon became harder and harder, as international crews started arriving and demanding air time of their own. So did navigating the complexity of satellite paths to London. But no live shot failed, and the viewers at home and around the world were given no idea of the difficulties of gathering news in the wake of an unthinkably large natural disaster.

The problems of keeping the team supplied became greater and greater. There were dead bodies lying in the ditches and fields and gardens all round them, so the local water supply was deadly. They could only drink bottled water; and because of the oppressive heat they each needed a lot of it. Peter soon noticed that every phone call he made to Malcolm Downing in London started and ended with the urgent question of water. Peter found a driver and paid him $200 to fetch food, water and fuel from Medan, not knowing whether he would ever see the man again. He did: the driver came back laden with all the necessities and the correct amount of change, so the team was able to eat, drink and run the generator which kept everything going. After that, regular convoys were established, and supplies arrived every twelve hours.

The work was immensely hard, and Peter and most of the others usually did twenty-hour days. All ten of them slept in one room, with their sleeping bags in a line down the middle. On various occasions they would be wakened by earth tremors, and had to run out into the road in their underwear. They lived on noodles and packs of army MREs – 'meals ready to eat' – but they had one luxury: thick Aceh coffee. Peter insisted that everyone had to make regular use of the anti-bacterial handwashes he had brought, but there were problems with the housekeeper. She had to be persuaded not to wash the dishes in the squat lavatory, which all ten of them were using. For washing themselves there was just a bucketful of brownish water that came from somewhere they preferred not to think about.

Each day, when they went outside, they had to cope with the powerful smell of death. The bloated bodies still lay uncollected in the broiling sun. Peter later wrote to me that even a short walk through the rubble was a sickening experience:

> Everything was gone, everything destroyed, killed. The word 'indescribable' kept being used – well, it was. It was a hell on earth that no-one could have imagined in their wildest nightmares. Our correspondents tried to find new words every day to try to convey the horror, and their resilience was amazing.

By now, given the insatiable demands of the BBC, Peter and his colleagues were producing material for four twenty-four-hour television and radio news services, plus innumerable programmes, day and night. Its set-up in Banda Aceh became a major focal point in town, with newly arriving journalists knocking on the door to ask for floor space, help or advice. Soon a mobile BBC satellite dish arrived, so that the engineers could get out on a flatbed truck and broadcast live from the ruins of the town, deep inside the massive zone of destruction. Peter even managed to borrow a helicopter from somewhere.

After two weeks of working flat out on four hours' sleep and often less, fielding calls by the hundred, coming up with the ideas for new stories, sorting out all sorts of logistical complications, and fighting the rival landlords who were each claiming to own the houses the BBC was renting, Peter was told he could stand down and go home. It had been a shattering experience for him: 'What will stay with me personally was discovering a dead baby just yards from our house, some ten days after the wave hit, the body rotting and crawling with maggots.' It was the kind of thing that someone less resilient might have needed counselling for.

But by the time he left, the value of what he and the other journalists in Banda Aceh had done was starting to show. Aid was starting to flow in, and the tone of the reporting was changing. The people of Aceh had lost everything: their homes, their families, their friends, their community groups and structures. Now, after those dreadful early days, the story the correspondents were able to tell was one of resurgence and new hope.

THE TRANSLATOR'S STORY

Madame Wu was tough. She was also, Clare Hollingworth decided, a true believer. Her hair was scraped back on her head, her little round glasses glinted with pride in the achievements of Chairman Mao and the Cultural Revolution, and she disapproved deeply of the decadent West.

'Faugh!' she would say. 'You've been eating cheese again. I can't take it.' And she would sit as far away from Clare as the office allowed, and glare at her.

It was the early 1970s, and Clare was one of a tiny number of foreign journalists who were allowed to work in the closed, threatening atmosphere of Maoist Beijing. Each day Madame Wu would translate the Chinese newspapers and prepare a long transcript from them. Each day Clare would go through it carefully, and note the things Madame Wu seemed to be leaving out. The Chinese newspapers were pretty much all the same, but if they mentioned any shortages or any accidents or disasters, Madame Wu's transcript would ignore them. The only way Clare would find out about them was by listening to the BBC World Service or ringing up the Reuters bureau.

'Have you seen anything about the landslide in Guangzhou?' she would ask Madame Wu.

The pattern was always the same. At first Madame Wu would deny that any such thing had occurred, and then she would snatch up the newspapers in a bad-tempered way and scan them again.

'There's nothing like you are talking about,' she would say eventually. 'Just a very small incident in the south of Guangzhou. It's not worthy of your attention.'

'Perhaps I should be the judge of that,' Clare would reply, and Madame Wu would hammer out a translation on her elderly Chinese-made typewriter, which for some reason had an Italian keyboard, her fingers making a particularly loud noise on the keys.

'There!' she would say in her sulky fashion, ripping the sheet of paper out of the typewriter carriage and throwing it across the desk.

Clare longed to sack Madame Wu and get somebody more congenial, but the ministry, which (however ineffectually) oversaw the needs of journalists and diplomats, would never have considered it. No foreigner could sack a Chinese citizen merely for having a bad attitude or being lazy.

It was a hugely exciting time to be in Beijing, and Clare knew she had been right to volunteer for the posting. The Cultural Revolution was starting to fade, and the question of Mao's successor was becoming more and more important. Lin Biao, Mao's close ally and minister of defence, was already considering his bid for power. Later the bid failed, and he escaped to Russia (which was probably pulling the strings) in a hijacked plane, but crashed into a mountain along the way.

Clare was reluctant to allow Madame Wu to get her down; and she had an impulsive, sweet side. One time, when she got back from Hong Kong, she presented Madame Wu with a box of chocolates. Madame Wu's eyes opened wide with surprise and pleasure when she opened it, and she popped one into her mouth immediately. She almost smiled; and then the habitual bad-tempered look returned to her face.

'Thank you,' she said mechanically, as though the chocolates meant nothing to her. But Clare noticed how carefully she closed the lid and put the box away in the shopping basket she brought to work every day.

She was never quite so hostile again, and when Clare came back from a trip to London with another present – a brooch – Madame Wu greeted her with an actual smile. It was brief and chilly, but there was no mistaking what it was. And the next day Madame Wu wore the brooch on her white shirt, underneath her Mao jacket, where no one could see it unless she pulled open the lapel. That created a small alliance between them: they each knew something about Madame Wu which the Chinese state didn't know.

She remained basically hostile, but when no one was around there were occasional little gestures which showed that a different relationship was developing between them. She no longer lectured Clare loudly on the superiority of the Chinese communist system. She even said she wished that Chinese people could dress in Mao suits of a colour other than black or dark blue. Once she actually laughed at something Clare said; and Clare had the impression that the laughter was pleasant, not scornful.

Life was difficult for Westerners in Beijing at that time. A Reuters correspondent told me how he and his colleagues decided that they had to try to speak to ordinary Chinese people just in order to maintain their self-respect as journalists. But it was very difficult – dangerous, even. They chose Thursdays as the day to reach out to the Beijing population. Each correspondent's turn only came round once every four weeks, and for three weeks, my friend said, you had plenty of other things to think about. But as your Thursday came irrevocably closer, you got more and more nervous; and then you were out on the street, facing whatever injury or humiliation the day might bring.

One approach was to stand in a bus queue and try to look inconspicuous; not easy, when everyone else was wearing Mao suits and the Reuters correspondents wore Western clothes. After a few minutes (the buses were slow and relatively rare) the correspondent would ask the person standing in front of them in Chinese where they came from. Sometimes they would answer. Sometimes they would start yelling immediately. Sometimes the correspondent would get a couple of questions in – more, perhaps. But it always ended up the same way. The police would be called, and would start laying about them with clubs. The correspondent might be arrested, or beaten up, or both. The bureau chief's Thursday was usually taken up with getting the correspondent free. My friend loved China and the Chinese, but he came to hate and fear Thursdays.

Clare Hollingworth wasn't expected to talk to people in the street, and Madame Wu increasingly became her conduit to the life of the city around her. She never revealed any secrets, and she remained outwardly loyal to the savage regime which had introduced the Cultural Revolution and its cruelties. Slowly, though, Clare began to realise that something else was going on behind those stern features. One day Clare started to show her some family pictures she had brought with her to Beijing: parents, cousins, nephews, nieces, a husband. It seemed to trigger something in Madame Wu. Clare knew she just had to wait until Madame Wu was ready to talk to her.

It happened the next day. Beijing wasn't like Moscow – there wasn't the money or the technological expertise to fix up microphones in the room. Even so, Madame Wu beckoned to her to come to the little windowless back room where they filed old newspapers. They sat on hard chairs facing each other.

Madame Wu had decided to open up. The tears were flooding down her face, and she reached out to hold Clare's hands in hers. She came, she said, from an old family of the upper bourgeoisie. At the height of the Cultural Revolution her father, who had been a professor of English literature, was beaten to a pulp by a gang of screaming Red Guards, and thrown out of a third-floor window. He took a long time to die, since no doctor or ambulanceman dared to come near him. Madame Wu had seen his body, but hadn't dared to come forward and kiss him or cradle his head as he died.

Now her own life was in danger, and she put up an elaborate front. She applied to the ministry for a job as a translator. They questioned her closely about how she came to speak English, but she insisted that she had learned it at school, and improved it on her own by listening to Chinese propaganda broadcasts to Hong Kong; she didn't mention her father, who had taught her good English. Perhaps the people from the ministry guessed, but they took her on because they needed English-speakers urgently.

Her husband, whom she married in the mid-1950s, came from a similar background, though his family had managed to escape persecution. They had two children, but knew they dared not trust them with any confidences about their past or the way they thought. Children were expected to inform on their parents as a matter of course if they saw any sign of nonconformity at home, and in many cases they were expected to take part in the savage punishments that were dealt out to parents who were exposed as political deviants.

Yet Madame Wu and her husband couldn't bear to cut them-selves off from their bourgeois past altogether. Once a year, on their wedding anniversary, they would put the children to bed with the aid of a sleeping draught. Then, when all their neighbours had gone to bed, they would turn off the lights and roll back the carpet in their living room. Madame Wu's husband had made a secret hiding place under the floorboards, where they kept a long card-board box. He would pull it out and open it. Inside, protected by tissue paper, lay a ball gown and a set of men's evening clothes. When they had got married, it was still permissible to wear clothes like this for the ceremony. Now it would be death if they were found to have kept them.

The couple would dress up in the clothes, and admire each other. Then they would take a turn or two round the floor, dancing a silent waltz, their footfalls as light as they could make them. It was just about the most dangerous thing they could conceivably have done. After a little more than a minute they would stop, take off the fine clothes, and pack them away for another year. It was, Madame Wu said, crying openly now, the one way in which the two of them could endure this terrible, cruel existence, where the children they loved were potentially their greatest enemies.

'And now,' said Madame Wu, still gripping Clare's hands in hers, 'you know my secret. I have put my life in your hands. Don't betray me.'

'*Jamais de la vie,*' said Clare, profoundly moved herself; never in life. And she never told anyone until the Cultural Revolution was over and done with, and life had become a little better and a little freer, even for descendants of the old bourgeoisie. In fact, Clare said, I was the first person she had ever told.

THE CAMERAMAN'S STORY

Cameramen (a term which is nowadays used to include the increasing number of women who operate cameras) are more important to television news than even correspondents or producers. True, a first-class writer can make up for poor pictures, but never to the point where badly shot pictures can seem good. A first-class producer can provide all the right conditions for a cameraman to work well, but it's the person with their finger on the button and their eye on the viewfinder who has to frame the action correctly and follow it as it develops. A lesser cameraman alongside Lyse Doucet at the assassination attempt on Hamid Karzai would have certainly got some good pictures, but they would mostly have been confused and unfocused. It was Phil Goodwin's steadiness in filming while the action was going on around him which ensured that his and Lyse's report was so good.

Cameramen are like the rest of us: they can be nervous or over-imaginative, they can see danger round every corner, they can have wives or husbands who insist angrily that things are getting too difficult and they must take on safer work in future. But there are plenty who just carry on and do the business, whatever that business may be. And when it becomes really dangerous, they still keep filming. Sometimes correspondents explain away their cameraman's steadfastness by saying that they have a more restricted sense of danger because the world they are seeing is a little rectangle of black and white objects in the viewfinder, while the rest of us are seeing the real thing in full colour. There are, of course, examples of cameramen and photographers taking pictures of the gunmen who are in the process of shooting them, which does argue a certain detachment from reality. But in general I don't believe the notion that, unlike the rest of us, some cameramen lack the natural instincts of self-preservation. I think they're just doing their job properly, and the rest of us are trying to explain away our timidity.

It's been my good fortune for half a century to have worked with, and sometimes against, some magnificent cameramen. Several of them have become close friends: Bob Prabhu, Tony Fallshaw, Joe Phua, Nigel Bateson and four or five others. Among them is Duncan Stone, a big, young-looking chap of around fifty who was trained by Mike Davies, one of the best picture editors I've ever worked with, in the days before cameramen edited their own pictures, and who reminds me of Mike both physically and in manner, as he was in the days when we roamed the world together.

My abiding picture of Duncan is of him standing on a high mound of earth beside a road – *the* road, indeed, which runs right across the country of Libya from west to east, fringing the sea. It is during the uprising against Colonel Gaddafi in 2011, and Gaddafi's planes are attacking a group of rebels whom we've briefly joined up with. Every now and then a bomb drops, but Duncan doesn't budge. He looks like an immoveable object, with his camera on a tripod, turning his head to hear where the next attack is coming from. Behind him stands a former SAS man who is working with us as a security adviser. And behind them I'm standing, because it's bad form to let your cameraman stay out in the open, taking the risks, if you're not prepared to take them too. I feel horribly exposed.

'You'll be sick tonight,' the adviser said confidentially to me later, after another bomb had landed unpleasantly close to us. The dust was still hanging in the air. 'In a country like this they shit by the sides of the road, and you're breathing it all in.'

This wasn't something I'd considered before, but stopping breathing didn't seem to be an option. That night I was indeed sick. So was the adviser.

Duncan endured it all, and his pictures were excellent. You might think that covering a war would automatically provide you with good pictures, but unless you are right where something important is going on, with your camera running at the moment it is happening, you can spend entire days putting yourself at risk without actually getting any video that is worth looking at. Lots of men in uniform rushing around don't themselves necessarily make good pictures. Guns and bombs going off do, but you have to be lucky as well as constantly alert to film them.

A combination of technical ability, physical strength and an endlessly positive attitude to work had ensured that Duncan Stone was a senior cameraman. Accordingly, in 2003, he was at the heart of the BBC's operation in Baghdad as the American invaders neared the city. It's one of my lasting regrets that I wasn't there with him. He and the rest of the BBC team, headed by a wonderfully irascible friend of mine, Paul Danahar, were based at the ugly, rather sinister Palestine Hotel. Danahar never minded what he said, which made working with him a difficult but definite joy. Once, when some tactful editor warned him over the open phone from London that people had been writing to the BBC complaining that the coverage from Baghdad had been too pro-Iraqi, Danahar yelled down the phone for all the Iraqi spooks and minders to hear: 'Pro-Iraqi? We HATE the fucking Iraqis.'

Duncan had set up his camera on the balcony of a room on the seventeenth floor of the hotel, with a superb view across the River Tigris towards Saddam's palace: a natural target for the Americans. Just before midnight on Wednesday 19 March the first undoubted sign came that the war was about to start: satellite phone signals were cut, as a way of protecting the incoming American planes from electronic counter-measures. A few minutes later, midnight struck and it was Duncan's birthday.

'That made it certain,' he said. 'Of course they'll start a war on my bloody birthday.'

Air-raid sirens began to wail, far away at first then nearer and nearer, until all Baghdad itself resounded to the noise. It was an eerie moment, and everyone knew that their lives were now in serious danger. Soon, wave after wave of American missiles were flying in and striking targets across the city: power stations, military facilities, government ministries. Duncan, standing out on his balcony in his body armour, felt the force of the explosions in his lungs, making him gasp for air. It seemed to be raining high explosive. Saddam's palace went up in flames. Directly the flights of missiles stopped, Duncan rushed down to the main BBC office, a room on the thirteenth floor, and they started editing a package for the BBC's overnight bulletins.

A pattern emerged. During the day there was rarely any action, and the correspondents did live reports on camera and re-used the pictures from the previous night. Directly it was dark, they waited for the extraordinary picture show to start. Key buildings and installations were hit again and again, night after night: soon Duncan worked out how to anticipate the missile strikes. The entire team was working twenty-four hours a day, with occasional snatched pauses for sleep.

One particular morning, Duncan became aware of a new set of sounds. He leaped out of bed in his underwear and raced out to start filming. Waves of American A-10s, known as Warthogs because of their stumpy shapes, were flying in low, almost on a level with him as he stood on his balcony, firing their 30mm cannons at particular targets along the banks of the River Tigris. The following day things became even more surreal. For once they'd had a quiet night, with no aerial attacks. They'd heard explosions which didn't sound like bombs. Now Duncan could see American tanks in the distance, firing at the positions Iraqi soldiers had dug for themselves on the far bank of the river. Iraqi soldiers, terrified, were running away; and Duncan, filming them in his underwear, got some memorable close-ups of an Iraqi escaping in *his* underwear.

More and more American tanks started to arrive, moving very slowly along the river bank from left to right across his field of view. Their objective was the al-Jumhuriya Bridge, to the far right as

Duncan saw it. He had fixed up an immense video cable, 200 metres long, from his camera on the thirteenth floor down to a satellite dish far below on the mezzanine floor. This meant that he could send London live pictures of one of the tanks as it manoeuvred onto the bridge in full daylight. Through the viewfinder, Duncan could see the turret of the tank moving round towards the hotel. He wasn't worried, because the journalists in the Palestine Hotel, several dozen of them, had hung sheets out onto their balconies with 'TV' and 'PRESS' marked out on them in grey gaffer tape. Many foreign desks had told the Pentagon that their teams were in the hotel, and its image and name had been repeatedly mentioned in articles and television reports over the previous three or four weeks. There didn't seem to be anything more that needed to be done to safeguard the journalists there.

A company of the 4th Battalion, 64th Armor Regiment, had stationed itself on the western end of the bridge, looking across in the direction of the Palestine. The battalion had been told to expect a mortar attack at some point, and a soldier on an A Company tank reported seeing someone on a balcony on a tall building to the southeast who seemed to be observing them 'with some kind of optics'. The tank commander concluded that this was an enemy spotter. He requested permission to open fire, and received it.

Duncan Stone watched the tank's turret turning towards the hotel, and caught a glimpse of fire belching out of the tank's gun. He threw himself onto the floor just as the round hit the far end of the hotel two floors above. The entire building shook, and there were screams and falling plaster everywhere. The shell had hit the Reuters office: a cameraman, Taras Protsyuk, was killed, and three others wounded. José Couso, a cameraman from the Telecinco channel of Spanish television, was on the floor below and was also killed. Duncan jumped up immediately and started filming again. The other BBC cameraman, Andrew 'Killa' Kilrain, a calm, easy-going but gutsy Australian, went running upstairs to film what was happening where the shell had hit. He got some shocking pictures of Prostyuk's body being brought out, and the injured people being given first aid.

'We were really worried,' Duncan Stone said later. 'We felt that up to now we'd survived the American bombardment because they knew where we were and what we were doing. But now – what the bloody hell was going on? Maybe they were going to pepper us with shells. Later, it turned to anger that they should have done this. But for now, we were scared.'

General Buford Blount, who was in command of the 3rd Infantry Division, made it worse by saying that his tank had shelled the hotel because the Iraqis had fired at them from there. This was patently untrue, and Duncan's pictures showed that the tank's gun had been aimed at the Palestine for minutes before it fired. There was no question of its returning fire.

American gunners had ignored obvious signs that they were attacking Western journalists before. An investigation by the Committee to Protect Journalists found that the killing of the two cameramen in the Palestine Hotel had not been deliberate, but it had been avoidable. Usually in cases like these, the US military carries out a cursory inquiry, which almost always accepts the argument that its forces have an inherent right to self-defence. This means that any American who says he fired because he thought his life was in danger will not be punished. In the town of Tikrit, a couple of days earlier, an American soldier beside me had aimed his rifle at an old man on a nearby rooftop who was hanging a carpet up to dry. 'Sniper!' shouted the soldier. I'm proud to say I whacked him across the back with the walking stick I was carrying, and stopped him firing.

There was an even more worrying attack by two American missiles on the Al Jazeera office in Baghdad, which killed a Palestinian reporter, Tareq Ayyoub. He was broadcasting live from the roof of the building at the time. The US Department of Defense had often accused Al Jazeera of hostile reporting. During the American bombing of Kabul two years earlier, the Al Jazeera bureau had also been attacked. The shelling of the Palestine Hotel might perhaps have been a mistake; but could two attacks on Al Jazeera in successive wars have been a coincidence? It was hard to think so.

A couple of days later, the BBC people in the Palestine were told that American soldiers were now within the city limits, only a mile or so from the hotel. With considerable courage, given what had happened at the Palestine, Duncan Stone and Paul Danahar decided to go out and meet them. Usually a correspondent would go out on such a dangerous expedition as a matter of course, but in this case it didn't happen. Stone and Danahar walked in parallel about six feet apart, holding a white hotel bedsheet with 'TV' marked out on it in gaffer tape – much like the ones hung out of the windows at the Palestine, which had proven useless. Duncan carried his camera slung over his shoulder, with his free hand in the air, and they walked slowly towards a group of several American tanks halted in front of them. When they were about fifty yards away they were told to halt.

'Welcome to Baghdad,' Danahar shouted, his voice sounding distinctly croaky.

An officer waved his pistol at them, beckoning them to come closer. They identified themselves, and the Americans reacted in friendly fashion, grinning and shaking hands with them. Their orders were to head into the centre of town. Danahar asked if they could film them as they went in, and the Americans were happy with that.

It made superb pictures, which were of course exclusive; that was the reason Danahar and Stone had taken such a risk.

'What's the point of being there at a time like that,' Duncan asked later, 'if you're not prepared to stick your neck out a bit?'

But immediately afterwards he added: 'I still feel a bit shaky when I talk about it.'

THE PHOTOGRAPHER'S STORY

I admired Don McCullin the moment I met him. He was gentle and humorous and introverted, and not at all given to grandstanding. We were in the sitting room of our hotel in Londonderry, and outside in the darkness stretched the slums and violence and terror of a city that was out of control. The year was 1971.

McCullin was there because the *Sunday Times*, at that stage the finest newspaper in Britain, wanted a war photographer's take on the street violence which happened every day in Derry. He was one of the world's best-known photojournalists, who had made a huge reputation for himself with his photographs of the Vietnam War. And now he was sitting drinking Irish whiskey with us as though he was just another hack.

I had never been anywhere interesting before I got to Derry; I had never seen a war, and I had been rather mollycoddled by family life and the BBC. It had taken a big effort just to come here to Northern Ireland, and I'd already been scared out of my wits more times than I liked to remember.

The differences between Don McCullin and me were almost too many to recount. Even leaving his considerable experience aside, he was nine years older, from a poor, working-class background, dyslexic, hugely talented and insanely brave. Yet the extraordinary thing was that he treated me as though I was on a par with him, and with the journalist-adventurers he worked with in Southeast Asia. I had scarcely any stories to tell him, except how lucky I had been to escape with my life when a Provisional IRA gang decided I must be a British spy (it was, I think, my shiny brown brogues that did it, plus the fact that I'd forgotten to bring my BBC pass). They had just decided to put a bullet through my head in a corner of a Belfast cemetery when a colleague saw what was happening and rescued me.

Don had so many stories that I felt I could listen to them for hours. But he never patronised me. And after I'd told him about the cemetery incident he said he thought reporting from Northern Ireland was more dangerous than reporting from Vietnam. It wasn't true, of course, but it was intended to put me on a par with himself: the act of a gentleman. Can you wonder that I took to him?

During the years that followed, I rarely saw Don on my travels. He tended to avoid the big set-piece stories that attract the television cameras. The Ministry of Defence refused to take him to the

South Atlantic for the Falklands War, so the best-fought, short-
est and most intelligent military campaign of modern times went
unrecorded by the country's best war photographer. Presumably the
British government was scared that his pictures would be so searing
that they would turn people against the war. In one or two places –
the Amazon, Lebanon – I would come across his footprints: 'That
photographer, the famous one, Don somebody, – he was staying
here just last week. You should have been here.'

But for the most part we operated in different spheres; and
although he has always been too polite to say so, I suspect he dislikes
television, thinking it to be noisy, clumsy, overmanned and irreflective. As it is, of course.

Nowadays it would be my great joy to travel somewhere difficult
and nasty with Don; and although he's eighty and I'm seventy-one,
he still does this kind of work, just as I do. Recently he was in Syria
with the glamorous and cerebral American journalist Charlie Glass,
dodging across open ground under the eyes of machine-gunners,
snapping away at the horrors that the civil war there has given rise
to. Two or three years earlier, though, Charlie went to see Don as he
lay in the Wellington Hospital beside Lord's cricket ground, waiting for a quadruple heart bypass operation.

'Charlie, I must say, exhibited an immaculate bedside manner,' Don
writes in his beautifully crafted 2015 autobiography, *Unreasonable
Behaviour*. 'He even refrained from inviting me to accompany him
to a war zone, a sure indication of massive restraint on his part.'

It happened later, though, and off they went to the new most
dangerous place on earth.

Don's friends and experiences link him in to various of the other
stories in this book of mine: he was brother-in-law to Rick Beeston,
the charming and much-missed foreign editor of *The Times*, and
went to Syria with Anthony Loyd, one of the best writers among
foreign correspondents. When Nick Tomalin was killed on the
Golan Heights, it was Don who phoned for help. He was close by
when several other people I have mentioned were in danger or died.
He has lived out the best of newspaper journalism throughout his
life, clever, opportunistic, but not capable of anything spiteful or

shabby. If I didn't think he'd regard it as wanky, I would tell him that he reminds me of a particularly alert, sharp-witted character from Shakespeare's *Winter's Tale*: 'My father named me Autolycus, who being as I am littered under Mercury, was likewise a snapper-up of unconsidered trifles.'

Don has the ability to make the most unconsidered trifle thought-provoking or pity-inspiring. In Biafra in 1968 he photographed a twenty-four-year-old mother, waiting for death with her skeletal child on a hospital bed, her breasts as flat and stretched and empty as those of a woman of seventy. It's enough to make you weep; and yet her face has a serene beauty which seems to transcend everything else.

In 2012, when Don was seventy-seven, his brother-in-law Rick Beeston, by now dying of cancer, persuaded him to go to Syria with Anthony Loyd. Over lunch at a fish restaurant in St James's, the editor of *The Times*, James Harding, agreed to let Don travel if he would learn how to tie a tourniquet (something he had never done) and agree to wear a flak jacket (something he hadn't done since Vietnam). Don agreed.

McCullin and Loyd decided to go to Aleppo, where there was fierce fighting between the Syrian rebels and the forces of the Assad regime. Both of them had been there various times before, as recounted in *Don McCullin*:

> As we arrived in Aleppo this time. . . we could hear no end of bother being caused by the 'boom, boom, boom' of heavy artillery. It was probably the point at which I should have said to myself, Are you wise to be doing this? But, in reality, I was just excited; elated to have made it into what was obviously a real war zone.

Anthony told him they would meet his friend Hakim Anza, 'the Commander', the next day. Before the war, apparently, Hakim had been an accountant; all this goes to show you should always be wary of accountants, especially those wearing camouflage. Loyd told Don that when someone had upset Hakim, Hakim had given him a serious beating. Then he told him he'd spare his life, but that he should take a car parked close by, drive off and not come back.

The man did as he was told. Hakim punched a number into his phone and the car blew up.

'I couldn't help thinking,' said Don afterwards, 'that with friends like Hakim, we might not need too many enemies.'

When they met him, though, Hakim turned out to be handsome, smooth and helpful. He arranged for them to visit the front line the next day; and when they got there, they found the front line lay all round a military base. The rebels were firing at it through loopholes in the perimeter wall. After that, Don and Loyd went to check out the hospitals:

> A car came screaming up, and we saw people dragging dead bodies out of it... Then a truck roared in, bringing an even bigger load of misery. It was really strange. There was a man sitting in the back, a really big guy, with black, curly hair, blazing eyes, and an overcoat on because it was freezing, and he was sitting surrounded by dead people. And I said, 'Why don't you help to get these people off instead of just sitting there? What is the matter with you?' And I got a bit closer, and realised he was also dead, apparently killed by a shell...

One day, Don climbed onto a roof to get a long shot. A soldier who spotted him decided he must be a spy, and more soldiers gathered. Then Hakim's people turned up and rescued him. Don was grateful to them, yet he couldn't feel comfortable in their presence. The rivalries between the different groups made things even more dangerous: 'I would rate Aleppo as being behind Phnom Penh in the murderous heyday of the Khmer Rouge,' Don said later, 'but not by very much.'

As they left, Don felt moderately pleased with his pictures, but thought he could have got better ones if they'd been able to stay longer. In fact his best shots came outside a refugee camp close to the Turkish border. He spotted a group of forty men with black headbands on a nearby ridge, looking down menacingly at the camp. One of the men spotted him and demanded to see his pictures. Fortunately Don had a digital camera with him as well, and with some sleight of hand showed the man the last picture on that: an innocuous shot of someone in Aleppo. The man with the black headband said 'No problem' and let him go.

It had not been the world's greatest newspaper assignment, but I wanted to go because I felt that the public were not sufficiently engaged with the conflict in Syria, preferring to look the other way. As for myself, I experienced one last time that amazing sustained burst of adrenalin at the beginning, followed later by the tremendous whoosh of relief that comes with the completion of any dangerous undertaking. In short, I felt very much more alive than I had done before.

As it turned out, it wouldn't be the last time Don went to Syria, or felt that burst of adrenalin: he soon returned with Charlie Glass.

Nor will it be the last time in this book that we will come across Commander Hakim.

THIRTEEN

Getting Involved

> You're not sent there to help people, but if you find that
> people need help when you are there, of course you have
> to give it. It would be quite wrong not to. Just don't make
> a habit of it, that's all.
>
> Charles Wheeler speaking to a BBC symposium, 1987

JOURNALISTS TEND TO GET uncomfortable if people praise them
for their humanitarian purpose, or the practical value of what
they are reporting, or the effect their work has had on public opinion. Of course they, like everyone else, want to look at themselves
in the mirror and feel they've done a good job; but for a great many
journalists the purpose of their work isn't to do good, it's simply to
present a certain set of facts and views as well and as honestly as
they can. The notion of journalism as a means of uplifting society,
of making people feel better about their lives or their government,
is something many of us would instinctively shy away from.

Most foreign correspondents would probably believe that one of
their chief functions in the job is to present the case for the people
they live among – to act as an advocate for them, so that outsiders
can see that they, like everyone else, are mostly decent and above all
interesting.

Is the purpose of journalism to do good? Most of us would feel
mildly uncomfortable about that idea too, though there are plenty
of examples where journalism has done remarkable amounts of
good, in revealing facts and uncovering corruption. At such times,
perhaps, journalists can take pride in their profession, and justly so;

but it's the fundamental instinct to place hidden facts in open sight that tends to come first.

Investigative journalism is a branch of the business which foreign correspondents don't often stray into. Most of them have their hands full just explaining what is going on in their territory day by day, without being able to take the time to go through the complicated details of some major scandal. Sometimes, though, you'll hear a case mentioned that you haven't come across before, an injustice which is crying out to be revealed to a wider audience; and it begins to get hold of you and force you to take it further, until finally you are able to reveal the full details and then, perhaps, have to take the consequences. There can be an element of obsessiveness about this process, but usually without it there would be no story at the end. Yet it's worth repeating that the purpose is usually to tell a story worth telling; the act of doing good, though praiseworthy in itself, is secondary.

Aleem Maqbool is a British foreign correspondent who is currently based in the United States for the BBC. I first became aware of him when he was reporting from Gaza: a difficult place, if you work for an organisation like the BBC which demands balance and a lack of judgementalism in its output. Gaza is a place that can outrage you very quickly, and turn you into an advocate rather than a reporter; and although there is certainly an important place for advocacy journalism, it isn't in the BBC. I watched and listened to Aleem Maqbool's reporting with some care and was impressed to find how even-handed his reporting was. He didn't ignore the ugly, shameful side of Gaza and its situation, but he was honest about it without preaching. He didn't have an axe to grind.

Maqbool's success there led to promotion, and he was later sent to the United States, a country where there is so much daily news to report that most foreign correspondents do not look for extra work. But Aleem was attracted by a particular murder case from long before, in which someone who seemed likely to be innocent had been sentenced to life imprisonment. So he started to look into it, while carrying out his normal day job.

His report for the BBC appeared on the BBC website in 2015. It started in a measured way: quiet, factual, free of histrionics, and, mercifully, with a minimum of adjectives:

America imprisons a higher proportion of its citizens than anywhere else in the world, and Louisiana more than anywhere else in America.

It is estimated that 14 out of every 1,000 adults in the state are in prison.

This is the story of one of them, Robert Jones, who was jailed in the 1990s for killing a young British tourist in New Orleans.

It was a crime another man had already been convicted of, but he was prosecuted anyway.

In the spring of 1992 a British couple, Julie Stott and her boyfriend Peter Ellis, were celebrating their engagement by travelling round the United States. By 14 April they had reached New Orleans. That night they went out to a restaurant, and finished up at the Café Brésil, listening to a Latin dance band. At 11.30 they were strolling back to their hotel through the French Quarter when a man jumped out and pointed a gun at them. He shouted at them to lie down, but they froze in panic. The next moment he fired twice at Peter Ellis, who threw himself down behind a parked car.

Then the gunman turned to Julie, who was still standing, paralysed, in the middle of the road. When at last she started to run the gunman fired a couple of shots, and she fell to the ground. He made for a nearby car, jumped in and drove off the wrong way down the one-way street.

Peter ran over to Julie, who was lying unconscious on the ground. Blood was flowing from her arm, and he used his shirt as a tourniquet, shouting out to people nearby to call an ambulance. But it was no good: the second bullet had hit her in the head and she was dying.

Twenty-three years later the local detective who was assigned to the case, James Stewart, showed Maqbool exactly where the shooting had happened. It was clear that Julie Stott's murder was the result of a botched robbery. Peter Ellis, the boyfriend, could give the police only a very sketchy description of the killer. But Stewart did have descriptions from witnesses of the car that was used in the getaway, and he had a bullet casing from the gun that had been used.

Stewart guessed there would be a lot of media attention, but he wasn't prepared for the frenzy which the British tabloids unleashed on New Orleans. Their involvement changed everything.

There were several other important leads. Just a few minutes before Julie Stott was attacked, and close by in the French Quarter, another couple had been robbed at gunpoint. And two hours earlier, there had been another street robbery by an armed man. In these two cases the description of the gun and the getaway car seemed to match. The car was described as burgundy red, with a white roof. The killer was believed to have carried out at least four recent attacks in New Orleans.

At this point the British press started exerting its influence on the investigation. The *Sun* offered a reward of $10,000 for information leading to the arrest of Julie Stott's murderer. Soon its front page was proclaiming: 'The whole of New Orleans last night praised *The Sun's* $10,000 reward to catch the killer of British tourist Julie Stott. One cop said "I hope this helps nail him – we want this murdering rat on Death Row".' The quote may of course have been accurate, though it sounds distinctly like what a British reporter might imagine an American policeman would say.

The result of the *Sun's* offer was a flood of calls to the New Orleans police. Most of the tips were discarded, but the police thought that one deserved further exploration: 'The caller identified some guys,' Stewart told Maqbool. 'He said they had all been in a bar talking about the murder and giving details that made him think they had been involved.'

One of the names the caller gave was that of Robert Jones, a nineteen-year-old from a poor black neighbourhood, who the police had suspected of selling drugs, though he had never been convicted of any crime.

By this stage, Stewart was under pressure from his bosses to make a breakthrough in a case which was receiving such media attention. Not surprisingly, he was getting desperate.

Soon after the tip was received, a woman who had been robbed, kidnapped and raped in a prolonged ordeal was brought into the police station. She was shown a series of photographs and after some uncertainty she chose the picture of Robert Jones. At 4 a.m. the police surrounded Jones's home. They forced their way in and forced everyone, including several children, to lie flat on the floor. Then they said who they were looking for. They took Jones away. He was later shown on television news bulletins being taken, bare-chested and handcuffed, to Orleans Parish Gaol.

Television news crews went round interviewing tourists, who said how relieved they were that Julie's killer had been caught. As for the *Sun*, it wasn't too worried about the presumption of innocence either. Its front page carried this story:

THE SUN TRAPS JULIE KILLER
The Sun was the toast of New Orleans last night for trapping
the crack-crazed killer of British girl Julie Stott.

Inside, a headline called Jones a 'Beast of the Jungle' and a 'junkie murderer' who had carried out a number of other rapes and robberies. The mayor of New Orleans was quoted as congratulating the newspaper for offering the reward, though Aleem Maqbool could find no evidence afterwards that it had ever been paid.

Detective James Stewart wasn't comfortable with all this, he told Maqbool. All they had in the way of evidence was the description of a car and a bullet casing, and Robert Jones wasn't tied to either of them. Worse, the very day the *Sun* was trumpeting its success, another young couple walking through the city were confronted by a gunman who made them lie on the ground and ran off with their jewellery. He got into a burgundy-coloured car with a white roof and drove off.

Soon afterwards, a car fitting that description was seen parked in a poor area of the city. When the police went round to check, an African-American who said he was the car's owner asked them what they were looking for. One of the detectives spotted that he was wearing a ring and a wristwatch reported stolen in one of the crimes, plus a medallion and chain stolen during the rape. There were more stolen items in the car. Curiously, the man had the same surname as Robert Jones: he was Lester Jones, thirty years old. They also found his gun – and it matched the bullet removed from Julie Stott's body. Later, people who'd been attacked identified him. The police had everything they needed. In August 1994 Lester Jones was convicted of murder and sentenced to life imprisonment. Detective James Stewart assumed the case was closed.

There was only one problem: Robert Jones still hadn't been released, two years after this new arrest. And in March 1996, nineteen months after Lester Jones had been found guilty of Julie Stott's murder, Robert Jones went on trial for the same murder, plus some of the robberies, and the rape as well. Extraordinarily, no one – not even his defence counsel – mentioned at the trial that Lester Jones was already serving time for several of these crimes. The prosecution claimed that Robert was Lester's friend, even though Detective Stewart had assured them he wasn't. The first charge of which he was found guilty was that of rape; after that the prosecution offered to downgrade the murder charge to one of manslaughter, if he would plead guilty to that and the remaining charges. Robert Jones agreed. The trial was over in less than ten hours.

With perhaps a touch of obsessiveness, Aleem Maqbool plugged away at the case, interviewing Robert Jones in his prison, Louisiana State Penitentiary. It was known as 'Angola' because it was built on a former slave plantation of that name. He later reported: 'To this day, prisoners (more than three-quarters of whom are black) work in the fields, often picking cotton under the watch of (predominantly white) armed prison officers.'

The judge at Robert Jones's trial, Calvin Johnson, was himself African-American. This didn't help Jones at all. When Maqbool interviewed him, years later, Judge Johnson admitted that the trials of many black defendants which he himself had presided over were manifestly unfair. The prosecutor's office regularly hid information which could help defendants, he said, and 'played fast and loose' with the truth. He maintained that the aim of the system he himself served was to put as many young, black men behind bars for as long as possible.

Neither of the prosecutors in the case would agree to be interviewed by Aleem Maqbool. In 2015 a memo written by one of them in 1996 was made public. It conceded that there was no admissible evidence against Robert Jones in the Julie Stott murder case.

In the end, in November 2015, the campaign to free Robert Jones succeeded. He was released twenty-three years and seven months after being arrested. Outside the gaol, waiting for him, were his elderly mother and his twenty-two-year-old daughter Bree, who was born eight months after he'd been dragged out of his family home in handcuffs.

Maqbool went to meet him in a local restaurant, and asked him what it had been like to be in prison for so long:

> 'A complete nightmare, a real nightmare. You can't find the words in the dictionary to describe the cruelty,' he said.
>
> How did he get through it?
>
> 'My faith in God. And it's a true saying that the truth will set you free one day, when you can find it. And that was a problem for me, just finding the truth. The truth was buried so deep, and God was able to reveal those things.'

At one point, late on in his imprisonment, the district attorney's office had offered Jones a deal: freedom if he would admit some of the charges. He turned it down. As a result, even though he had been freed from prison, he still wasn't completely at liberty. He had to observe a curfew, and was still being threatened with the ordeal of a retrial.

There are thought to be hundreds of innocent black prisoners still serving long terms in the state's gaols. Aleem Maqbool, patiently and with a touch of obsession, played a part in winning the freedom of one of them.

Did the *Sun* apologise for calling Robert Jones the 'Beast of the Jungle' and helping to imprison him for twenty-three years? What do you think?

―――――――

For a time – it seems to have faded now – there was a vogue among American journalists for regarding the reporter as a purely independent being, whose duty was to observe but not in any sense to intervene in what he or she saw. 'The I Am A Camera mythos', the writer and controversialist Christopher Hitchens scornfully called it. Inevitably, one or two British journalists started taking the same line. There were several occasions when photographers and cameramen, in particular, looked on at some disaster and simply took pictures without doing anything to help. That, of course, was their job, the reason their employers had sent them there. But when there was a fuss about it, the principle of the purely objective onlooker was invoked. Journalists, the principle seemed to say, were beyond mere involvement; they had a sacred calling to bear witness to the truth.

I always found that idea irritating. Of course it is incumbent on all of us to do our job as well as we can do it; the reason why a cameraman or a reporter is at the scene of some disaster is to record it. But no one is exempt from the basic duties of being a human being. One of my favourite photographs of a journalist in action shows Don McCullin helping to give first aid to an injured soldier in Vietnam: the picture captures the intensity of the moment, and the look on McCullin's face (though perhaps I'm being fanciful here) seems to say, 'This could be me.'

Nevertheless, the most effective thing any journalist can do is to bear witness to what he or she is seeing. To record, say, the effects of a rocket attack that has carelessly gone astray and killed civilians is to play some small part in putting pressure on the people who allowed it to happen. To report on the use of rape as a weapon of war is to help recruit further support for an end to the practice. There is no need to preach; the facts and the pictures are sufficient. 'I decided to open the matter up,' says Sherlock Holmes in one of the stories, and that is the basic job of any journalist.

Yet if someone comes running towards you, pleading for help, it seems to me that you have no right to turn them away. You aren't merely a camera; you are a human being who happens to be holding a camera. Sometimes, refusing to help isn't really an appeal to the principle of objectivity; it's just cowardice.

Marie Colvin, the American foreign correspondent who worked for the *Sunday Times* in many of the most dangerous places in the world, was very strong on this. In 1999, in East Timor, she found herself with a couple of dozen other journalists in a compound containing 1,500 women and children. They were being besieged by a particularly unpleasant force of irregulars who had the support of the Indonesian army. The only protection was provided by a small, unarmed force of UN soldiers. The journalists debated the position long and hard, and in the end those who argued that they could do their job better if they left the compound, won. It was the logic of the herd, and soon, having persuaded themselves that it was ethical to leave, the journalists wanted to leave as fast as possible. Even those who knew it was wrong were swept up in the desire to get out. It happens; and it's not right for anyone who wasn't there to be judgemental about it.

But there was of course one person who would never have left a story, or a group of vulnerable people, under those conditions. Marie waved goodbye cheerfully as the twenty-two other journalists left, then turned back to the women and children and the unarmed UN force which had the job of protecting them.

'So how shall we organise this?' she said.

Her own task was clear. She had a small satellite dish, and friends at various newspaper, radio and television organisations. After she'd written her despatch for the *Sunday Times* and sent that, she got on to the BBC and offered them a first-hand report on the siege. It made excellent radio. Soon she was broadcasting on BBC World TV and CNN. The siege lasted four more days, and at times things became very tense indeed. But because international opinion was starting to be invoked, the pressure grew on the Indonesian government to call off its supporters.

A former aide once said of President Bill Clinton, who was in office at the time, that if one of the rolling news channels started broadcasting pictures of some crisis, he wouldn't ask himself what he should do about it, he'd ask what people *thought* he should do about it: a subtle difference. In this case the answer was clear. The Indonesian government was given a talking-to, the siege was called off, the UN soldiers and the 1,500 women and children were free to go. It happened for one reason only: because Marie Colvin had stayed on and told the world what was happening.

'These are people who have no voice,' she said in one of her broadcasts. 'I feel I have a moral responsibility towards them, that it would be cowardly to ignore them. If journalists have a chance to save their lives, they should do so.'

After another particularly difficult experience, Marie wrote: 'What I want most, as soon as I get out of hospital, is a vodka martini and a cigarette.' Her tastes were fairly well known as a result. Not long after her experience in East Timor she went to New York and checked into a hotel there. She was awakened by a room-service waiter carrying a tray. On it was a big bottle of vodka, and all the makings of a good vodka martini: 'It had been fixed, God knows how, by the East Timor crowd, the people in the compound.'

Should journalists show themselves helping the people they're reporting on? That too is a difficult question. There will often be a suspicion in the viewer's mind, if it's done on television, that it's been carefully choreographed for show: to demonstrate, perhaps, that the correspondent in question has a heart of gold. Once, when I was covering the genocide in Rwanda in 1994, I went to film a psychiatric hospital that had been turned over to Hutu refugees. The doctors and staff had all fled, leaving the patients behind; and the refugees' plan for getting rid of the patients was to let them die of hunger and thirst, locked away in little cells.

One particular patient seemed to be in the last stages of insanity, singing and weeping and calling out for water. I couldn't bear it any longer, and told my crew I was going to fetch some food and water from our vehicle for him. I knew, as they did, that it was entirely pointless: when the food and water ran out, he would still be left to die of hunger and thirst. But I defy anyone to listen to that cracked voice, singing and croaking and laughing and calling for water, without feeling obliged to do something. The refugees were angry, of course, but I threw bottle after bottle through the gap at the bottom of the cell door, then threw in some food as well. The cameraman filmed all this, and we put it into a report we made that night from Rwanda.

The response in Britain and around the world was intense. Mostly, I was criticised for not freeing the man, though we had been warned that, if I did, he and we would be lynched immediately; and anyway, in the middle of a civil war, we couldn't possibly have driven round the country with a raving maniac, nor abandoned him somewhere. Others blamed me for not giving him *more* water and more food. A hardened few pointed out, rightly, that it was all a waste of time, and that the man would die anyway. And a large number accused me of doing it all simply in order to impress the audience with my (phoney) humanity. This level of judgemental anger is relatively unusual, in my experience, at least on a subject that doesn't involve Israel, immigration or the European Union, and the only reason I could think of was that the question I posed was such a stark one.

What should I have done? With hindsight, I think it is clear: I should have eased our anguish by giving the poor man everything we could spare, but not included that element in our report that night. It was simply too much strong meat for our audience.

Like Marie Colvin, NBC's chief foreign correspondent, Richard Engel, was brought up in New York; and unlike many foreign correspondents, he is a linguist, speaking and reading Arabic fluently, as well as Spanish and Italian. I once queued for an hour and a quarter in the hot Baghdad sun to get a place in the courtroom for the trial of Saddam Hussein, and only Engel's conversation made it bearable. He is thirty years younger than me, and has only been a correspondent since the invasion of Iraq in 2003, but his experience, humour and sharp intelligence made him an excellent companion. Once, President George W. Bush invited him to come and brief him on Iraq. He was too discreet to talk about the meeting afterwards, but if he gave Bush a tenth of his real views on the invasion and its aftermath, the president will have had an earful; far too late, of course.

In 2015 Engel, whose responsibilities now extended beyond the Middle East, was reporting on the refugee crisis in Europe. The right-wing government in Budapest had recently put up a barbed-wire fence along the Hungarian border with Serbia, and thousands of refugees from Syria who wanted to get to Germany and Britain were trapped by it. Hungarian police in riot gear, not by and large a very sympathetic group of people, fired pepper spray at a group which was trying to break through it. Engel is the kind of correspondent who likes to get stuck in, and he forced his way through the crowd of would-be refugees towards the front.

In all the pushing and shoving he encountered a woman who was having a fit of hysterics. He pulled her in front of the camera in order to speak to her, but she fell to the ground, with Engel standing over her, trying to protect her against the heaving mass of bodies: 'This woman just collapsed in front of me. She's breathing, they are calling to get her some water.'

'She's breathing, she's waking up. . . she's waking up,' he shouted to camera over the noise of the fighting.

Then, in commentary recorded later, Engel says: 'I tried to keep her head up. Leaning her against her bag, it was clear that she was pregnant. Afterwards people carried her off to a makeshift infirmary.'

Was this grandstanding, an attempt on Engel's part to present himself to an audience as a caring soul anxious to impress everyone with his humanity? I certainly didn't feel so. He found the woman in the crowd by chance, and the incident illustrated the stresses and terrors which she, like thousands of others, was going through. He was criticised back home, of course; there is very little that correspondents from the so-called mainstream media can do nowadays in America, and increasingly in Britain, without having their motives and characters impugned. But I thought it was all perfectly legitimate. A week before, Krishnan Guru-Murthy of Channel 4 News had taken some real physical risks in helping a group of refugees who were in an extremity of exhaustion as they reached the Greek island of Lesbos. That, too, seemed to me to be absolutely right. Guru-Murthy wasn't just a neutral observer, a kind of moral eunuch watching with interest while people nearly drowned. He behaved as you and I have a duty to behave anywhere on earth; it was just that, like Richard Engel, he did it on camera.

Did the two of them reveal a tendency to sympathise with the refugees in their battle with the authorities? These were people who were breaking the law, and Engel and Guru-Murthy were apparently siding with them. But if they did, it was only to save life and protect the vulnerable. The complaints would have been – should have been, indeed – a great deal harsher if they had stood aside.

In my five decades as a foreign correspondent, there has never been a time when broadcasters were under fiercer and more hostile scrutiny. The default assumption, in this age of social media, is that the public is being habitually lied to. A degree of scepticism is always good, of course; but now, it seems to me, the scepticism has turned to outright disbelief. What's more, the journalistic profession itself seems determined to pull down its own members.

At the end of 2012, Richard Engel and his five team members were kidnapped during a reporting trip to Syria. After a few days, they got free, thanks to the help of a different group of fighters. Engel then wrote an article for *Vanity Fair* saying he thought a group loyal to President Assad had captured them. For reasons which only the habits of journalism, a fierce dog-eat-dog business, can explain, Engel's account was then challenged by the online magazine the *Daily Beast*, citing those always questionable entities, 'unknown sources', which maintained that a group *opposed* to President Assad had captured them. Of course truth and accuracy matter more than anything; but Engel had never stated as fact that a Shabiha group had kidnapped his group: he merely believed it to be the case.

The effect of the *Daily Beast*'s intervention was to make people feel there was something questionable about Engel's entire experience. After that, with the bewildering obsessiveness which American newspapers sometimes show, the *New York Times* carried out dozens of interviews in Syria and elsewhere which appeared to show that Engel's captors had been a Sunni criminal group affiliated to the Free Syrian Army, Assad's enemies, rather than his supporters. NBC was obliged to put out corrections about Engel's reports, which must have diminished his authority. If someone from the *New York Times* had been kidnapped, would the *Daily Beast*, or NBC for that matter, have devoted similar amounts of time to investigating the finer details? I doubt it.

There are other areas where broadcasters, much more than newspaper correspondents, have to tread with the greatest care. Nowadays Russia and China are home to groups of dedicated people who write angry messages on internet stories critical of their governments. Anything to do with Israel and its armed forces is likely to cause difficulties too. In Britain there are said to be pro-Israeli groups who are organised to send concerted barrages of complaint to the BBC, ITN and Sky News about their reporting, particularly about Gaza and the West Bank. Orla Guerin, who came to the BBC from the Irish state broadcaster RTÉ, had a particularly bad time from these groups when she was the correspondent in Jerusalem.

Her offence wasn't that she was opposed to the state of Israel, or to Israelis, let alone to Jews in general – though she was accused of all these things, sometimes in the most offensive way. It was that she showed particular concern about victims. Sometimes the victims were Israeli; much more often, given the way the balance of events in the region lay, they were Palestinian. The complainants believed – or said they believed – that her reporting on the victims showed sympathy for the Palestinian cause. Time and again, watching and listening to her reports, I tried to understand the reason for the complaints; but it always seemed to me that the real cause was that she was sympathising with people who were suffering, and as far as I know there are no journalistic rules of balance which outlaw that. It was interesting, incidentally, to see how male-dominated many of the attacks on Orla Guerin were. The Sky News correspondent in Jerusalem at the time, Emma Hurd, also seemed to come in for more than her fair share of spiteful complaints. Could there have been some connection between the subjects they were reporting on, and the fact that they were women?

Back in 1982, I watched floods of Palestinians and Lebanese being brought into the hospitals of West Beirut, severely injured. Children as young as twelve were stationed in the corridors outside the doors of the operating theatres, and given the job of pulling out the larger and more obvious chunks of shrapnel from the patients' bodies with their bare hands. That allowed the surgeons to concentrate on operating to remove the smaller and even more deadly pieces affecting internal organs. At that time the Israelis dropped cluster bombs and phosphorous bombs, which were supplied to them by the US on condition they were solely for use against enemy soldiers, into the narrow streets of West Beirut. If you are close to a phosphorous bomb when it explodes and inhale its fumes, they will continue burning your lungs and air passages for up to seven hours before you die in agony. These things were observable, filmable facts, not biased opinions.

Yet even in those days, long before the writing groups were established, there were complaints about our reporting of them. Nobody, as far as I know, suggested that I and my colleagues were making them up; it was simply that they were unpleasant to hear about, and reporting them did damage to Israel's image in the world.

Orla Guerin is a deeply conscientious journalist, determined to make sure that everything she says is factually correct. Someone more duplicitous might have found a way to steer clear of the regular reporting of civilian sufferings; maybe that's what the critics would prefer. But it wouldn't be accurate reporting, and it wouldn't be balanced and unbiased.

———

After the tsunami hit Aceh province in Indonesia, Ben Brown was sent in to join the BBC team there. Ben was one of the earliest correspondents I recruited to the BBC's newly established World Affairs Unit in 1988, and I was always filled with a sense of pride, not to mention self-congratulation, as I watched his career advance.

He was the correspondent in Moscow during the turbulent period that followed the fall of Marxism-Leninism. For years he raced around the globe as a special correspondent – the title which people like William Howard Russell and Archibald Forbes once bore – and in January 2005 he was sent in to Banda Aceh. There he came across someone whose plight seemed to embody everything he had witnessed.

Her name was Rohati, and she had lost her four children and her home. Ben had found her scrabbling away with her bare hands at the sand where her house had once stood. Now, as he wrote to me, it covered everything:

> I interviewed her in the way TV news crews interview countless victims of wars and natural disasters – and yet somehow Rohati was different. As she answered my questions, she reached out to grab my arm, and then pulled me towards her. She had no one else to comfort her then, and since I had appeared from nowhere with a microphone to talk to her, I would have to do.

Ben put his arm round her lovingly, and the camera caught the action. He was 'crossing the line': not just listening to the story of her pain and loss, but doing what little he could to ease it. Some of his colleagues criticised him for this, but for the most part the audience didn't:

> I was stiff and awkward, the classic English public schoolboy uncomfortable with big shows of emotion. But that strange scene on the *Ten O'Clock News* seemed to help viewers empathise not only with Rohati, but all the other victims. People at home almost felt she was clinging to them. They wrote letters in great numbers to tell me what an impact Rohati had had on them.

In the weeks and months that followed, Ben couldn't forget Rohati, and six months after the tsunami he went back to Banda Aceh to see what had happened to her. News reporters are so often accused of cashing in on people's pain and then forgetting them, that the trip seemed thoroughly worthwhile.

But it proved difficult to find her. She had lived in a town called Meulaboh, where 30,000 people had died. Many of the survivors had left. Those who had stayed lived in sprawling tented camps which flooded every time it rained. A few were living with friends or relatives. Ben and his team printed stills from their interview with Rohati six months earlier, and handed them round to everyone they came across in Meulaboh. At last someone recognised her picture, and introduced them to Rohati's brother. He took them to a house where she had been staying, some miles outside the town. But when they got there they found she had moved on, to the house of another relative.

She wasn't around when they found it, and they were starting to think the whole thing was a wild-goose chase. Eventually, though, she turned up, and remembered Ben instantly. She hugged him and started to cry almost as heartbreakingly as she had when her losses were just new. To his horror, Ben realised that he was making everything worse for her all over again.

'Life is so hard for me,' she said. 'Can you imagine what it is like to lose so many children?' She held up four fingers.

He asked her what help she had received from the authorities and aid agencies. It hadn't been much: she had slipped through the net, perhaps because all her children were dead. She used the small amount of money the Indonesian government had given her to buy some old clothes, which she sold again in the market.

Ben stayed talking to her for almost an hour, but he knew the moment when he would have to leave was getting closer. She had bared her soul for him on two occasions, and both times he had listened with the greatest sympathy, then walked away.

'Take me with you back to England,' she begged him. 'Please – either find a home for me here in Aceh, or take me back to your country.'

It was impossible, naturally. All he could do was to give her money: a considerable amount by Indonesian standards, possibly even enough for her to buy a house. But it wasn't really money she wanted, and it wasn't even a house; it was some emotional link to help compensate in a small way for everything she had lost. And that was something Ben Brown couldn't give.

She waved goodbye to them as they left. But she was still pleading with them to take her with them.

————

The reporting of big humanitarian crises can often seem impersonal and broadbrush: footage of vast crowds of faceless people, relieved by the occasional individual detail, gathered hastily by a harassed journalist anxious about the approaching deadline and jotting down a few quick names and stories before heading back to the hotel for the night. Haste generally has a deadening effect on good reporting. '*La presse, toujours pressée*,' a French cameraman I used to work with would say when I talked to him of deadlines: the press, always pressed for time.

Weekly correspondents, by the nature of their work, don't have quite these pressures. They have others, though: if you work on a Sunday newspaper or a weekly programme you can dedicate yourself to the pursuit of a good story, only to find that some daily journalist stumbles over it and breaks it a day before you. Often their story will be inferior to yours, with much less detail and understanding; but it will still kill yours stone dead. And when that happens you find yourself bitterly envying the daily journalist's freedom and scope.

Christina Lamb of the *Sunday Times* long ago learned how to master the particular demands of weekly reporting. She looked for stories which were closely related to the big issues of the day, but were sufficiently separated to ensure that she wouldn't read about them in Saturday's *Guardian*. And she showed an enviable ability to find people to write about whose stories weren't simply emblematic of the wider issues, but were important and interesting in their own right. Christina's reporting of the refugee crisis in Europe in 2015 stood out from the rest because she knew her paper didn't simply want a longer version of everything that had been written during the week.

In October that year she spent time on board a rescue boat out of Malta, the *Phoenix*: one of four private craft helping the navies of several countries to stop the flow of would-be refugees from Libya. The weather had been bad all that week, and Christina had had four rough days at sea.

'The smugglers know these seas – they won't put boats out in this,' the captain had told her; not the kind of thing you want to hear if you've invested so much time in a story. There was a force five wind, and a seven-foot swell. But just before six in the morning, the captain spotted a refugee boat. 'They must be desperate,' he said.

> We were about one and a half hours away and for a long while I strained to see anything. Then, there it was – a tiny, dark oblong on the horizon, rising and falling in and out of sight with the waves. As we got nearer, I could see it was a grey dinghy, perhaps 28ft long, packed with more than 100 people, their faces twisted into a mixture of hope and despair. It was perilously low in the water. At the front was a woman holding up a baby.

The second-in-command set off towards them in an inflatable RIB, with a couple of crew members and a doctor from Médecins Sans Frontières. They manoeuvred to the back of the dinghy and the second-in-command shouted: 'Can anyone speak English?'

'Yes!' came the reply.

'You're safe now!' he yelled back.

But they weren't.

The passengers stood up and some tried to jump into the RIB.

'Keep calm!' shouted the 2-i-c. 'Sit down, don't stand!'

Immediately, everyone started standing up and trying to jump from the back of the dinghy, nearly capsizing it.

'Keep calm!' he shouted. 'Sit down, don't stand!'

The crew handed out bright orange life jackets, then started to take off the refugees from the stern. They had been on the open sea for more than eight hours, all through the night, and all of them were wet and shivering. Some were wearing Manchester City or Chelsea football shirts, and Christina noticed that many of them had soiled themselves out of seasickness and fear. Often they just fell on the deck of the *Phoenix* and lay there. Some were vomiting from all the sea water they had swallowed. Several were limping, their feet cut by the nails in the planking on the floor of the dinghy.

They mostly seemed like economic migrants rather than refugees – people who wanted to make the dangerous crossing to get jobs, rather than because they were in fear of their lives in their own countries. Soon, though, Christina realised how unclear these divisions were. Almost all were men and mostly Gambians and Senegalese, where they had fallen foul of the government. One woman said she had escaped to avoid female genital mutilation. There were four Syrians who had fled from their city, Idlib, when Muslim extremists took it over. They had been travelling for eight months.

One of the men said he had paid a group of traffickers nearly £600. They took him to the Libyan capital, Tripoli, then to the coastal town of Garabulli to wait for a boat in a big compound with more than 200 people.

'I heard of drownings, but I couldn't see any other way,' he told Christina. 'It's like if your house is burning, and the only way out is to jump from a high window, even if you might die in the fall. We could see the boat was too small, but they were beating everyone to get on. Lots of people fell in the sea and couldn't get on, particularly the women. The boat was small, going up and down.'

The body of a woman lay in the dinghy. The rescuers zipped it up in a dark blue body bag and conveyed it to the *Phoenix*, where it lay on the deck. Christina couldn't stop looking at it and speculating about her. Her name was Omo Festus. She was twenty-three years old and from Nigeria. Her older sister, Jennifer Arebeyu, had survived the journey, watching helplessly as Omo drowned, lying in the bottom of the boat. The two sisters had left their home in the north of the country the previous year, after their parents were killed by a Boko Haram bomb. For a while they had tried to scrape a living baking cakes, but Jennifer had a young daughter, and someone told them they could have a new life in Europe.

They survived the perilous 2,000-mile journey to Libya across the Sahara desert. In Tripoli, they worked for a while as cleaners, crowded in a room with four others, trying to avoid the attentions of militia fighters. Through all of this, the dream of living in Europe kept the sisters going, and then, in early September, they had been taken with hundreds of others to a smuggler's compound to wait for a boat.

After a week's wait, they put to sea in a cheap rubber dinghy (the promised fishing boat had failed to materialise). The waves were so high, everyone was quickly soaked. Lying on the floor of the dinghy, overcome with seasickness, Omo drowned in the water that covered her.

Christina Lamb's sharp eye noticed a blonde Italian woman in rubber boots, her hair tied back under a baseball cap, clambering around among the migrants and checking their needs. Regina Catrambone, aged thirty-nine, had no need to be there; she and her American husband lived in Malta, and they could just have stayed there, enjoying themselves. Instead, Regina Catrambone spends her time cleaning up vomit on the ship and giving people who have soiled themselves clean clothes which she gets from collections at church. She and her husband have spent a fortune in buying and fitting out their rescue boat. Just keeping the *Phoenix* going costs half a million Euros a week.

Why should they do this? Christopher Catrambone made a great deal of money insuring and protecting expats who work in dangerous places like Afghanistan, but he learned something about homelessness and loss when his house in New Orleans was destroyed by Hurricane Katrina in 2005. In 2013 he chartered a luxury yacht for a holiday in Italian waters, and they stopped on the island of Lampedusa. Something was floating in the water. Catrambone asked the yacht's captain what it was, and the captain told him it must be a coat from a dead migrant.

'This moral dilemma started to sink in,' Catrambone told Christina. 'We're out here enjoying our holiday in these waters, which are a paradise for us, but for others they are hell.'

Their first rescue came a year later, when they had bought the *Phoenix* and fitted her out. They were called in to save a dinghy full of Africans. But while they were doing so they spotted a small fishing trawler nearby which seemed about to capsize.

'There were so many people hanging out, you couldn't see the boat,' Catrambone said. 'Women were holding out babies and pleading, "Please take them!"'

Their first passenger was a one-week-old baby.

'That day changed my life,' said Catrambrone. 'I was so happy we were able to save everyone. Not one dead or injured. It was 227 people, but it felt like a million.'

On the island of Lampedusa, Christina Lamb went to a ceremony for the migrants who had died. There had been so many of them that Lampedusa had run out of room for the graves, and the bodies had to be transferred to Sicily for burial. But the mayor was determined at least to give them the dignity of a religious ceremony:

> While I was there, she held one for Omo Festus, the body now in a coffin. She held her arm around Jennifer, who wailed, 'Why, why?' as the priest blessed the coffin.
>
> 'I'm alone now,' Jennifer sobbed into the mayor's arms.

Christina Lamb's article was the first I had read which made me feel I understood something of the fundamental daily realities of the refugee problem: from the sister of the woman who lay on the floor of the dinghy and drowned in the bilge water and the man who had scraped together £600 for this hellish journey, to the millionaire who cared enough about his fellow human beings to throw millions away to save their lives, and his wife who cleaned up their shit and vomit. Only long-form newspaper journalism could achieve this; and long-form newspaper journalism is as endangered nowadays as the lives of desperate migrants in an overcrowded dinghy.

FOURTEEN

Sacrifice and Survival

> One day Danny came home [from school] with a book-
> let full of new safety instructions. Among them we
> found one popular rule of the 1970s: 'Do not talk to
> strangers'. . .
>
> Little did we know then that 'talking to strangers'
> would become Danny's hobby, then his profession, and,
> eventually, his mission and ideology. . .
>
> He talked to peasants and rulers, rabbis and mullahs.
>
> He talked to winners and losers, to special strangers
> and to ordinary strangers.
>
> Little did we know that 'talking to strangers' would
> one day invite this tragedy.
>
> Judea Pearl, at the memorial service for his son
> Daniel, 10 March 2002

THE LIFE OF A foreign correspondent can be remarkably stimu-
lating and deeply rewarding: not financially, for the most part,
but intellectually and emotionally. I have no regrets at all about
deciding, on that day in 1968, that this would be my future.

Still, it would be pointless to deny that the correspondent's
life comes with a price tag attached. There is, of course, the effect
it has on personal relationships and family life. But if you are
obliged to witness scenes of violence and suffering, the personal
damage can be serious too. I feel I've managed, over the years, to
cope fairly effectively with the flashbacks and the bad memories.
Talking them over, writing about them, has proven to be an effective therapy. After watching the botched execution of three men

in Kabul in 1996, I remember thinking that this was something I would never get out of my mind; yet I wrote a script for a television report about it ('Don't forget,' the editor of the day told me over the phone nervously, 'you can't even show the ropes and the victims in the same shot'). Then I wrote a detailed piece about it for a Sunday newspaper. 'You poor thing,' said a motherly copy-taker in London after I'd dictated it to her, 'I'm sorry you should have had to go through all that.' But writing, reporting, talking, are all useful. I've had a lot of troubled, disturbed nights over the years since then, but the faces of those three dying men haven't intruded on my sleep, nor (mostly) have those of the other dead and dying people I have seen.

Such things can be part of the foreign correspondent's life, as much as the fascination of travel and the pleasure of succeeding. The best writer to have put the occasional horror of the job into words is my colleague, Fergal Keane. He covered the genocide in Rwanda in 1994, as I did. Like me, he slept on the floor of a chapel in the capital, Kigali, the one place we could find late at night, only to realise in the morning that half the floor was covered with a sea of drying blood. Twenty-four hours earlier the church had been a place of execution.

Fergal's book *Season of Blood: A Rwandan Journey*, written soon afterwards and published in 1995, makes painful reading; yet somehow, by the end, I felt obscurely comforted by it. Surely, I thought, nothing can be worse than this, and the thought was almost uplifting:

> I do not know what dreams ask of us, what they come to collect. But they have come again and again recently, and I have no answers. I thought that after the bad nights of last summer the dead had abandoned me, had mouldered into memory. But the brothers and sisters, the mothers and fathers and children, all the great wailing families of the night are back, holding fast with their withering hands, demanding my attention. Understand first that I do not want your sympathy. The dreams are part of the baggage on this journey. I understood that from the outset.

After all, four years in the South African townships had shown me something of the dark side, and I made the choice to go to Rwanda. Nobody forced me or pressurised me. So when I tell you about the nights of dread, understand that they are only part of the big picture, the first step backward into the story of a journey that happened a year ago...

As late as the start of the 1990s, foreign correspondents were loosely regarded by governments and political movements alike as being, if not exactly neutral, then at least useful sounding boards to help project their views and arguments. This certainly didn't guarantee their safety, but it did mean that they stood a reasonable chance of survival. In wartime, of course, the bets were off: shells and bombs were as indiscriminate as they always are. But armies and guerrilla groups would usually let you live, in order to get the word out. Each side in the Cold War believed that the other's journalists were spies, but for the most part they were tolerated. The worst that generally happened was that they were tossed out on their ear at short notice.

This relative feeling of security came to a sudden end with the fall of the Berlin Wall. As the wars in the former Yugoslavia quickly showed, everything was different now. In Sarajevo especially, many Western journalists took sides as strongly as their predecessors had during the Spanish Civil War, and the Bosnian Serbs came to regard them as little different from the civilians of Sarajevo: they were potential targets. The collapse of central authority gave everyone with a gun the power of life and death.

One morning in December 1992, my team and I, who included a brave Croatian woman translator, stopped at an artillery position in the hills outside Sarajevo. It was manned by an already drunken group of Bosnian Serb Četniks, and directly we stepped out of our heavily armoured Land Rover it was obvious that they were hostile. Within a couple of minutes I shouted a warning to everyone to get back into the vehicle as fast as possible, and we drove off. Afterwards, when we listened to the soundtrack from the brief pictures the cameraman had been able to shoot, we heard the instruction that one of the senior Četniks had called out to the others in Serbian, off camera: 'Keep the girl – we can fuck her. Shoot the men and throw them over the cliff, and we'll sell their camera gear in the market.'

We had entered a world of banditry, and the old expectation that your status as a journalist gave you a certain measure of protection was finished.

In some places the forces of the state themselves behaved like bandits. The most savage war of all was in Chechnya, where the Russians actively targeted journalists of all nationalities, on the grounds that they were likely to be sympathetic to the Chechens. Given the huge Russian firepower, no journalist was safe; and the government of Vladimir Putin would always back its soldiers and airmen, no matter what they did.

The United States had always been more tolerant of journalists, even those from hostile countries or organisations. That seemed to change in 2003, when the United States and its allies invaded Iraq. After the 9/11 attacks a new mood of angry self-pity often char-acterised the American forces, and the Pentagon proclaimed a new doctrine: you are either with us or you will be seen to be against us, it said in effect. If we accept you as worthy of being embedded with us, we will provide you with everything you require to do your job to the full: transport, power, security, food. But if you ignore this offer and range around the battlefield on your own, you will be putting yourselves in grave danger and we won't be responsible for what happens.

As we have seen, working for Al Jazeera, which the Americans regarded (usually wrongly) as being biased against them, became disturbingly dangerous. Journalists are often difficult, cussed types, unwilling to fall into line, and many of us dislike being embedded, preferring to operate on our own in no man's land. The result was that in Iraq, the new American approach, and the reaction to it, led to the deaths of a number of journalists, and of the people who worked alongside them.

Back in the 1980s various people including Terry Waite, Brian Keenan and John McCarthy, a journalist for the video agency UPITN, were taken prisoner by Muslim groups in Lebanon, but although they endured a long and terrible imprisonment (five years in McCarthy's case), much of it in solitary, blindfolded confinement, they were finally released when the necessary deals were done. Some Western governments were prepared to pay a cash ransom for their nationals, but the British and American governments refused, on the grounds that this would simply increase the number of kidnappings.

In March 2007 an organisation called the Army of Islam kidnapped the BBC correspondent Alan Johnston in Gaza. Johnston's reporting on conditions in Gaza had been widely praised, and some of the strongest demands for his release came from Gaza itself. His captors seem not to have realised that he was an independent-minded man who wasn't in anyone's pay. The leadership of Hamas, at the request of the British government, started to put pressure on the Army of Islam – which was in fact thought to consist of a few dozen not very intelligent extremists – and let it be known that if they didn't let Johnston go, Hamas would hunt down every single member of the group and kill them all. A little less than four months after his kidnapping, Johnston was released.

But there were already new heights of brutality against journalists, starting in 2002 with the abduction of Daniel Pearl of the *Wall Street Journal*, a dedicated, humane and charming man. He had travelled to Pakistan from his base in Delhi to investigate links between the American so-called 'shoe bomber', Richard Reid, and al-Qaeda. Pearl was kidnapped, imprisoned, and beheaded on 1 February 2002 by a senior al-Qaeda member, Khalid Sheikh Mohammed, who confessed to the murder in Guantanamo Bay after prolonged torture by the Americans.

Now correspondents were not merely in harm's way: they were regarded as useful targets, no different from enemy soldiers or airmen. The coming of Islamic State meant that correspondents and aid workers were slaughtered in disgusting ways in order to showcase IS's total lack of concern for human life. The job of the foreign correspondent had never been so dangerous. Patrick Cockburn of the *Independent*, one of the bravest and most perceptive of contemporary foreign correspondents, wrote in an April 2016 piece entitled 'The First Draft of History':

> Friends and colleagues who have been killed, such as David Blundy in El Salvador in 1989 and Marie Colvin in Syria in 2012, were very experienced journalists. Once I had imagined that it would be young and over-enthusiastic freelancers trying to make their name who would be killed. In the event, it turns out to have been the veterans who lost their lives more frequently – not because they made any great mistakes, but because they went to the well too often, and got away with it so many times that they took one risk too many.

Not, of course, that reporting has ever been a safe profession.

On the morning of Wednesday, 17 October 1973, Nick Tomalin of the *Sunday Times* was in Israel, covering the Yom Kippur War. It had entered its second difficult week, and he had decided to write a political piece from Tel Aviv for the following Sunday. Then a German photographer, Fred Ihrt, told him he was heading out to the Golan Heights, between Israel and Syria, to see the fighting. He had a spare seat in his hired car; did Tomalin want to go with him? Tomalin decided he did. A personal view of the front line would add to the strength of his piece.

Ihrt's car was white, but he had plastered it with mud to prevent it from showing up too much in the sunshine. Tomalin was driving.

He pulled up near a bunch of destroyed tanks a few miles south of the ruined town of Kuneitra. The fighting seemed to be over here, and Ihrt wanted to get some pictures of a battlefield which had been abandoned.

He got out. So did the Israeli press liaison officer who was accompanying them. Tomalin stayed in the car, and drove slowly after them as they walked up the rough path towards what seemed to be an empty bunker.

It wasn't. The Israeli soldiers inside were keeping their heads down, because they knew – as Ihrt, Tomalin and their Israeli escort didn't – that the battlefield hadn't been abandoned at all. The Syrian artillery opposite had simply gone quiet for a while. The Israelis didn't warn the three of them because, they said afterwards, they hadn't even noticed them. They certainly weren't expecting a civilian car to turn up in what turned out to be a brief lull in the battle. The Israeli escort officer was just a reservist, who knew as little of the situation as the journalists he was accompanying.

After a few minutes, Ihrt decided he'd got enough pictures. He and the Israeli officer walked down the path again, and Tomalin put the car into reverse and drove backwards down the path. He didn't want to turn because there could be mines on either side of the path. He was heading back to the crossroads, and would turn round there. At that moment Ihrt spotted something flying slowly through the air, a few feet above the ground. It was a Soviet-made Sagger anti-tank missile, guided by wire and fired by a Syrian less than a mile away. It struck the car and blew it up, and the petrol tank exploded an instant later. Nick Tomalin didn't stand a chance.

The photographer, Don McCullin, forever close to the action, was nearby. He too was working for the *Sunday Times*, and with typical courage went forward to see what had happened. In less than an hour he had contacted the paper's foreign desk to break the news. There was shock and genuine grief, and not only from Tomalin's colleagues. In the House of Commons, a motion of regret was tabled. A committee of the United Nations observed a minute's silence. A number of governments sent messages of sympathy. One of the world's finest journalists was dead at the age of forty-one.

No one was really guilty, not even the Syrian soldier who fired the missile. To him, the hired car must have seemed like a legitimate target. Just being near the front line was dangerous, and Tomalin knew that as well as anyone. You can cover a war from your hotel in the capital, or from the ministry of information, but that isn't war reporting; it's just acting like a one-man newsroom, safe and sound. Funnily enough, that's what your foreign desk would often prefer you to do. They don't want you to get yourself killed, and they just want to get hour-by-hour coverage. The decision to go out or to stay in safety lies with you. If you want to report a war properly, you have to take risks and see for yourself what is going on. Nick Tomalin took the risk, and it killed him.

When I planned this book, I wanted to deal in some detail with the deaths in combat of a whole group of journalists, several of them friends of mine. On reflection, though, I have realised that recounting so much pain and suffering might well have a dulling effect, reducing sympathy rather than awakening it. I have decided instead to concentrate on a few cases instead.

One is that of Abed Takkoush, a driver and fixer in Lebanon, amusing and fearless, and a great admirer of women. On 23 May 2000, Abed was with Jeremy Bowen on the border between southern Lebanon and Israel when, like Nick Tomalin twenty-seven years earlier, he stayed in his Mercedes while the others got out and started getting pictures. An Israeli tank fired a shell at the Mercedes, and Jeremy watched Ahmed climb out of the window, his clothes on fire, then fall head first to the ground. An Israeli machine gun opened up on Jeremy and his cameraman, Malek Kanaan.

Later, filled with guilt and anger over Abed's death, Jeremy wrote with painful honesty in *War Stories*:

> I shouted his name but he didn't answer. Maybe he was hoping we would come and rescue him. If life was like a film I would have run up to him, bullets zinging off the gravel around me. I

would have got to him and comforted him, and even if I had not saved his life he would not have had to die alone. But I decided I could not save him and that I had to save myself. The ending was not happy. Life is not a film.

The day after Abed was killed, Kurt Schork of Reuters died in an ambush on a road through the bush in Sierra Leone.

Sometimes, reflecting on these things seems like living in the opening lines of the Henry Vaughan poem:

> They are all gone into the world of light!
> And I alone sit ling'ring here...

So many people I have known and liked, and some whom I've loved, have died. They wander past in the mind, a random succession of smiling faces and pleasant memories: David Blundy, clever and self-possessed, shot dead by a sniper in El Salvador in 1989; Rory Peck, a wonderfully brave and charming cameraman who died in Moscow in 1993, also the victim of a sniper; John Schofield, murdered by Croatian soldiers in August 1995 aged twenty-nine, at the time the seventy-sixth journalist to die in the wars of the former Yugoslavia; Terry Lloyd, who was killed on 22 March 2003 when troops at an American checkpoint fired at his vehicle as it was fleeing from an Iraqi tank; Paul Moran, a freelance cameraman for ABC Australia, killed the same day by a suicide bomber; Gaby Rado, a Channel 4 News correspondent, who fell from the roof of his hotel in northern Iraq; Simon Cumbers, a gentle, pleasant Irish reporter and cameraman, murdered by Islamic extremists in a suburb of Riyadh in June 2004.

There was the dreadful day, 2 April 2003, when my colleague Jim Muir stopped his car in northern Iraq to ask a local commander if he could park his car on a nearby patch of grass. The commander nodded. But someone had planted mines there, and one went off. Kaveh Golestan, a delightful, highly intelligent Iranian BBC cameraman, assumed they had come under shellfire and jumped out of the car directly onto a mine. It blew up, and he was thrown onto another mine which exploded too. Stuart Hughes, a sharp-minded BBC producer, also got out and detonated a mine; he lost part of his foot, and eventually his leg needed amputation. Jim, a brave, intensely thoughtful Scotsman, had to drive his car back to their base alone that night, a journey lasting several hours, with Kaveh's mangled body lying on the back seat.

Four days later, my team was the victim of an American friendly-fire attack, when a US special forces captain on the ground radioed the pilot of an American warplane flying over-head the coordinates of our position and those of a nearby Iraqi tank which was shooting at us. Instead of hitting the tank, the pilot dropped a 1,000-pound bomb right into the middle of our group. It was never established who had made the mistake, the special forces captain or the pilot. Nineteen people died, many of them burned to death. Every one of my colleagues received minor injuries, but our charming, courtly Kurdish translator, aged only twenty-five, had his feet sheered off by a big piece of shrapnel. He died of blood loss, after trying to fight off our producer, Tom Giles, who was comforting him.

'You know, there could be real danger if you work with us,' I had told Kamran a few weeks before, when I gave him a job as my main translator.

'Yes, I realise that,' Kamran answered, 'but I have seen you on television and I want to work with you.'

So by hiring him I killed him. I didn't do it on purpose, but my decision led directly to his death, and I had to explain his death to his elderly mother with his blood still on my clothes. Not a day passes without my thinking of Kamran, and the way he shouted out and struggled as he lay dying, and the bewildered words of his mother, 'But he wasn't doing anything dangerous – he said so.' He had decided not to tell her about our daily trips to the front line. Afterwards, back in my hotel room, I sat with my head in my hands, tears running down my face, saying again and again, 'I'm sorry. I'm so sorry.' And that isn't the only time this has happened.

As Jeremy Bowen put it, life isn't a film. It isn't neat, and the endings can't necessarily be relied on to be happy.

All in all, then, I'd prefer not to dwell too much further here on all the other deaths and the way they happened. But one has to be described in detail.

In February 2012, Marie Colvin went back into Syria under cover: characteristically, she rode on the back of a motorbike, heading for the Baba Amr district in the west of the city of Homs. The shelling of civilian areas by the Syrian government forces was intense, and on the evening of 21 February she broadcast her account of it by satellite phone on each of the British television news programmes and on CNN; a very considerable achievement. She described how the Syrian forces were indiscriminately shelling and sniping at the civilians in the area.

But the calls, which she made from an impromptu media centre, seem to have brought about her death. The Syrians tracked the phone signals. She and two photographers, a Frenchman, Rémi Ochlik, and Paul Conroy, a British freelance, spent the night in the centre. In the early morning a series of explosions rocked the building. Conroy, who had served in the Royal Artillery during the 1980s, realised that the Syrians were bracketing it: straddling it with their shots in order to hit it more precisely.

A rocket landed directly in front of the media building, and a chunk of shrapnel went right through Conroy's thigh, leaving a gap he was able to put his fist into and out the other side. He made himself a tourniquet with an ethernet cable, then lay helplessly in the rubble for a short while.

After that, he discovered the bodies of Marie and Rémi. The shell had landed only two yards away from them. Mercifully they wouldn't have known anything about it, or suffered any pain. He later wrote in *Under the Wire: Marie Colvin's Last Assignment*:

> I couldn't see Marie's face. Her head and legs were covered in fallen rubble and I recognised her only by her blue jumper and belt. . . Marie, with whom I had shared a thousand adventures; Marie the sailor; Marie who had given a face and voice to millions of people whose lives had been torn apart by war; Marie, the Martha Gellhorn of our generation, who now lay motionless

in the ruins of Baba Amr. I gently laid my hand on her chest and checked she was dead. Farewell, Chechen queen.

———————

Easier, perhaps, to concentrate on those who've survived, and have surmounted their experiences.

Frank Gardner was sent to Saudi Arabia at the start of June 2004 to cover the aftermath of the murder of a British citizen. Simon Cumbers, a journalist and cameraman who ran a production house of his own, went with him. Not long before, Simon had sent one of the cameramen who worked for him to cover a story in Baghdad; characteristically, because he disliked sending other people into dangerous situations, he decided that this time he would go himself.

Saudi Arabia is a difficult place for a television news team to work: highly bureaucratic and defensive at the upper levels, while junior officials have a tendency to be slow, unwilling and bad at keeping time. Frank asked permission to film three things: police checkpoints, an interview with a senior counter-terrorism official, and shots of the area towards Al-Suwaidi in the south of Riyadh. Six months earlier there had been a shoot-out there between the police and an Islamist leader, Ibrahim Al-Rayyes, who had been killed.

Even this limited shopping list seemed to be pretty unlikely, and the response of the ministry of information was discouraging. Like all government ministries in Saudi Arabia, it closed down for the day at 2 p.m., and Gardner assumed that their trip was finished. He and Cumbers went back to their hotel and planned to return home the next day. They were surprised when the ministry phoned that afternoon to say that they could, after all, film in Riyadh, and even in Al-Suwaidi.

A government vehicle arrived to take them. The driver was a Saudi of African descent called Mubarak; their ministry of information minder was a man called Yahya, pleasant, round-faced and relatively open; my wife and I had worked with him on a filming trip to Riyadh some time earlier and rather liked him. Yahya told them they could go where they liked, but they couldn't film any checkpoints. The vehicle set out for Al-Suwaidi.

It turned out to be the usual poorer Saudi neighbourhood: flat-roofed, usually one-storeyed buildings lining either side of the road, with basic shops, food stores, cheap restaurants and garages selling car parts: 'People were just starting to emerge on to the streets after the mid-afternoon siesta; a few of the men, I noticed, wore the short robes and long beards of devout fundamentalists. One could sense this was a poorer part of town, but the poverty was not extreme.'

Al-Suwaidi seemed like every other outer suburb in the Gulf: villas surrounded by high walls, usually with climbing plants of some kind growing on the tops of the walls, the buildings separated from each other by patches of litter-strewn waste ground. They had been told that the area was calm now, but even so they didn't want to go into it, just to film it from a distance. Some children turned up, as they always seem to, and asked them to film them.

The rule in difficult places like this is that you shouldn't stay for more than fifteen minutes; that, theoretically, being the time it would take some hostile character to spot you, get on the phone to his friends, gather up some weapons, and go out to get you. The fifteen-minute rule has served us well in really dangerous places like the streets of Baghdad during the height of the kidnapping period, from 2004 to 2008. But Yahya seemed relaxed, and there was no hint of danger, so Frank did a number of takes of a piece to camera, strolling across the waste ground and pointing out the area where the shoot-out had happened six months before. As he wrote in *Blood and Sand*, they were just about finished when a car pulled up beside the minivan and a young man got out:

> Like every adult male Saudi, he wore the traditional white *thaub*, essentially a smart shirt that extends all the way down to the ankles. He looked very young, perhaps still in his teens, and had a kindly face with a hint of a smile, almost as if he knew us or our two Saudi escorts. Was he coming to ask directions? Perhaps he knew the driver and had come to chat.

331

He called out the usual Muslim greeting, '*Assalaamu aleikum*', peace be upon you. Frank, who spoke Arabic, replied in the traditional polite fashion.

> The man paused, a curious look on his face, then with no sign of haste he reached his right hand into what must have been a specially extended pocket sewn into the breast of his *thaub*. I did not need to see the weapon to know what was coming next. It was like a film with a predictable ending.
>   'No! Don't do this!' I shouted instinctively in Arabic.
>   He pulled out a long-barrelled pistol. Oh my God, I thought, this cannot be happening.

Frank turned and ran towards Al-Suwaidi. The man fired a shot at him, hitting him in the shoulder. For a moment Frank thought he had got away, but there was another shot and Frank fell on his face on the ground, hit in the leg. A second group in a minivan had driven round to cut him off. Now they were jumping out of the van and heading towards him:

> They appeared very different from my first attacker; they had made no attempt to disguise their jihadi appearance. Their thin, pale faces were framed by wispy, unkempt beards in the style of most extremists and they had the look of people who spent all their time indoors.

They wore scarves wound tightly round their foreheads, like the jihadis in countless suicide videos:

> In that instant I glimpsed faces driven by pure hatred and fanaticism. I pleaded with them in Arabic, as so many hostages have done in Iraq, while they held a brief discussion as to what to do with me. It did not take long.

A gunman stood over him and pumped three more bullets into him:

> I don't remember it hurting at the point of impact, just a deafening noise each time he squeezed the trigger and a sickening jolt

as the bullets thudded into my guts. Each time he fired it was as if a giant hand had picked me up and slammed me down on the tarmac...

The sole thought he had in his head was to survive all this for the sake of his wife and daughters:

I closed my eyes and kept as still as I could, face-down on my front. The shooting had stopped and there was a discussion going on in Arabic. One of the terrorists was getting out of the van and walking towards me.

Frank held his breath and played dead. The man reached into the back pocket of Frank's trousers and took out the radio microphone which Simon Cumbers had given him. Then he tried the other pocket. It contained a miniature copy of the Koran.

For a few seconds nothing happened. Then Frank heard the attackers' car starting up and driving off. There was utter silence. No one came to his rescue:

I flipped over on to my back, supporting myself half upright with extended arms so I could call out more effectively for help.

As I turned I felt my legs roll over like two dead logs, my feet flopping flat and lifeless against the ground. My right leg was bent in and out at crazy angles and I could feel nothing below the waist.

Slowly, a crowd gathered round him, but still no one did anything. It was half an hour before the police turned up, but they too just stood around for a while. One of them asked if he'd got the number plate of his attackers' car.

Eventually they picked him up and put him in the back of their patrol car, but he was too long for it and his head and shoulders stuck out through one of the back windows. He was in great pain by now, yet he had to keep his hand on the car roof to stop his head banging about.

They took him to the Al-Iman hospital, which didn't have much of a reputation. Before someone at last gave him a painkilling injection and he sank into unconsciousness, he saw a look of panic on the surgeons' faces.

Frank's life was saved by a combination of factors. He had managed to phone the British embassy in Riyadh and ask for help. The ambassador, Sherard Cowper-Coles, was alerted, and got straight on to the royal court and the governor of Riyadh. They in turn sent a highly qualified team from the King Faisal Hospital, the best in the country, to take care of him. One of the surgeons who operated on him was a South African who had previously worked in Baragwanath Hospital in Soweto, where people were treated for serious gunshot wounds every single day; he knew precisely what to do, stage by stage. Frank's life was saved, but he would never be able to use his legs again.

In all of this, there was no mention of Simon Cumbers. He had run when Frank did, but had been hampered by carrying his camera – the natural instinct of the cameraman – and he found himself eventually in a cul-de-sac. A gunmen shot him in the head at close range.

Simon was one of the gentlest-natured people I have ever worked with, and his loss was widely felt. At the BBC newsroom in London there was an unusual outpouring of sorrow when the news of his death broke. He was only in Saudi Arabia because he didn't feel he should ask someone else to put themselves into harm's way. In an obituary she wrote for him, Orla Guerin, the BBC's Middle East correspondent who, like Simon, was Irish, quoted his motto, as positive and cheerful as the man himself: 'Give it a go, give them a smile, and if they let you in, get the story.'

Mubarak, Frank and Simon's government driver, drove off in the ministry car with Yahya, the government minder, directly the killers arrived. There was inevitably suspicion that they had somehow been involved, and Yahya simply disappeared afterwards; no one at the ministry of information would say what had happened to him. I personally did not think that he had been in contact with the militants; he didn't seem the type. He certainly didn't behave like an Islamic sympathiser himself. Yet someone seems to have tipped off the killers. Could it have been another official inside the ministry?

Possibly. But the most likely explanation is the simplest: they were spotted by an extremist in Al-Suwaidi as they recorded the piece to camera, and whoever it was that saw them quickly summoned up a group of gunmen.

Simon Cumbers's family was devastated by his loss. Frank Gardner's family gathered round him and supported him as he recovered; which he did triumphantly. He will never walk again, but he has continued working as a correspondent specialising in counter-terrorism with great effectiveness, reporting in the studio from his wheelchair or standing with a frame, and on occasion flying to places like Afghanistan. For Frank, the story of the years since 2004 has been immensely difficult, but on the whole it has been heartening and positive.

Having to face up to horrors and react to them humanely without going crazy in the process isn't easy. Caroline Hawley is a gentle, slightly built woman whose job as a foreign correspondent has forced her to witness some of the worst things human beings have done to each other in recent years; and she has survived.

After studying Arabic and Persian at Oxford, her first job was a plum: *Newsweek* took her on as its Jerusalem correspondent. From there she joined the BBC, and became its Baghdad correspondent – only to be thrown out of Iraq in 2002, during the last months of Saddam Hussein's rule. She returned to Baghdad immediately after the American-led invasion, and saw for herself the gross stupidities of the coalition's rule: the across-the-board sackings of all officials who had been members of the Ba'ath Party (since membership had been virtually mandatory under Saddam, not many civil servants remained), the disbanding of the old Iraqi army, many of whose Sunni officers promptly joined the resistance to the coalition, and the grotesque looting of government ministries and the world-famous archaeological museum in Baghdad, while American soldiers looked on because they had no orders to intervene. We were in the era of 'stuff happens': the words the US

335

defence secretary Donald Rumsfeld used when challenged about the spoliation of the country.

Right from the start, Caroline saw things that were deeply disturbing: the evidence of the kind of torture the Saddam regime had used, and the increasingly frequent attacks carried out by the insurgents in Baghdad. The BBC bureau was rocked by bomb explosions from time to time, some of which broke windows in the house where we worked. She was caught up in a number of bombings and shootings in the streets of the city. And there was the sheer stress of the things she had to witness. Ten years later, she wrote for BBC news of one early example:

> It was heartbreaking to watch women clawing through the earth at mass graves, desperately trying to find any remnant of their sons. Any bone or scrap of clothing was enough – they just wanted some part of their child to bury. A decade on, it is equally distressing to think how many horrors and burials, kidnappings and bombings lay ahead.

Conditions were hard for everyone. The coalition proved incapable of ensuring proper supplies of water or electricity in Baghdad, so the BBC bureau, like everywhere else, regularly had to endure the full heat of the summer or the chill of winter. Once when I was there, I rang the BBC in London in a rage because the demands of live broadcasting had kept Caroline standing out in the sun on the roof of the building for nearly an hour in a temperature of forty-eight degrees centigrade.

For the people on the desk in London it was just another story; for Caroline it was draining and exhausting, and potentially dangerous. She didn't ask me to complain to the producers in London; in fact she'd probably have preferred me not to. She was the daughter of an ambassador, and I used to feel that it was her sense of public duty that kept her going through these intensely difficult years. After she had left, a young, healthy and ambitious male correspondent gave up only a year into the job, because he found the physical and psychological demands too much to take. Caroline served three full years in Baghdad: the worst years. In November 2005, almost at the end of her time, she took a few days off with her boyfriend in Amman, the capital of neighbouring Jordan. While they were there, there was a series of coordinated bomb attacks in three hotels, including theirs. Altogether sixty people died and 115 were injured.

Caroline endured all these things, and soon returned to work. One of her best reports was an investigation into a British company which supplied fake explosive detectors, the ADE651 and the GT200, to countries like Iraq and Afghanistan. In 2013, as a direct result of her reporting, the founder of the company, Jim McCormick, was sentenced at the Old Bailey to ten years in prison; though the security men who guard the street where the BBC office still operates continue to check cars with the useless detectors. Caroline Hawley's story is one of real, if unreported, devotion to duty; and instead of crumpling under the strain, she survived and overcame it.

A few chapters ago, the *Times* correspondent Anthony Loyd was musing on a severed head outside the Iraqi town of Fallujah. That he should have been back in the Middle East reporting on a story which concerned war and Islamic extremism is one of the more remarkable examples of courage and the determination to survive which this book contains.

It was 8.30 a.m. on a May morning in 2014. Loyd, the *Times* photographer Jack Hill, and two Syrians had just left the house of a local rebel commander, Abdel Hakim al Yaseen. He was the man who had beaten up someone who had angered him, then told him to get into a car and promptly blown it up as it drove away. Now Loyd and Hill were kidnapped, and Hakim was responsible.

Loyd had known and trusted him for two years – had, indeed, regarded him as a friend. In his account of the ordeal that followed, Loyd writes in *The Times*:

> I can barely write the words now, four months later, without feeling my face twist with loathing at the depth of his deception.
>
> We had dined with him under his roof, met his newborn daughter, played with his son, discussed dead and absent friends,

337

the course of the war against the regime and the conflict between rebel groups and Isis.

We had slept as guests in his home. He had even ensured that we did not depart for Turkey without first being given breakfast and coffee. And behind all that, he was all the while planning our downfall, manoeuvring to have us abducted and sold as hostages: a fate that guaranteed lengthy captivity in abysmal conditions, heartbreak for our families, possible beheading.

Like every journalist working in Syria and Iraq, Loyd was frightened of becoming a hostage of Islamic State. Eighteen months before, IS had kidnapped the American correspondent James Foley, who worked as a freelance, and had beheaded him. An IS video showing his murder in disgusting detail had been shown on the internet. Steven Sotloff, another American journalist, was also killed in the same fashion. A British journalist, John Cantlie, had been captured around the same time. Though he hadn't been killed, he had been ill-treated and forced to make videos praising his captors. Nothing more has been heard of Austin Tice, another American journalist who was captured and held by IS.

Anthony Loyd and Jack Hill now seemed in danger of facing the same fate. They were driven to an abandoned farm where they were blindfolded and handcuffed. A guard tried to take a silver chain round Loyd's neck which bore his daughter's name. He had two other things on him which he called his 'war magic': a little silver fish engraved with the word 'Hope' and the date of his marriage, and a small brass container which carried a few of the ashes of his friend and mentor Kurt Schork of Reuters, the author of the report on the Romeo and Juliet of Sarajevo who was killed in Sierra Leone. Anthony Loyd is the first person to admit that he's weird, but anyone who has worked in a war zone knows how important things like this can be. Now, as the guard tried to grab the chain, he called out 'daughter, daughter', and said the Arabic version of her name. The man let go. Anthony had held on to his talismans.

They were moved somewhere else by car. He could hear a banging noise coming from the boot, and then sounds which he assumed were those of Jack and one of their Syrian friends being beaten up. Then the car door was wrenched open, and Jack was mumbling at him through his gag to run for it. Jack had managed to get out of the boot, and had attacked one of the guards. Loyd sprinted away, and climbed up one wall then another despite his shackled hands. He knew where he was now – back in Tal Rifaat, Hakim's town. He could hear shouting in the street, and looking down saw Jack, fighting two men and yelling. He'd been caught by the rest of the kidnap gang, though the two Syrians had managed to grab a motorbike and had escaped.

As Anthony Loyd looked over the edge of the roof, one of the men Jack was fighting lifted his head, and Anthony recognised him:

. . . the man I looked down upon, Judas in the street, was Hakim.

Motherf***er. I spat it. Never did a word fit a man so well.

Yet there was no aftermath to that bolt of fury. Jack's fate was unfortunate, but I could do nothing to help him. Hakim? A regrettable betrayal. I continued my run.

But he was spotted within minutes and recaptured. Six men started beating him, and he blacked out. When he came to, he was being dragged towards a crowd, and Hakim was shouting that he was *jazoos*, a spy, probably assuming that they would lynch him. But the crowd didn't react. Loyd yelled out that he was a British journalist from *The Times*.

Hakim swung round to look at me. His eyes were feral and glittering. He looked faintly desperate, too. There was silence as I was pushed towards him until we faced one another.

'Hello, Hakim,' I said, as coolly as I could. 'I thought we were friends.'

'No friends,' he rasped, as his silver pistol arced across his chest and down towards my feet for the traditional punishment shooting.

He blasted two bullets into me at almost point-blank range.

Fortunately, the shots didn't do as much harm as they might have. The first hit the leather of Anthony's boot and smashed part of his ankle bone. The second bullet stuck his ankle higher up, then turned round on itself and broke his heel. It was bad, and very painful, but it could have been even worse.

Anthony was pushed and shoved into a room crowded with armed men. There was another prisoner there, with a badly battered face: Jack Hill, the photographer.

The two of them were valuable commodities who could be traded for cash, as long as they survived. So instead of being killed, they were taken to a hospital. Even there they weren't safe from harm; a couple of degenerates took turns in kicking Anthony's injured ankle.

Soon, though, a commander from an important rebel group arrived.

'It's OK,' he said. 'We know who you are. You are safe.'

Anthony was in a bad way. He'd been shot and beaten, and one of his eyeballs had been haemorrhaging. Now he was taken to a field hospital in the town of Marea, in serious pain. A Syrian doctor stood over him and offered him the use of his mobile phone. Anthony used it to call his wife, but he didn't tell her he'd been shot. He just said he'd escaped, and was now with the good guys.

He handed the phone back to the doctor. In the bed beside him lay a rebel who'd been badly injured and hadn't yet been treated. The doctor's eyes kept shifting from Anthony to him.

'We have some morphine,' the doctor said. 'Unless, of course, you think you can handle it?'

Anthony knew exactly what he meant: they were short of morphine, and the man beside him needed it more than he did: '"Thanks, doctor," I said, after a while, trying to sound cheerful and decent. "I don't want your morphine. I can handle it."'

AFTERWORD

> I now think that the act of keeping the record straight
> is valuable in itself. Serious, careful, honest journalism is
> essential, not because it is a guiding light but because it
> is a form of honorable behavior, involving the reporter
> and the reader.
>
> Martha Gellhorn, *The Face of War*, 1959

FOR AROUND FIFTY YEARS, from the 1920s to the 1970s, the *Daily Express* boasted one of the world's great stables of foreign correspondents. As late as 1968 thirty-five correspondents were still based around the world for the *Express*, and although many of them were used to dig out stories that gave backing to the views of their proprietor, about the iniquities of the European Common Market and the benefits of trade within the Commonwealth, they still reported the news in the lively and readable fashion which had made the *Express* a real force in British life.

By the early nineties the *Express* had one solitary figure who produced, wrote and edited its foreign coverage: an urbane, crinkly-haired, finely turned-out figure called John Ellison, who seemed to be emblematic of the entire tribe of foreign correspondents, past and present. Whenever he could persuade his bosses, he would (as foreign editor) send himself (as chief and indeed only foreign correspondent) to cover a particular story. He had a secretary, to whom he would send his stories.

Eventually John Ellison had to go too; but before that happened I bumped into him one morning at Heathrow Terminal Four, dressed in a linen jacket and panama hat. He was on his way to one hot and difficult place, I was going to another. We shook hands and grinned, and he passed a few acerbic comments about the current management of the *Express*, and we headed off to our different departure gates. Even at the time I remember thinking I was saying goodbye to the last old-style foreign correspondent, of a type which has cropped up again and again in these pages: shrewd, literate, good at languages, stylish, distinctly steely beneath the civilised exterior.

Of course foreign correspondents were an expensive luxury, and for years the American networks, in particular, wasted huge amounts of money on their foreign bureaux. According to an unappealing character called Andrew Lack, who was president of NBC News from 1993 to 2001:

> The dirty little secret. . . was that those people were not very productive. I was at the old CBS Paris bureau and the old CBS London bureau and there were an awful lot of guys sitting around and going to Savile Row and buying fancy-looking suits. . . There was a noblesse oblige in the bureaux system that was a waste of. . . money, and bullshit. . . That level of waste was pulled out of the system.

There's something quite distasteful about those words; and, as it happens, among the guys in their Savile Row suits were distinguished figures such as Tom Fenton who added genuine lustre and class (what Lack presumably meant by 'waste') to an otherwise not very impressive operation. And when people like him were 'pulled out of the system', the quality of CBS News fell accordingly. Another, more sympathetic president of CBS News later wrote: 'Tom is the embodiment of the wise and worldly CBS News correspondent. . . In a world where civility is increasingly a casualty of competitive pressures, Tom holds steady to that most old-fashioned of virtues: he's a true gentleman.'

Andrew Lack was no doubt a pleasant enough character at home, and he was probably kind to animals; but it's hard to think that someone would write an encomium along these lines about him. And yet there was a good deal of truth to what he said. The American networks did indeed lavish ludicrous quantities of money on their overseas newsgathering. Even more was spent after the assassination of President Anwar Sadat of Egypt at a military parade in Cairo in 1981. An ABC crew was on hand to film the whole thing; but the NBC and CBS crews had decided that the next location was likely to prove more promising, so they left before the shooting started. The subsequent sackings of NBC and CBS staff, like the assassination itself, was a bloody business, and none of the networks forgot it. It was now in almost everyone's interest – the entire editorial, planning and foreign staff, and all the bureaux everywhere – to protect their positions by lavishing coverage on every potential story, just in case something big might happen. Only an infinitesimal proportion of this formidable body of work ever saw the air, but no one dared take the chance of failing to cover something that New York might later show an interest in.

Even so, nothing much seemed to have any great importance to New York apart from a few stories in Israel and Russia, terrorism in Lebanon and occasionally in London, and the doings and wardrobe of Princess Diana. In the late eighties, an extremist threw a hand grenade at the conference centre in Luxembourg where the leaders of the European Community were gathered for a summit meeting. No one was hurt, but it was a big story at the time. An excellent and gutsy NBC producer, Tira Shubart, with whom I was living at the time, raced around getting pictures of the aftermath, then phoned New York to gauge the interest.

'Any big shots there?' a world-weary voice asked her.

'Not unless you count the prime minister of Britain, the German chancellor and the president of France,' she answered.

'Oh, OK,' said the voice. 'Think we'll take a rain-check.'

Of course, the people who should have been sacked when the time of reckoning came were those who had overseen the unlikely combination of grotesque overspending and sharply dwindling interest in what was going on in the outside world. Instead, hatchet men of the calibre of Andrew Lack chose to sacrifice the talent – and there was still a good deal of that in those days – rather than the managers and the programme producers who were responsible

343

for the shrinking of the networks' world view. The pattern was crystal clear: the less you tell people about what is happening, the less they'll know, and the less they'll be interested in. The downward spiral gets progressively tighter and tighter until it vanishes altogether.

In the 1960s, when Tom Fenton first went into the reporting business, he found that the CBS style book contained a magnificent (BBC people would call it 'Reithian') statement of principle by the then-president of CBS News, Richard Salant: 'He said that we won't give the viewers what we think they want to see, or what some expert tells us they want to see, but what we, in our best news judgment, think they need to know. That attitude has totally disappeared.'

The reason it disappeared was because CBS, like the other networks, came to regard the profit margin, rather than broadcasting quality, as the sole guide to value. Another hero of this book, Dan Rather, wrote angrily some years ago in the *New York Times* after yet another cull: 'CBS Inc. is a profitable, valuable Fortune 500 corporation whose stock is setting new records. But 215 people lost their jobs so that the stockholders would have even more money in their pockets. More profits. That's what business is about.'

Newspapers, at least in Western countries, have long ceased to be profitable businesses. A report on the future of the foreign correspondent, written by a friend and former boss of mine, Richard Sambrook, for Reuters Institute for the Study of Journalism at Oxford noted that newspapers in twenty out of thirty-one OECD countries faced declining readerships. In 2016 the *Independent*, which as late as the 1990s was arguably the world's best newspaper, brought its print edition to an end and became simply an online entity. Perhaps this doesn't matter: many of us read a selection of the world's newspapers online every morning and feel thoroughly well informed without ever stepping out to buy a single physical copy. At least the *Independent* still exists, and, in contrast to many of the world's other news outlets, it remains what its title proclaims: independent. If the world has changed decisively, there is no real point in our weeping over it or constantly wishing the old days back.

———

But it's part of a much wider change. The authority figure, whether in politics or journalism, is now often regarded with contempt and derision. The comments which readers leave online under any given newspaper article nowadays show a breathtaking combination of cynicism, spite, ignorance and misspelling; and it sometimes takes an effort to remember that these savage remarks aren't necessarily a genuine reflection of public opinion, but merely the kind of irreflective dross which would scarcely have registered before the coming of the internet.

So what can those of us who care about such things do to shore up the standards which seem to be slipping away before our eyes? We can, for a start, acknowledge that quality doesn't come cheap, and that decent writing and reporting costs money – though not necessarily an awful lot of it. Fifty pence a day for reading a newspaper online, fourpence a day for watching or listening to the BBC: it's scarcely a fortune. We can demand more from our sources of information. We can make a fuss about declining standards. We can resolve to give more support to media outlets whose standards aren't declining; and there are plenty of them.

What won't work is to adopt the approach of the Confucian scholar and keep our heads down among our books, in the hope that one day a better emperor will come along. Nowadays better emperors are in distinctly short supply. The unrestricted play of market forces has already done immense damage to the supply of honest, open information; what has happened over the past half-century to CBS in America or the *Daily Express* in Britain is clear evidence of that. Crowd-funding alone won't save the situation, though if people were prepared to pay more for their news it would certainly help. Over the years the European Union has toyed with ideas of setting up a fund to support news organisations which meet certain clear standards. It's a disturbing thought to some people – suppose those standards included supporting the European project? – but a licence-fee system for broadcasters has worked right across Europe, most notably with the BBC, so maybe it could work for newspapers. Anything, surely, is better than watching the continuing decay of once-decent sources of information into propaganda sheets or sub-porn for a few wealthy owners.

I'm writing the last pages of this book in Uluru, or Ayers Rock, in the Martian landscape of central Australia; and something about this place makes me determined not to end on a gloomy note. Looking out at that numinous sandstone prodigy, the colour of dried blood, rearing up in the broiling afternoon sun, inclines one towards grand and general thoughts; not, in fact, the kind of things that foreign correspondents are particularly good at. Traditionally the people in the field have always preferred to leave the big strategic thinking to the editorial writers back at headquarters.

If 400 years of foreign corresponding since the time of Nathaniel Butter and Ben Jonson's Emissary Buz are drawing to an end, it's only fair to say that they have helped to form the lives and characters of some pretty remarkable people, from William Howard Russell, Martha Gellhorn and Clare Hollingworth, right through to Marie Colvin and Anthony Loyd. The combination of moral purpose and adventurousness is a heady one, and thoroughly worth celebrating.

But what does such an existence do to you as a person? I suppose it strips away your illusions: think of Anthony Loyd and his friend of two years, Hakim; or Marie Colvin left alone by her colleagues among the refugees and the unarmed UN people in East Timor; or Fergal Keane dreaming of the people he had seen killed in front of him; or Alistair Cooke remembering the woman shouting: 'Stinking country, no, no, no, no' after the murder of Robert Kennedy. Not all memories are good ones, by any manner of means. Think too of John Cantlie and Austin Tice, who as I write this are still the prisoners of men in Syria who take a pleasure in the savage killing of Western journalists.

But does the life of a foreign correspondent lead you to expect nothing but cruelty and cowardice and betrayal from your fellow human beings? No; as Oscar Wilde said at one of his trials, 'There are marvellous exceptions.' There are indeed. There is Dith Pran, who remained with his friends and colleagues in Cambodia when he knew it was likely to lead to an ugly death. There is also the Tutsi woman I came across in Rwanda during the worst of the genocide, who hid her Hutu neighbour in the water-filled ditch between their houses, gave her a reed to breathe through during the times when the Tutsi mob was hunting for her, then smuggled her into her house and fed her when the hunt died away. The good moments don't, alas, match the ugly ones in purely numerical terms, but they help to keep you going if your job is to tell people about all the bad things that are going on.

Richard Sambrook ends his lapidary essay on the future of the foreign correspondent, 'Are Foreign Correspondents Redundant', like this:

> From William Howard Russell in the Crimea, to the beaches of D-Day. From Baghdad, Kabul, the streets of Tehran or Tiananmen Square or the genocide in Rwanda, eyewitness reporting has been and will remain of crucial importance. There is no substitute for being able to say 'I was there and this is what I saw'. It is the heart of international journalism.

And he quotes a present-day foreign correspondent, Allan Little, renowned for his thoughtfulness and good writing:

> Eyewitness journalism is in one sense the purest and most decent work we do. It has the power to settle part of the argument, to close down propaganda, to challenge myth-making.

This book has been full of stories of people who, when it counted, did this job decently and sometimes with real courage. But, as Marie Colvin said, the last time I saw her, when someone (it may have been me) was getting a bit too solemn and worthy: 'We also have a great deal of fun, you know.'

BIBILIOGRAPHY

Adie, Kate, *The Kindness of Strangers*, Headline, 2002

Atkins, John Black, *The Life of Sir William Howard Russell, The First Special Correspondent*, 2 vols, John Murray, 1911

Becker, Elizabeth, *When the War was Over: Cambodia and the Khmer Rouge Revolution*, Simon & Schuster, 1986

Beeston, Richard, *Looking for Trouble: The Life and Times of a Foreign Correspondent*, Brassey's, 1997

Bowen, Jeremy, *War Stories*, Simon & Schuster, 2006

Bowles, Thomas Gibson, *The Defence of Paris, Narrated As It Was Seen*, Sampson Low, 1871

Boys, Jayne E. E., *London's News Press and the Thirty Years War*, Rochester, 2011

Buerk, Michael, *The Road Taken*, Hutchinson, 2004

Cockburn, Patrick, *The Broken Boy*, Jonathan Cape, 2005

Colvin, Marie, *On the Front Line: The Collected Journalism of Marie Colvin*, HarperPress, 2012

Conroy, Paul, *Under the Wire: Marie Colvin's Last Assignment*, Quercus, 2013

Cooke, Alistair, *Letter from America: 1946–2004*, Penguin, 2005

Crawford, Alex, *Colonel Gaddafi's Hat*, Collins, 2012

Cutforth, René, *Korean Reporter*, Allan Wingate, 1952

Deedes, William, *At War with Waugh: The Real Story of Scoop*, Macmillan, 2003

Delmer, Denis Sefton, *Trail Sinister: An Autobiography*, Secker & Warburg, 1961

Di Giovanni, Janine, *Madness Visible*, Bloomsbury, 2004

Fayehun, Adeola, *Keep it Real*, Facebook, 2015

Fisk, Robert, *The Great War for Civilisation*, Fourth Estate, 2005

Frayn, Michael, *Towards the End of the Morning*, Harvill Press, 1967

Gardner, Frank, *Blood and Sand*, Bantam Press, 2006

Garrett, Patrick, *Of Fortunes and War: Clare Hollingworth, First of the Female War Correspondents*, published privately, 2015

Gellhorn, Martha, *The Face of War*, Simon & Schuster, 1959

Goodman, Alan, John Pollack and Wolf Blitzer, *The World on a String*, Holt Paperbacks, 1997

Grant, James, *The Newspaper Press: Its Origin, Progress, and Present Position,* London, Tinsley Brothers, 1871

Harmsworth, Harold, 1st Viscount Rothermere and William Collin Brooks, *Warnings and Predictions*, Eyre and Spottiswoode, 1939

Hastings, Max, *Going to the Wars*, Macmillan, 2000

Hawley, Caroline, BBC News Online, April 2013

Jonson, Ben, *The Staple of News:Regents Renaissance Drama series*, ed. Ben Kifer and Desmond Rowland, Edwin Arnold, 1976

Keane, Fergal, *Season of Blood: A Rwandan Journey*, Viking, 1995

Labouchère, Henry, *Diary of the Besieged Resident in Paris*, Macmillan, 1871

Lamb, Christina, Report in *Sunday Times*, October 2015

Loyd, Anthony, Reports in *The Times*, 19 May 2014 and 12 March 2015

Makbool, Aleem, Documentary, BBC Online, 10 December 2015

McCullin, Don, *DonMcCullin*, Jonathan Cape, 2001

Moorhead, Caroline (ed.), *The Letters of Martha Gellhorn*, Chatto & Windus, 2006

O'Kane, Maggie, *Looking for Karadžić, A Maggie O'Kane Investigation*, BBC2, 19 May 2002

Robinson, Henry Crabb, *Diary, Reminiscences and Correspondence*, Macmillan, 1869

Russell, William Howard, Reports in *The Times*, 1841–71

Sambrook, Richard, 'Are Foreign Correspondents Redundant? The Changing Face of International News', Reuters Institute for the Study of Journalism, Oxford, 2010

Schork, Kurt, Report of 23 May 1993, Reuters news agency

Snow, Edgar, *Red Star Over China*, Victor Gollancz, 1937

Snow, Jon, *Shooting History: A Personal Journey*, HarperCollins, 2004

Stanley, Henry Morton, *How I Found Livingstone,* Dawson Brothers, Montreal, 1872

Steer, George Lowther, Nicholas Rankin, *Telegram from Guernica: The Extraordinary Life of George Steer, War Correspondent*, Faber & Faber, 2003

Stevens, Philip Pembroke, reports in *Daily Express*, 1932–5

Swain, Jon, *The River of Time*, William Heinemann, 1995

Todenhöfer, Jürgen, Interview with Abu Qatadah, published on
YouTube, 20 November 2015

Tomalin, Nicholas, Report for *Sunday Times*, 5 June 1966

Ward Price, George, *Extra-Special Correspondent*, Harrap, 1957

Ward Price, George, *I Know These Dictators*, Harrap, 1937

Waugh, Evelyn, *Scoop*, Chapman & Hall, 1938

Wells, H. G., Report in *New Statesman*, 27 Octobr 1934

COPYRIGHT ACKNOWLEDGEMENTS

INDEX